Compiled and edited by
Julie Ann Godson

Memories of the

Vale

*Life in the countryside
before the railway came*

Alley Cat Books

Published in 2023 by Alley Cat Books
Copyright © Julie Ann Godson

First Edition in this format

Julie Ann Godson has asserted her moral right under the
Copyright, Designs and Patents Act, 1988, to be identified
as the author of this work.

A CIP catalogue record for this title is available from the British Library.

Front cover: "Mr Garne's Cotswold Sheep, Northleach"
by Richard Whitford, 1866, Royal Agricultural University.
Drawings on pages 60, 70, 77, and 90: *Victoria County History*.

Part One

A BERKSHIRE VILLAGE,

ITS

HISTORY AND ANTIQUITIES

BY THE

REV. LEWIN G. MAINE

CURATE OF STANFORD-IN-THE-VALE

Oxford and London,

JAMES PARKER AND CO.

1866

Drawing by Miss Wordsworth

TO THE VENERABLE

CHRISTOPHER WORDSWORTH, D.D.,

ARCHDEACON OF WESTMINSTER,
VICAR,

MR. HUNTER, AND MR. PUSEY,

CHURCHWARDENS,

AND THE PARISHIONERS OF
STANFORD-IN-THE-VALE

THIS LITTLE

History of their Parish

IS AFFECTIONATELY INSCRIBED.

CONTENTS.

Rev Lewin G. Maine
1828–1897

PREFACE.

First published in 1866 as "A Berkshire Village: its history and antiquities", this little collection of memories and true tales from the Vale of the White Horse has charmed generations of readers. At a time of rapid change in the English countryside, local curate Reverend Lewin G. Maine sought to record for posterity rural people's recollections of a lost way of life.

I discovered Reverend Maine's treasure trove of information and anecdotes concerning the way of life in the Vale of the White Horse a few years ago when I was writing "The Water Gypsy: how a Thames fishergirl married a viscount". Upon her marriage to 2nd Viscount Ashbrook in 1766, my true-life heroine Betty Ridge moved into her marital home of Shellingford Castle. Reverend Maine's book provided the perfect picture of what Betty would have experienced around her in the villages of the Vale in the 18th century—the red cloaks of the women, the white smocks of the men, and the sound of the cowherd calling on his horn every morning to summon the cattle.

The vogue for Victorian clergymen to record the oral histories of their parishes has provided the modern historian with a source of information that is taken increasingly seriously these days. By recording the memories of elderly residents recalling what they had been told by *their* grandparents in their youth, Reverend Maine accessed testimony reaching back to the middle of the 18th century. I felt that the result is still as absorbing and informative as when it was first written, and deserved to be given a new lease of life by means of this latest edition.

Of course, the original title is now somewhat misleading; following the county boundary change of 1974 the Vale of the White Horse finds itself in Oxfordshire, not Berkshire, hence the change to "Memories of the Vale". Otherwise I have changed very little, preferring to allow Rev Maine's sometimes old-fashioned spelling and punctuation to prevail since it forms part of the fabric of what is now a historical document in its own right.

The distinction between a "manor" in the legal, landholding sense, and a "manor" in the sense of the domestic headquarters of the lord of the manor, the manor *house*, continues to be a tricky one. A particular lord of the manor may never even have visited a manor, let alone resided in its manor house. In the case of Stanford-in-the-Vale, the *Victoria County History* wisely makes no identification, but says of Manor Farm: "The Manor Farm, north of the church, is a square building of about 1700." This is clearly too late for a medieval manor house, but of course it does not preclude the existence of a former building on the site. Of Stanford Park Farm, east of the village, the *VCH* says: "There are traces of a considerable mansion at Stanford Park Farm, in the east of the parish, near Stutfield Brook. Near it is a spot laid out originally as a pleasure ground, called the Island, surrounded by water, formerly, perhaps, constructed for a fish-pond." The reader may choose.

Julie Ann Godson
Easter, 2016

THE following pages contain the substance of two Lectures upon Stanford and its neighbourhood, delivered during the winter of last year. They are printed at the request of some who heard them in the hope that others may be induced to imitate that which has here been imperfectly executed, and to give to the world the rich materials which abound towards the compilation of the history of our county. All agree in saying that it is high time something was attempted for every writer upon Berkshire makes the same complaint, viz., that old customs are being forgotten, and local traditions continually passing away. Thus the author of "Tom Brown's School Days" tells us that "the present generation know nothing of their own birthplaces, of their own lanes, and woods, and fields; that not one in twenty knows where to find the wood sorrel or bee orchis, or is acquainted with the country legends, the stories of the old gable-ended farm-houses, the place where the last skirmish was fought in the Civil Wars, or where the parish butts stood."

And Lord Carnarvon, in his excellent little address on the Archaeology of Berkshire, tells us that "local traditions and legends are the most precious heirlooms of archaeology, because, in an especial degree, they breathe the life, the habits, and the faith of our ancestors. These," he writes, "are year by year perishing from amongst us, and day by day, as it is deferred, the difficulty of obtaining materials for a county history becomes greater and more formidable." In the hope of contributing something, however small and imperfect, to such an undertaking, this little work is given to the public, in which, together with other matter by way of illustration, I have endeavoured to preserve the current village traditions.

Rev. Lewin G. Maine
Easter, 1866

A BERKSHIRE VILLAGE:

ITS HISTORY AND ANTIQUITIES.

THE village of Stanford or Stanford-in-the-Vale, can hardly lay claim to be called a picturesque village. On the contrary, when I first approached it by way of the fields from the railway station, on a hot and dusty July day in the summer of 1859, I must confess that my first impressions respecting it were anything but favourable. There was a certain old tumble-down barn which met the eye after crossing the little bridge over the Ock, which seemed to give a character to the whole— an appearance of poverty and decay by no means pleasing. The approach to the bridge, too, seemed sadly in want of the mason's care; and I mentally inferred that the village of Stanford had great need of a local surveyor. One redeeming feature, however, encouraged a hope that there was a better side to all this: viz., a handsome church tower peeping out from amid trees, on a slight elevation above the houses of the village. And when, on entering the church path through Football Close, the Manor Farm, with its old grey buildings and crowded rickyard, appeared on the right, I began to think even a tumble-down village was not altogether devoid of beauty.

And certainly it has proved so on further acquaintance, for although I have often grumbled at the absence of trees, the hot dry dust in summer, the excess of mud in winter, and the level country in the immediate neighbourhood, I have learned to love it for its own sake, to look with pleasure on the beautiful Berkshire hills in the distance, and to enjoy the glorious sunsets which never seem more lovely than at Stanford.

It is no doubt a great thing to live in a vale, and that vale the Vale of the White Horse. As Mr. Hughes observes in his famous novel, entitled "Tom Brown's School Days", "I pity people who weren't born in a vale. I don't mean a flat country but a vale, that is, a flat country bounded by hills. The having your hill always in view, if you choose to turn towards him, that's the essence of a vale. There he is, for ever in the distance, your friend and companion; you never lose him as you do in hilly districts." Now Stanford, be it ever remembered, lies in the very midst of the Vale of White Horse, which is the richest district in all Berkshire. It lies midway between two ranges of hills, and, although in itself a little wanting in picturesque character, is in the neighbourhood of fine scenery. Standing either on the White Horse Hill or on the Faringdon range, a view may be obtained over many counties of England. Our own village has a special claim to represent the glories of this famous district, for it is called after the vale; and all who hear its name become acquainted with the fact that Stanford is Stanford-in-the-Vale.

The Vale of White Horse is full of historical memories; not only famous for Backsword Play and Scouring the White Horse, but famous for the part played by its inhabitants in many a drama of English history. There is scarcely an historical period which is not in some way connected with this part of Berkshire. To connect some of these periods with the history of our parish and its immediate neighbourhood, is the design of this lecture. It is an humble endeavour to interest you as well as myself in the memorable events of which this village has been the witness, and in which numbers of those who now slumber in our churchyard were the living agents. Should any be inclined to think such knowledge profitless, I would reply to them in the words of Bishop Kennett, "I am sensible there be some who slight and despise this sort of learning, and represent it to be a dry, barren, monkish study. I leave such to their dear enjoyments of ignorance and ease, but I dare assure any wise and sober man that historical antiquities, especially a search into the notices of our own nation, do deserve and will reward the pains of any English student, will make him understand the state of former ages, the constitution of Governments, the fundamental reasons of equity and law, the rise and succession of doctrines and opinions, the tenures of property, the rites of religion, and, indeed, the nature of mankind."

There are indications within a few miles which carry us back into a hoary antiquity, and connect this neighbourhood with the very dawn of English history. Many of you must have visited that singular group of stones on the White Horse Hill made famous by Sir Walter Scott's novel of "Kenilworth," called Wayland Smith's cave. In the middle of a clump of trees

Wayland's Smithy

you may see a large flat stone raised on seven or eight others. This is an ancient Cromlech, and connects the place with the heathen worship of the ancient Druids. It speaks to us of a time when the early Britons roamed over these hills, and worshipped Him whom they called the Unknown. The name of our little river, the Ock, is another trace of early British rule, for it bears a Celtic name, the language of the first inhabitants of our island.

But if in many places we can find indications of British occupation, our own parish carries us a link further in the chain of history. On the farm in the occupation of Mr. Penstone at Chinham we have evidences of these very lands having been trodden by the Roman legions. For Chinham has been identified with Julianum, a Roman settlement, and on its site is found what is called the "Chinham money" on which you may read the superscription of the Caesars. A large number of these coins was lately in the possession of Mr. Penstone, they were given by him to the late Bursar of Brazenose College, Oxford. Another collection, now belonging to Mr. Kimber, has been lent to me, and amongst them I find several coins of Constantine, and one of Trajan and Nerva. Remains of Roman building have also been found in a field, on the farm lately occupied by Mr. Henry Penstone, and traces of a road reaching across the country to Sparsholt have been also discovered. But, in speaking of the times of the Romans, I must not omit to mention the Camp on the White Horse Hill. It is one of the finest specimens in England. You may trace its gates and ditch and mounds all in perfect preservation; and within it you may find, as Mr. Hughes has observed, "most beautiful green turf with tender blue bells, and gossamer, and thistledown, together with the pleasantest breeze that ever blew." But the chief evidence of these lands having been trodden by the Roman legions is to be found in the old Roman roads called the Ridgeway, and the Ickleton or Icknield way, which run for miles along the White Horse Hill. It was by means of these roads the Roman soldiers marched, and doubtless by them Christianity was first introduced into this island, and perhaps into this parish. The first martyr of these islands, St. Alban, was, we know, a soldier in the Roman army.

The hamlet of Goosey, which, since the Reformation, has been joined to this Parish, advances us another link in the chain of history. It speaks to us of those who next became the masters of this island, viz., the Saxons. And here we stand on firmer ground, being able to show by actual existing documents that Goosey was known by the same name that it bears at present, in the middle of the eighth century. This information is gained from an ancient Latin record, entitled "The Chronicles of Abingdon", which, since the dissolution of monasteries in the 16th century, has remained in the custody of the Queen's Master of the Rolls. From this we learn that Offa, King of Mercia and Wessex, whose name survives in the name of the neighbouring village of Uffington, or Offa's Town, gave to the monks of Abingdon the Manor of Goosey in exchange for a large tract of meadow-land near Abingdon, called Andresey, or St. Andrew's Island. This grant of the Manor of Goosey connects our parish with the times of the Saxons, for Goosey is essentially a Saxon village, its name signifying Goose Island; being probably so called from the large flocks of wild geese frequenting Goosey Mere. But, indeed, the whole country round about us teems with traces of our Saxon forefathers. The White Horse cut on the hill commemorates the famous victory obtained by King Ethelred and his brother Alfred, afterwards called Alfred the Great, over the Danes, in the year 871. This is called the battle of Ashdown. The Danish army was in two divisions, one commanded by two of their kings called Bergseeg and Aldene, the other commanded by two earls. The Danes had the advantage of position, for they occupied the higher grounds, that is Uffington Camp and the slope beneath. The Saxon army was likewise divided into two parts, the one under the command of King Ethelred, and the other under that of his brother Alfred. Whilst King Ethelred was engaged in his tent in prayer and receiving the Holy Communion, the Danes began the battle. Seeing the danger of delay, Alfred, without waiting for his brother, formed his men into a dense phalanx and led his troops against the enemy. But Alfred's troops, fighting with disadvantage of ground and numbers, began to be discouraged and give way, when King Ethelred came up, and charging the enemy with great fury, turned the fortune of the day. According to the old Saxon chronicler whose words I transcribe, "There was also a single thorn-tree of stunted growth which we ourselves with our very eyes have seen. Around this tree the opposing armies came together with loud shouts from all sides, the one party to pursue their wicked course, the other to fight for their lives, their dearest ties, and their country; and when both armies had fought long and bravely, at last the pagans, by the Divine judgment, were no longer able to bear the attacks of the Christians, and having lost great part of their army, took to a disgraceful flight. One of their two kings and five earls were there slain, together with many thousand pagans, who fell on all sides, covering with their bodies the whole plain of Ashdown."

Such was the great victory obtained by the Christian Saxons over the heathen Danes, of which the White Horse, cut on the hill, is the sign and memorial. There it has been for nearly a thousand years.

Another memento of Saxon times remains in the name of Wayland Smith's Cave. It is true it is a British cromlech, but the name by which we know it, is Saxon. Wayland the Smith,

The Uffington White Horse

was one of the Teutonic demigods, and traditions of him are found throughout Europe. According to Anglo-Saxon legend, he was a cunning goldsmith and magical farrier. The local tradition is, that an invisible smith, called Wayland, had his abode on this spot, who would shoe a traveller's horse, if left here for a short time with a piece of money for payment. Certain it is that this group of stones has borne the same name since the time of the Saxons, for it is mentioned in the Abingdon Chronicle as a landmark under the name of "Welandes Smiththe."

But, indeed, everywhere in the Vale we find unmistakable indications of our Saxon origin. Many of our familiar names are Saxon. Thus Wic means a dwelling-place in the old Anglo-Saxon, and we have Goosey-wick and Charney-wick. Mere is Saxon for a lake, and we have Goosey Mere. Croft is Saxon for a meadow, and we have Sheepcroft, and Horsecroft. The name of our parish, and, indeed, that of all the neighbouring parishes, is Saxon. Stan is Saxon for a stone, and ford is Saxon in its derivation, perhaps meaning when put together "the ford by the quarry" for Stanford, we know, abounds in quarries of stone. The termination "sey" in Goosey, Charney, Pusey, Hanney, Childrey, means Island, and is Saxon in its origin. It shows that the country in those times was much covered with water, and that these were places so surrounded by it as to obtain the name of islands. Anyone may well understand this who has ever been to Hanney or to Goosey in the winter. In Uffington, as we have said before, we are reminded of a Saxon king, whose town it was. In Buckland we seem to have reference to the Saxon distinction of land into "folc-land" and "boc-land". Land which belonged to the state or community at large, was called "folc-land," that is, the people's land. Stanford had folc-land, or, as it was called, "Stanford common field". Bocland was land held by book or charter. Boc is the Saxon for beech, and books or charters were written on beechen tablets, and so the word "boc" came to signify book.

But, indeed, we have still more familiar traces of Saxon times in the very language spoken amongst us. Some of the best judges pronounce the dialect of our Vale to be the purest Anglo-Saxon now spoken. To mention some few words amongst many. We say *housen* when we mean houses. We speak of a *heisch* day. We call a gate, a *geat*. When we are lonesome or solitary, we say we are very *unked*. When we are vexed or put about, we say, we are *caddled*. We say, when wheat comes up very early, it is *fromm*. We say, when we are very hungry, that we are very *leer*. We say, when a child is brisk and lively, that it is *peart*. We speak of staying in a place as *biding* in a place; and when we talk of moving, we say *wagging*. From this word *wag* is formed the word waggon—that is, something which wags or moves on. A man came to my house, the day after New Year's Day, selling oranges, from the Saxon town of Wantage, who pleaded as a reason for my purchasing some, that I had not given him a *hansel* this year; *handsel*, in Saxon, meaning a New Year's gift.

We often make use of old grammatical forms. Thus we use the personal pronouns *he* or *she* to express objects without life. Thus I heard a lad remark one day to another who had given him an apple, "Who ever gave you *he* to give to *I*?" Such was once the manner of speech amongst all. Such expressions are not bad, but only antiquated English, and prove that once our forefathers spoke pure Anglo-Saxon.

Moreover, traces of the time in which those hardy Norsemen, the Danes, disputed with the Saxons the possession of this country, survive also in the tradition connected with the horn by which Mr. Pusey of Pusey holds his land. This horn bears the inscription,

> *"Kyng Knoude gave William Pewse*
> *Yys horne to holde by thy Londe."*

About this horn there has been some dispute. The tradition about it is called a fabulous legend by one historian of Berkshire; and perhaps it may be that the inscription is of later date than the horn itself; but certain it is that King Canute was a great deal in this neighbourhood, for he is mentioned in the old Latin Chronicle of Abingdon as a considerable benefactor to the monastery. Holding lands by cornage, or the service of a horn, was common in early times. He who held land by a horn, it is said, was bound to blow a horn when any invasion of an enemy was perceived.

The name of Pusey will ever be honoured and respected in Stanford. There is scarcely a cottage which does not contain the portrait of the "old Squire" and he well deserves to he honourably mentioned in any account of our parish; for he was a man of genial humour, varied information, practical ability, and sterling worth. He set a good example to the gentry of Berkshire in residing much on his property. He was the president and founder of the Agricultural Society, and for some time worthily represented this county in Parliament. Both he and Lady Emily, his wife, are remembered with affection by many of the labourers and their families.

But not only are we reminded of the Danes by the Pusey horn, but also by the camp, about half a mile from Pusey, called Cherbury Camp. This has been called a British camp; but the tradition about it is, that it was at all events used by the Danes. The present Lord Carnarvon, a relative of Mr. Pusey's, in a little work on the Archaeology of Berkshire, published in 1859, relates that this is the camp into which Alfred the Great penetrated in disguise as a minstrel, in order to learn the plans of the Danes. The story told by the Saxon chronicler Ingulf is, that "the king, feigning to be a glee-man, took his harp, and went into the camp of the Danes, where, being admitted into its most private places, he saw all the secrets of his enemies; and, when he had gratified his wishes, withdrew without being found out."

Thus, in all parts of the Vale we are reminded of the great Alfred. Wantage, or Wanting—that is, "the place of moles"—was his birth-place, and at Ashdown he gained his great victory. Well may those who live in the Vale think with pride of Alfred the Great, for a great and good king he was. His great desire was to benefit the English nation; and for this purpose he translated much of the Scripture into English; and in order to encourage the clergy of his own and future times to the earnest performance of the pastoral office, he translated a famous book called the Pastoral of Gregory the Great, a copy of which, together with a golden pen, he sent to every bishop in his kingdom, that it might be preserved for ever in their churches. The whole of this neighbourhood is connected with

King Alfred

the residence of the Saxon kings; for both at Wantage and at Faringdon there were royal palaces. In one of them, at Wantage, Alfred was born; and in the other, at Faringdon, Edward, his son, called Edward the Elder, died in 925. Thus the antiquity of this neighbourhood and its connexion with the several races which from time to time obtained the mastery in England can be proved without dispute; but if we would form a perfect idea of the life of those early days, we must strive to comprehend something of that monastic life which was led by so many in this immediate neighbourhood.

The monastic life does not seem a state recommended to us by the life of our Blessed Lord. He taught us rather, while we seek for seasons of retirement, to mix among men and leaven by Christian example the mass of sin about us. The monastic life began about the middle of the third century, during the Decian persecution. Many persons then formed themselves into communities, and lived apart from the world. No sooner had religion made any progress amongst the Saxons, than many monasteries began to be built all over the island. This was natural, for Gregory the Bishop of Rome, who sent forth a mission to convert the heathen Saxons, was himself a monk, and the person he selected to undertake their conversion was Augustine, a monk from his own monastery.

One of the first monasteries built in the south of England was that of Abingdon, some few traces of which may still be seen. There are the remains of a gateway, and in an adjoining brewery some ancient rooms still exist. The Arms of the Abbey, with the Royal Arms, may yet be seen over the gateway. This Abbey was built about the year 675 by Heane, nephew of Cissa, king of the West Saxons. Some idea of its extent may be gathered from the number of in- and out-door servants employed in it, which were more than a hundred in number.

At its gates the poor were continually relieved. It was the *hospital* for the whole district, for all the knowledge of medicine possessed in those days was enjoyed by the monks. It was the *school* of the neighbourhood, and here William the Conqueror left his son to be educated. It was the *alms-house* of those days, where the aged servant and the decayed labourer retired to a home neither uncomfortable nor humiliating. Again, the monasteries were the *inns* of the country, where all wayfaring men were lodged and fed on their journeys. The brethren of Abingdon spent their time partly in prayer and

Remains of Abingdon Abbey

partly in labouring in the fields. They were the great farmers of their day, and greatly promoted agriculture.

The food of the monks was at first very coarse and simple, but afterwards greater indulgences were permitted them. In later times pork or bacon was allowed once a day. Each monk had also half a quartern loaf and half a pound of cheese, with beer twice a day. On feast-days they had other indulgences, such as hydromel, a drink made from water and honey, and wine was allowed on the great festivals. In Lent, instead of cheese, they had each one large eel. Milk and eggs were largely consumed, for their own manors were bound to furnish them with 29,000 eggs yearly.

I have dwelt upon these details because the hamlet of Goosey was a manor belonging to the Abbey of Abingdon. Here in all probability the monks had a farm, for Goosey is mentioned in the Chronicle as supplying the Abbey with cheese. At Charney they had another farm, from which also the monks drew a further supply. Doubtless that very form of cheese which is made so extensively in this neighbourhood is fashioned after a recipe which originally emanated from the dairy at Abingdon. In imagination, then, we may people the fields of Goosey with the lay brethren of the monastery engaged in agricultural pursuits, busied in the hay field, cutting wood, milking cows, or driving them to pasture. Nay, we may think of this labour as sanctified by religion, and hear the matin bell calling them to early prayers, and the vesper, or evening, bell inviting them to devotion and repose. True, in many respects, it was a corrupt religion which they professed; but their piety in this respect contrasts somewhat favourably with that of the 19th century.

The dress of the Benedictine monks of Abingdon, and therefore of Goosey, was a long robe of black serge with a hood to cover the head. The head was partially shaven, and in their hands they carried a book of prayers. Such figures must have been very familiar to the inhabitants of Stanford in past years. The Abbey at Abingdon was destroyed by the Danes, but its ruined fortunes were restored by King Athelstane. He bestowed on it many manors, and amongst them that of the neighbouring village of Shellingford. And it happens that the gift of Shellingford to the Abbey is connected by a remarkable link with our own parish church. Athelstane, as the Chronicle of Abingdon relates, kept the feast of Easter in the year 939 with his whole court in great state at Abingdon. Whilst there, messengers arrived from Hugh Capet, king of France, with valuable presents of gold and jewels and holy relics, to ask from the English monarch his sister's hand in marriage. Amongst the relics was a finger of St. Denys of Paris. This St. Denys was one of a company of seven who were sent from Italy in the time of the Decian persecution to relight the lamp of faith in Gaul. He preached most diligently, and is called the Apostle of Gaul. With two others he suffered martyrdom, and was buried in Paris at a spot called Montmartre, that is, the *mount of martyrs*. A magnificent church was built in his honour, in which, for many centuries, the French kings were buried. It is the Westminster Abbey of France. St. Denys is looked upon as the patron saint of France, and the French soldiers used to shout his name for their battle cry, as the English that of St. George. Now it is to this holy saint and martyr our parish church is dedicated, for the festival of St. Denys of Paris was held on October 9th, the very day on which Stanford feast falls, these feasts being the anniversaries of the dedication of the church.

Now our present church was built at a later date, but yet there are tombs in the churchyard which show there was a church on the present site about 800 years ago. It seems more than probable that about this time, the time when Shelling-ford came into the possession of the monks, that a church was built in Stanford and dedicated to the memory of St. Denys of Paris.

The naming of the church was doubtless owing to the fact of a finger of St. Denys being possessed as a famous relic by the monks of Abingdon. While, then, we condemn that superstition which the veneration of relics brought upon the Church of God, let us remember that he to whom our church is dedicated was indeed a saint and martyr—one who, at the hazard of his life, preached the blessed Gospel of the living God during a time of persecution.

It was only by degrees that corruptions crept into the Church. In the times of the Saxons, there was much pure religion practised in England. It was not until much later in the history of our nation that the reading of the Bible was discouraged. The learning of the four gospels by heart was a necessary acquirement for all who took Holy Orders; and the Saxon homilies—i.e., sermons composed to be read in churches—exhort the people with much earnestness "to the frequent perusal of the Scriptures" and enforce the advice from the great benefit of that exercise, saying "that the mind was refined, and the passions purged by this expedient; that this was the way to refresh our greatest concern upon us, and make heaven and hell have their due impression. That, as a blind man often stumbles in his motion, so those who are unacquainted with the word of God are apt to make false steps and miscarry[1]."

Laws, too, were made at successive councils, exhorting the clergy, parents, and godparents to instruct children, and commanding the sanctification of the Lord's Day.

But to return to the history of our own parish. Its history, so far as it is known from authentic documents, cannot be traced until after the Conquest. From the evidence of ancient charters referred to in Lyson's History of Berkshire, it seems that the Manor of Stanford was given by the Conqueror to Henry de Ferrars, Earl of Derby, in whose family it continued for 200 years. This nobleman held no less than twenty-two manors in Berkshire, he being the greatest lay proprietor. During the time the manor was in the possession of the Ferrars, Earls of Derby, a market was granted to the parish, in the

1   Cp. Collier's Eccl. Hist., vol. i. p. 201.

year 1230, in the reign of Henry III. Stanford was a market town down to the time of the Reformation; for it is called a town in the Churchwarden's accounts of the 16th century; and traces of this may be found in the language used respecting strangers—viz., that they are *out-towners.*

At this time also a fair was granted to Stanford, which was held at the time of Stanford feast, and which still lingers in the annual appearance of a few travelling shows and gingerbread stalls. A fair was a very different matter once, being attended by persons from all the country round; for in old times there were few shops, and such opportunities of obtaining needful merchandise could not be lost. Our market was held on Thursdays, perhaps on Church Green; and then the neighbours from Shellingford, Pusey, Charney, Goosey, and other villages, would bring wool, honey, poultry, butter, and eggs. Occasionally, perhaps, a lay brother from Goosey would offer for sale some of those cheeses so much appreciated by the monks.

Stanford was lost by the Ferrars family in 1266. On account of the part taken by Ferrars, Earl of Derby, against Henry III and his son, this estate was forfeited, and was given by the king to Clare, Earl of Gloucester, whose arms may be seen in the chancel window of the church. The church was in all probability built whilst this nobleman possessed the manor. The architecture, which is of the style called Decorated Gothic, leads us to think it was built about the beginning of the fourteenth century. The windows are exactly similar to some in the chapel of Merton College at Oxford, where the arms of the De Clares are also to be seen. A brass in our chancel tells us that Roger Campedene was Rector of Stanford, and that he died in 1398. Perhaps he was the first rector of the new church. From the Clare family the Manor passed by female descent to the family of De Spencer, then to that of Beauchamp, and after that, to the Nevilles. And this brings us to a very interesting period in the history of our country, to an event rendered still more famous by the pen of Shakespeare. For this Manor, we have seen, belonged to the Nevilles, and from thence it passed to the Crown. How this happened we may gather from the south porch of our church, which is of later date than the rest, and has carved upon it the rose and fetlock impaling the ragged staff. This points to the porch being built about the time of the marriage of Lady Anne Neville with the Duke of Gloucester, afterwards Richard III, by whose orders it is said the two young princes were murdered in the Tower.

This lady was a daughter of the famous Neville, Earl of Warwick, sometimes called the King-maker, who played a prominent part in the Wars of the Roses. Her first marriage was a very unhappy one. She was married to that Prince Edward, son of Henry VI, who was stabbed to death by the Dukes of Clarence and Gloucester, after having been taken prisoner at the battle of Tewkesbury—the horrid deed which Shakespeare, in his play of Richard III, has fitly made one of the phantoms that haunted the death dream of Clarence.

> *"Then came wandering by*
> *A shadow like an angel, with bright hair*
> *Dabbled in blood; and he shrieked out aloud,*
> *Clarence is come—false, fleeting, perjured Clarence,*
> *That stabbed me in the field by Tewkesbury:*
> *Seize on him furies,—take him unto torment[2]."*

But the second marriage of Lady Anne Neville was a still more miserable one; for she was sought out from concealment by Richard Duke of Gloucester, one of those who stabbed her husband, and induced or forced to marry him. Shakespeare

2   King Richard III, Act i. Scene 4.

Lady Anne Neville

has woven some incidents of this sad history into the same play. He represents the corpse of King Henry VI being borne towards Chertsey, and Lady Anne following as a mourner:—

"Poor key-cold figure of a holy king!
Pale ashes of the house of Lancaster!
Thou bloodless remnant of that royal blood!
Be it lawful that I invocate thy ghost.

To hear the lamentations of poor Anne,
Wife to thy Edward, to thy slaughtered son[3]."

On the road to Chertsey she is met by Richard, who endeavours to persuade her to marry him. At first she rejects his suit with the most bitter scorn, but at last is seemingly persuaded to consent. It is not improbable that the south porch of our church may have been erected by the King, as a kind of penance for sin, for in such a manner sorrow for wrong done was often shown in those days.

The building of the south porch is the last link I am able to supply in the history of Stanford until the date of the Reformation; but it may not be without interest to mention that only a few days ago a silver penny of the time of Richard III was found in the mould of the churchyard. The reign of Richard is not perhaps the one which is most pleasing to remember in connection with Stanford, but still it was a most eventful period, and may serve to remind us of the stormy times through which our ancestors—those who worshipped in the same church—have passed. It is only fair to say that it has been contended that the popular notion of Richard's character is a party delusion, a matter of Lancastrian prejudice fomented by Shakespeare; but although it is possible the dark side of his character may have been exaggerated, there must without doubt have been some foundation for it. Shakespeare has a fine passage, where he makes Richard express remorse before his death. He has an agitated dream on the eve of the battle of Bosworth Field. There, rising from his sleep, harassed, haggard, and disturbed, he explains to his attendants the change which had come over his spirit, and the hauntings of his guilty conscience:—

---

3   Ibid., Act i. Scene 2.

"My conscience hath a thousand several tongues,
And every tongue brings in a several tale,
And every tale condemns me for a villain:
Perjury, perjury in the high'st degree,
All several sins, all used in each degree,
Throng to the bar, crying all—Guilty! guilty!
I shall despair. There is no creature loves me,
And if I die no soul will pity me.
Nay, wherefore should they? since that I myself
Find in myself no pity to myself;
Methought the souls of all that I had murdered
Came to my tent, and every one did threat
To-morrow's vengeance on the head of Richard[4]."

May we not hope that Shakespeare has only in this preserved a tradition of the qualms of conscience felt for his deeds by Richard before his death? Such conscientious qualms perhaps may have moved the king to the erection of our church porch; and may we not trust, that perhaps within the walls of Stanford Church, the king may have sought pardon and forgiveness for his great sins from the mercy of God, a pardon which we know is not withheld on sincere repentance even to the greatest of sinners.

At this period of war and bloodshed in the State, there was much corruption in the Church; but even before, and at that time, some there were who set a bright example of Christian living. This may be learned from the poetry of Chaucer, who, it is alleged, lived at Donnington Castle near Newbury in this county, where, under an oak in the park, he composed, according to tradition, many of his poems. His son was Lord of the Manor of the neighbouring villages of Buckland and Hatford in the year 1436. In one of his poems, Chaucer has

---

4   King Richard III, Act v. Scene 3.

left us a description of a parson of his day, which, if true, abundantly testifies that at that time there were, at all events, some parishes where faith was not altogether extinguished. He speaks of:—

> *"A poor Parson of a town,*
> *But rich he was of holy thought and work;*
> *He was also a learned man, a clerk*
> *That Christe's Gospel truly would he preach.*
> *His parishers devoutly would he teach.*
>
>   .   .   .   .   .   .
>
> *Wide was his parish—houses far asunder,*
> *But he neglected nought for rain and thunder;*
> *In sickness and in grief to visit all.*
> *The farthest in his parish, great and small.*
> *Always on foot, and in his hand a stave,*
> *This noble example to his flock he gave.*
> *That first he wrought, and afterward he taught;*
> *Out of the Gospel he that lesson caught.*
> *And this new figure added he thereto.*
> *That if gold rust, then what should iron do."*

But in the same poem from which this description is taken, Chaucer shows us that many corruptions were rife in regard to religion. A wicked traffic was carried on in pardons which the Pope pretended to grant, and which were sold for money by his agents in England. Then, also, pilgrimages were made to the shrines of the saints, as if by this, sin could be atoned for. All this was fostered by the denial of the Scriptures to the people, and by the use of Latin in the public prayers, which, therefore, the people could not understand. Much corruption, moreover, grew out of the monastic system. The monks persuaded the lords of manors to make over the churches on their estates and the tithes with which they were endowed, to their own monasteries, they, meanwhile, undertaking to provide for the ecclesiastical duties; and thus parishes were left without resident pastors, the Church services being performed by monks from the neighbouring monastery. The monastic system again interfered with the healthier parochial system in other ways. It drained off the resources of religious zeal into one channel, and prevented the erection and endowment of bishoprics and parishes. This abuse was foreseen by Bede, a learned Saxon monk, who died in 735. Even in his day, he foresaw the evil which would arise from too great an increase in the building of monasteries; and advised that some of them should be suppressed, and their estates applied to the erection of bishoprics.

Another evil arising from the monastic system was the false view it propagated in regard to religion, a corruption which is illustrated by the word religion itself. "A religious person in the times of the monks did not mean anyone who felt and allowed the bonds that bound him to God, and to his fellow men; but one who had taken peculiar vows upon him, a member of one of the monkish orders. A religious house did not mean a Christian household, ordered in the fear of God, but a house in which these persons were gathered together, according to the rule of some man. 'Religious' was a title which might not be given to parents and children, husbands and wives, men and women fulfilling faithfully and holily in the world the several duties of their stations, but only to those who had devised such a self-chosen service for themselves.[5]"

No one who has not carefully studied the history of those times can conceive the great revolution which at the dissolution of monasteries passed over this country. The first great change in this neighbourhood must have been the dissolution of the great abbey at Abingdon. This abbey must have been a

5   Trench, on the Study of Words.

source of wealth and temporal benefit to the whole neighbourhood. No doubt the system of which it was the representative was productive of much spiritual evil; but this evil was mixed with much that was good, and the temporal benefits which it dispensed were very great. For, at the gates of the abbey, as I have said, the poor were largely relieved. It was an asylum for the aged and infirm, for the sick and the destitute, the hospital and dispensary for the whole neighbourhood. But now all this was swept away.

King Henry VIII at two several times confiscated the whole of the monastic property to the service of the state. He is said to have lost at a game with dice the great bell of St. Paul's to one of the courtiers. By the sale of the abbey lands, and from the plate and jewels of which the monasteries were despoiled, an enormous sum of money was obtained. The excuse for this was the corrupt state of many of these monastic houses, but there is every reason to believe this was exaggerated. No doubt much of the land had been given to the service of religion under false notions of penitence, but still much of it must have been given through motives of piety; and, indeed, no one could be sure what were the inner springs influencing men to bestow their land and treasure.

These lands and this money did not belong to the monks absolutely. The monks were only the trustees for religion and the poor. Granting that the trustees were evil, they should have been removed, but not the trust confiscated. Thus a great wrong was done, and a great sin committed. Archbishop Cranmer and Bishops Latimer and Ridley earnestly moved the king to give some of the monasteries as schools of learning, and to endow them with their revenues, and to allow some to remain for better religious purposes, And the king certainly at one time had some intention of doing this, for there exists in his own handwriting a scheme for erecting thirteen bishoprics out of the spoils of the monasteries. But this scheme was never carried into effect. Out of the whole of the immense revenue that accrued to the Crown from the abolition of the monasteries, a fraction of about £8,000 per annum was bestowed upon the endowment of six new bishoprics, and the substitution of canons for the disbanded monks in several of the old cathedral churches.

The whole of this neighbourhood must have been deeply affected by the dissolution of the monasteries, for both Cistercians and Benedictines had religious houses in the vicinity. There was a cell at Faringdon, an offshoot of the Cistercian Abbey of Beaulieu in Hampshire, a record of which remains in the old barn at Great Coxwell; and at Abingdon there was the great Benedictine monastery. Stanford, it is probable, had frequent intercourse both with Cistercians and Benedictines, for Faringdon is only four miles distant from Stanford, and there still remain traces of an old road or track leaving this parish near that part of it which is called Bow, and running through Charney field in a straight line for Abingdon.

Intercourse with these places must have greatly promoted the breeding of sheep, and the tillage of land, for the Cistercians were the great wool-growers of the country, and the Benedictines the promoters of agriculture. Much wool was doubtless brought to Stanford Market, for it is plain from Mr. Fawconer's will, in which mention is made of wool weights, that tithes were paid in wool, and several published wills of the Unton family at Wadley, about the time of the Reformation, prove the staple production of this neighbourhood to have been wool. It is highly probable that Stanford may have had a considerable manufacture of jersey cloth, which was produced in many Berkshire towns, a trade which was ruined by the civil wars. Together with this trade, considerable attention must have always been paid to agriculture and dairy farming.

The cheese supplied by Shellingford, Goosey, and Charney to the monastery of Abingdon, sufficiently proves that attention was then, as now, paid to the feeding of cows in the Vale. The methods of farming were very primitive. No carts were known, and manure was carried in hampers or panniers on the backs of horses; and, indeed, this custom is still remembered by some living, who affirm that this was so in the village of Goosey until a very late date.

At the Reformation Stanford had to wish good-bye to her old neighbours, the Cistercians and Benedictines, and accustom herself to a new order of things, to exchange monkish landlords for lay proprietors. In order to reconcile the leading persons in every county to the sale of the Abbey lands and tithes, they were allowed to purchase them at easy prices. Thus it was said, "Popish lands made Protestant landlords." In these times the poor were great sufferers, for a vast proportion of the population were turned adrift without employment, and so great was the distress that in Oxfordshire there was a serious rebellion.

This parish was then, as indeed it continued until the last generation, entirely unenclosed. From Faringdon to Oxford, was one large sheep-walk. Ancient charters give us some idea of the state of the country round. Thus in the Wadley property in Wyke, that is, part of Faringdon and the whole of Hatford, the land was proportioned as follows:—There were 1500 acres of arable, 600 acres of meadow, 1000 acres of pasture, 100 acres of wood, 500 acres of jampnorum, that is, gorse or furze, being 2100 acres of grass land to 1500 of arable. Thus we see that the rearing of sheep was found more profitable than keeping the land in tillage. Indeed, Bishop Burnet shows that much land was turned into pasture, and many enclosures removed for the sake of breeding sheep, the wool of which fetched a very high price. Through this fewer labourers were employed, and land

was let at a dearer rate to yeomen. These ancient charters prove the existence of many woods which have now wholly disappeared, and show us that much land has been reclaimed, once altogether waste. Within the memory of many living, there were many acres of common covered with furze between this village and that of Buckland, and a large tract of land called Hatford Downs. The furze probably supplied the poor in old times with fuel, and when the making of bricks was introduced into the Vale, it was with furze that the furnaces were heated.

Anciently Stanford was peopled by many substantial yeomen. The name of yeoman may be read on many old gravestones, and constantly occurs in the Church registers. There still exist many old farmhouses, none of them of very large size. These are still known by the names of their former owners, whose families for many years inhabited this parish. Thus we have Spinage's, Ducket's, Stone's. There are the remains of one of these old houses of the yeomanry on Second Common, which, though now turned into cottages, presents a very ancient and picturesque appearance. It is said that large numbers of yeomanry are peculiar to Berkshire, and that at the beginning of the present century the number of yeomen farming their own land in Berkshire was greater than in any other county of the same size. None of these, in all probability, farmed a larger number of acres than forty, fifty, or at the most eighty, but then they had the right of pasturage on the common or "folc land" of Stanford[6]. In illustration of this we find Bishop Latimer in a sermon mentioning that his father was a yeoman having no lands of his own, but renting a farm of the annual value of 3*l.* or 4*l.* This, he says, he tilled, employing half a dozen men; but then, we are told, he had walk for an hundred sheep, that is, right of pasturage for so many. He was a substantial yeoman for those days, for he sent his son to school, and afterwards to the University of Cambridge. He was able to portion his daughters with 5*l.* apiece, and "he kept hospitality for his poor neighbours, and some alms he gave to the poor." However, this was before the Reformation, for Latimer complains in 1549, that the same farm for which his father paid 3*l.* or 4*l.* was then let for 16*l.* by the year.

The yeomanry at this time in England usually lived in dwellings of timber, the walls being formed of wattled plaster, but it is probable that in this neighbourhood stone would be very generally used from the abundance to be found in the parish; but all dwellings must have been of ruder construction than at present, for now the farmers of Berkshire occupy the

---

6   I remember the late Mr. Cowderoy telling me that his father was accustomed to relate that, before the Enclosure Act, the cows belonging to the different yeomen were gathered together each morning by the blowing of a horn, the cowherd calling loudly on the inhabitants to send out their cows to pasture, that this man had the charge of them during the day, and in the evening gave notice of his return in the same manner by blowing his horn.

old Manor Houses of the gentry. Houses at that time were not all furnished with chimneys; the monasteries and manor houses had them, but they were not common in the 16th century.

The yeomanry mostly lived together with their labourers in their kitchens, the fire being made against the wall or reredos, the smoke finding its way out at a hole in the roof. Many only slept on straw pallets covered with a canvas sheet and coarse coverlet. Then, perhaps, instead of a bolster, they had a good round log. Sometimes the father or goodman of the house would have a mattress or flock bed, and a sack of chaff to rest his head on. Oftentimes their servants had no sheets at all, but lay on the straw. Then, all ate off wooden trenchers, and drank their beer out of wooden bowls, called biggins or piggins, the beer being drawn for use in deep black leathern or wooden pitchers called jacks. The sign of the ancient inn near the present railway station, called "The Leathern Bottle," illustrates this custom.

Few of the yeomanry had more than four or five pieces of pewter in their possession. For seats, they had rough stools, such as any man could make with a chopper, and sometimes settles—seats with a back oftentimes opening and forming a box. Joined or joint stools, that is, stools made properly by a joiner, were more luxurious. The tables were formed by boards laid on tressels, so that they could he easily removed, as appears from an expression in "Romeo and Juliet", where Capulet exclaims:—

"A hall! a hall! give room and foot it girls;
More light, ye knaves, and turn the tables up[7]."

The food of the Reformation period was coarser, and much

7   "Romeo and Juliet," Act i., Scene 5.

less varied than it is now. Only the gentry could afford to eat wheaten bread throughout the year. Servants and poor people ate bread made of barley or rye. Sometimes it was even made of beans, pease, and oats. There were then no potatoes, nor was it until the end of Henry VIII's reign that any salads, carrots, turnips, or other such like roots were produced in England. When Queen Katharine wanted a salad, she was obliged to despatch a messenger to Holland on purpose[8].

Salt meat was eaten throughout the winter. Cattle were slaughtered at Martinmas, and the meat salted for winter consumption. It may be inferred that much of the meat consumed by our ancestors was bacon, from the word *larder*, which is derived from the Latin *laridum* or *lardum*, and the monks of Abingdon called their receptacle for cold meats *lardanarium*. The names by which we call many of the rooms in houses at the present day throw light on old customs. Thus parlour is of course from *parler*, for people lived in kitchens or halls a kind of public life, surrounded by their servants; but they had a room in which they went aside to *parley*. It certainly was not a sitting-room at this time, even in the houses of the gentry, for in the great house at Wadley we read of a bed in the parlour, and so also in the Vicarage at Stanford.

FitzHerbert, who wrote a book on husbandry in 1522, speaks about the duties of farmers' wives. In those days the housewife spun the wool and flax produced on the farm. Respecting this custom, FitzHerbert tells us that it is not profitable for a woman wholly to devote herself to the distaff, but, he remarks, "it stoppeth up a gap, and must needs be had." According to this writer, farmers' wives in the 16th century must have been patterns of diligence and industry. It was their duty to measure out the quantity of corn to be ground, and see that it was sent to the miller. They took care of the poul-

8   See Hume's History of England. Henry VIII.

try and pigs, and superintended the brewing and baking. The garden was especially the care of the yeoman's wife. She had to depend upon it for various herbs which are now no longer in use, but which could not be dispensed with in times when spices were rare and costly. Besides pot-herbs, strewing-herbs were required for the chambers, and herbs possessing medical virtues. A knowledge of herbs still lingers in this neighbourhood, but principally amongst aged women of the labouring class.

The principal materials for clothing were obtained by the industry of each family. Sole-leather was kept in farmhouses, with which shoes might be mended as occasion required. Every yeoman moreover was expected to know how to make yokes and plough gear. Such work afforded profitable employment in the winter evenings.

Thus the Stanford people in those days must have fulfilled that ideal picture which the poet drew of the habits of the ancient Romans, whom he represents in the nights of winter drawing round the fire:—

"When young and old in circle,
Around the firebrands close;
When the girls are weaving baskets,
And the lads are shaping bows.
When the good man mends his armour
And trims his helmet's plume;
When the good wife's shuttle merrily
Goes flashing through the loom."

Certainly in those days people in the country did not lead an easy, idle life.

A writer in Queen Elizabeth's reign relates that, "In times past men were contented to dwell in houses builded of sallow, willow, &c., but now these woods are rejected, and nothing but oak anywhere regarded. And yet see the change. For when our houses were builded of willow then had we oaken men, but now that our houses are made of oak, our men are not only become willow, but a great many altogether of straw. Now we have many chimneys, and yet our tenderlines complain of rheums, catarrhs, and poses. Then we had none but *rere-dosses*, and our heads did never ache, for as the smoke in those days was supposed to be a sufficient hardening for the timber of the house, so it was reputed a far better medicine to keep the goodman and his family from the quack or posse, wherewith as then very few were acquainted."

It is said that local peculiarities are wearing out in Berkshire, but one I rejoice to record has not yet departed, namely, the early and industrious habits of the inhabitants of the Vale. There is scarcely a farmhouse in this neighbourhood where the duties of the day do not commence at the very earliest possible hour. For cows must be milked, and dairy-work attended to. The universal Stanford dinner-hour among all classes is half-

9   "Lays of Ancient Rome."

past eleven, and the hour for tea half-past three. Fifteen years ago the children in the parochial school assembled at eight o'clock, and even now they meet at half-past eight, half an hour earlier than is usual in most schools. The necessary dairy work of the Vale is the means of training a hardy, useful, and industrious people, and of fostering the wholesome custom of early rising.

An interesting document relating to this village is preserved amongst the parish archives, viz. the will of Mr. Fawconer, vicar of Stanford in the time of the Reformation. He held also the living of Shalburne or Chalburne, in Wiltshire. He died in 1592, leaving a legacy of 2*l.* to every man, woman, and child living in Stanford and Goosey. This legacy suggests how greatly the population of the country has increased. It has done so particularly in Stanford, into which strangers have flocked from neighbouring villages. It is probable that the population of Stanford, at the time of Mr. Fawconer's death, was less than half its present numbers. We may infer this by comparing the population returns of 1801 with those of 1861. In 1801 Stanford had a population of 607, but, in 1861, it had increased to 1075.

This will, and the wills of the Unton family of the same date, published by the Berkshire Ashmolean Society, show us how customary it was in those days to bequeath articles of clothing. Mr. Fawconer divides his clothes amongst his friends and amongst the poor of his parish. Thus we find entries as follows: "I give and bequeath to Mr. Thomas Pincke, curate of Shulburn, my best gown, and my best coat furred with floynes." "I give and bequeath to Edmund Whitehorn my old frieze coat, one pair of my hose, a doublet, and a shirt." "I give and bequeath to Sir Roger Wollaston, a poor priest, my rugg gown, and in money twenty shillings, and do forgive him the debt that he oweth me." This last bequest illustrates the history of the times, and shows into what distress the Reformation had plunged many of the clergy. Numbers, it is said, at this time became carpenters, and tailors, and even keepers of ale-houses. Others were forced to go to service as domestics, to turn clerks of the kitchen, surveyors, or receivers. Another legacy left by Mr. Fawconer is one of 3*l*. 6*s*. 5*d*. to poor scholars. "I give and bequeath 3*l*. 6*s*. 8*d*. to be distributed by mine executors' discretion to ten poor scholars in Oxford that be towardly in learning and good condition." This legacy reminds us that although learning afterwards revived, yet for a time it received great discouragement from the dissolution of the monastic schools, and indeed it is said that immediately after the Reformation the Universities were almost deserted.

Another bequest, namely a sum of money, the interest of which was to be applied to the keeping up the highway between Stanford and Wantage, shows us the bad state of the roads at that time. The soil of the Vale is a strong grey loam, mixed with large quantities of vegetable mould, and the stone quarried at Stanford, and used for many years for making and repairing the roads is limestone, in the stratum of which fossil shells, and other marine productions, are found in abundance. This stone, however, is by no means the best for road-making, and a great modern improvement is the importation of harder stone from the neighbourhood of Bristol. Stanford doubtless, in Mr. Fawconer's day, must have been what it remains at present, a muddy place, and it must have been hardly possible to distinguish in the dusk the highway from the unenclosed heath on either side.

Another legacy consisted of five shillings apiece, and coats and gowns to a large number of Mr. Fawconer's godchildren, amongst whom were the names of Franklin, Tyrrold, Spinage, Lambourne, Whitehorne, Cox. A legacy to John Cox was as follows: "I give and bequeath unto John Cox, sometime my servant, in money 20s., and 20s. 5d. that Thomas Barlow the butcher oweth me for a pig, and a heifer that the said John Cox sold him." Another bequest was one by which Mr. Fawconer's name is still thankfully remembered in Stanford, for he leaves money "to portion poor maydes on their marriages, born within the parish of Stanford." Mr. Fawconer endeavoured to remember every one in his will; neither did he forget the poor of the neighbouring parishes, for he left ten shillings to each of the villages of Shellingford, Pusey, and Buckland. He left the residue of his property, after his debts were paid, to be divided into three parts, one was the poor maydes' portion, one that which was to go towards the repair of the highway, and the third he directed to be spent for the relief of poor prisoners abroad.

Before the Reformation the church at Stanford was served by three clergymen, a priest, a deacon, and sub-deacon. From the "Inventory," taken in 1553, a copy of which is given in the Appendix,[10] we find that it was very rich in plate and vestments. The interior of the church presented a very different appearance to that which it does at present. At the point where the chancel is divided from the body of the church, there was, near the roof, a gallery in which were placed a Crucifix, and on either side figures of the Blessed Virgin and St. John. The Crucifix was called the rood, and the gallery on which it stood the rood-loft. The ancient staircase leading to this gallery is now to be seen at the east end of the present aisle. In the rood-loft there were altars, as is shown by entries in the Church-wardens' Book, at which masses were said, and in it *"before the rood"* a light constantly burned. This gallery was removed at the Reformation, and in the "Inventory" mention is made

10   See Appendix, p.93. This inventory is to be found at the beginning of a valuable volume—the original record of the accounts of the church-wardens of Stanford from the year 1553.

of the Church possessing *"a bybull, 2 bokes of Comon Prayer, a Salter all in English."* These entries mark a change for which we cannot be too thankful, whereas the service was before in Latin, a tongue not understood by the people, henceforward all were enabled to worship God in their own language. In the place of a mutilated mass, men were now permitted to communicate after the practice of Apostolic times. Again, this "Inventory" records the vessels which were brought again to light, to be used according to the old fashion, in Mary's reign, and of certain costly vestments worked by the hands of Dame Dorothy Phetyplayse Voy, one who clung to those ceremonies to which she had been accustomed.

One of the corruptions which had grown up in the Church, and which made reformation so necessary, was the strange mixture of religious ceremony and worldly amusement. This is seen by the manner in which fairs were held. They were often opened in the immediate vicinity of the church, sometimes in the churchyard. Inscriptions were raised calling upon men to deal honestly with each other, not to steal, not to cheat, not to go beyond or defraud a brother in any matter. Wandering friars often preached on these occasions to the people, and the church doors were left open inviting men to enter and worship. Many abuses, however, grew up in connexion with these fairs, and in Henry III's reign the Papal legate reminded Englishmen that churches were built for purposes of prayer, and decreed that no market should be held in churches. Again, in Edward I's reign, an Act of Parliament was passed forbidding fairs and markets being held in churchyards. In the old Stanford Churchwardens' Book we meet with entries of money *"received for the gaymes of the May ale."* This was sometimes called Whitsun ale. It was a parochial feast said to be derived from the love feasts of the early Christians, and it was so called from the Churchwardens' buying and laying in from presents a large quantity of malt which they brewed into beer, and sold out in the church or elsewhere. The profits, as well as those from sundry games (there being no poor rates), were given to the poor, for whom this was one mode of provision. The Churchwardens' Book also makes continual mention of the Church House. There was one of these in every parish, to which belonged spits, crocks, and other utensils for dressing provisions. Here the people met, the young people engaging in dancing, bowling, shooting at butts, &c., the elder sitting by. A tree was erected by the church door, where a banner was placed, and maidens stood gathering contributions. An arbour also, called Robin Hood's bower, was put up in the church-yard. These meetings often led, as might be supposed, to great desecration of the church and churchyard, and a canon made in the reign of James I enacts that "the Churchwardens, or Questmen and their assistants, are to suffer no plays, feasts, banquets, suppers, church ales, drinkings, temporal courts or lete, lay juries, musters, or other profane usage to be kept in the church, chapel, or churchyard."

Again, the Churchwardens' Book contains entries of *"money received for the font."* This was a collection made by two young women at Whitsuntide from house to house, part of the proceeds of which was spent in buying the figure of a dove, which was suspended from the roof of the Church in order to represent the Holy Spirit, and the remainder of the money collected was given to the poor.

Another custom alluded to in this same book is the ringing of bells on the eve of All Saints' Day. We find entries as follows: *"Received from the maydes at All Hallowtide towards the belles."* This refers to the custom of certain young women walking about the parish dressed in black, ringing a dismal tolling bell, and calling upon all persons to remember the souls in purgatory, and to give them the aid of their prayers. Another entry in the book is as follows: *"For watching the Sepulchre."* This alludes to the practice of placing the crucifix wrapped in linen in a recess formed on the north side of the altar on Easter Eve, to represent our Lord's burial. There it was watched by certain appointed persons till early on Easter morning. Then the crucifix was uncovered with certain ceremonies, the priests and deacons asking questions of one another, acting over, as in a play, the Gospel account of the Resurrection. For instance, several would come stealing towards the tomb, as if looking for something; then one at the sepulchre would begin singing in a soft voice, "Whom seek ye?" to which would be replied, "Jesus of Nazareth." To this the other would answer, "He is not here; He is risen." Then they replied, "Alleluia, the Lord is risen!" The other then, as if calling them back, sang, "Come, and see the place," and then rising would raise the cloth, and show them the place without the crucifix, and the linen clothes in which it was wrapped[11].

---

11 For account of this and other ancient customs see Fosbroke's Antiquities.

Other entries in the Churchwardens' Book are interesting. Thus we have sums of money *"payd for Smoake farthings."* This was a yearly rent paid by the inhabitants of a diocese at Whitsuntide when they made the customary procession to the cathedral or mother church, which, in the case of Stanford, was that of Salisbury. A farthing was collected from every house as a composition for the customary dues. Again there are entries such as *"a booke of Collects to pray for Pope Julius;" "Paid for the Paschal taper;" "Payd for the Rode lyghte, the holy oil and Chrism, for frankincense, for mending the censers;"* and a yearly sum of four shillings paid *"to the Dogwhipper."* Respecting this office of dogwhipper, it is stated in Lyson's Environs of London that he anciently wore a vizard and a cap. His duty, it is evident, was to prevent dogs, of which in the absence of a dog tax there must have been many, straying into the church. He, as also the parish clerk, is a very ancient officer of the Church. The late dogwhipper at Stanford, who still lives, was John Plummer, a pensioned sergeant of dragoons. After serving with distinction in the Peninsular war, his latter days have been spent in guarding the church from the incursions of the Stanford boys. His white head and tall person, his scrupulously clean and neat Sunday apparel and white doe-skin gloves, will long be remembered in this village.

Parish clerks were anciently really poor clerks or clergymen. From the time of Henry III parish clerks formed a guild or fraternity, and were celebrated for their skill in church music, an accomplishment in which they are still required by the canon to be learned, if it may be. Their ancient duty at church was to assist the priest at the altar, sing with him, and read the epistle. In some places they read the lessons. Upon working days they attended the schools[12].

---

12 Since this lecture was commenced our Parish Clerk, Joseph King, after many years of faithful service, has been taken from us.

In the porch or south door of churches parishioners used to meet to settle law disputes, pay rents, &c., and over them was often a room used as a school or as a repository for books. One of these may be seen over the porch in Uffington Church, in which there is an original fire-place and chimney. Another, now destroyed, might have been seen some years ago at Denchworth. Over the porch there was a room erected in 1693, containing about one hundred and twenty volumes of books, principally on divinity, in folio and quarto. These books were attached by long chains to their cases, and were intended as a theological library for the successive vicars of Denchworth. The porch has been removed, but the volumes still remain, many of them with their chains in the custody of the present vicar. Amongst the books is a copy of Cranmer's Bible, the works of St. Thomas Aquinas, the works of Barrow, &c. The room was built by Mr. Geering, and the books were the gift of Mr. Geering, Mr. Ralph Kedden, vicar of Denchworth, and Mr. Edward Brewster, stationer, of London. Mr. Geering was lord of the manor of Denchworth, and a member of the Honourable Society of Gray's Inn.

The old parish church of Stanford was restored about ten years ago through the exertions of the present Vicar, under the direction of Mr. Street. Considerable judgment has been shown in retaining all its really ancient features, whilst all that was unseemly has been swept away. It is to be regretted that such like restoration did not earlier take place in many of the churches of this neighbourhood. It must be a subject of regret that so many memorials of the past have been suffered to perish, such for instance as the ancient glass which formerly adorned many of them. Some of the most interesting churches in the Vale are those of Childrey, Hanney, and Charney, which, unless a timely restoration is effected, must suffer greatly in consequence. It is, however, a matter of congratulation that the greater number of churches in this neighbourhood have been carefully renovated. It is now very rare, though still sometimes a church is to be met with, like that described by Bishop Home in 1787. "In a certain village," he writes, "within sight of the church, there stood a gentleman's seat, which was laid out with all the elegance that could be bestowed upon the house and grounds. The churchyard joined to the park. Having surveyed every thing, it being Sunday, I went into the church, to which one miserable bell, much like a small porridge-pot, called half a dozen people, which number comprehended the congregation. The churchyard itself was low and wet; a broken gate the entrance; a few small wooden tombs and an old yew tree the only ornaments. The inside of the church answered the outside; the walls green with damp; a few broken benches, with pieces of mats, dirty, and very ragged; the stairs to the pulpit half worn away; the communion table stood upon three legs; the rails worm-eaten, and half gone. Who can expect," he asks," that the young and gay will prefer this scene to the pleasures of the world? It is not in general to be expected. Would but the rich and great in every village who lavish sums of money on their own persons, furniture, houses, grounds, &c., would they but bestow a little of it towards making the house of God, if not equal with their own habitations, at least decent and cheerful, very great indeed would be the effect on multitudes. We naturally call to mind the uneasiness felt and expressed by the royal prophet on considering the magnificence of his own house, and the little or no care taken of the Ark of God[13].

Stanford Church[14] still consists of its original Nave, Chancel, and Aisle, and it has a roof of dark oak. The chan-

---

13 Bp. Horne, Olia Polrida.
14 For the sketch of Stanford Church in the frontispiece, I am indebted to Miss Wordsworth.

cel is paved with Hinton's tiles, and is fitted with handsome oak stalls. Behind the altar is a reredos in coloured tiles, on which are embossed ears of corn, alternately with bunches of grapes. Over it is the text, "Come unto Me, ye that labour and are heavy laden, and I will give you rest." There is a large east window, in the lights of which are depicted, in stained glass, different events in our Lord's public ministry. At the top some ancient glass still remains, representing the living creatures and the wheels in Ezekiel's vision.

Three windows on the south side of the chancel contain the arms of the De Clares and the royal arms, together with some modern glass. At the bottom are placed the versicles from the Te Deum, "To Thee Cherubin and Seraphin continually do cry, Holy, holy, holy. Lord God of Sabaoth: The Father of an infinite Majesty; Thine honourable, true, and only Son; Also the Holy Ghost the Comforter." There is an aperture or *hagioscope* in the north chancel wall, through which the altar may be seen from the aisle. On the north of the altar there is an ancient awning, and on the south a piscina, and over it a canopied tabernacle.

The nave and aisle are fitted with open seats, and at the west end of the nave is the tower, in which is placed a wooden font lined with lead. In the tower there is a small pointed window, filled with stained glass, representing our Lord as the Good Shepherd bearing a child in His arms. A beautiful effect is produced by the rays of the setting sun falling upon the window, which reflect its subject perfectly on the wall. At the west end of the aisle is a window filled with stained glass in three compartments, representing the Annunciation, the Message to the Shepherds, and the Adoration of the Magi. This, also, when lighted by the setting sun, is very beautiful, the angels appearing as if lifting up their wings in an attitude of adoration. The ancient custom still lingers in Stanford Church of the men and women sitting on different sides, and I have seen an aged woman curtsey at the Gloria.

The communion plate in use at Stanford has been used for many years. The cup, which is furnished with a cover, bears the date 1585. The paten and flagon are both interesting memorials of individual piety. The paten was dedicated by John and Elizabeth Hutton, December 8th, 1711, plainly as a thank-offering for past mercies, for on it is engraven, "I will pay Thee my vows which I promised with my lips, and spake with my mouth when I was in trouble." This Mr. Hutton became about that time vicar of Stanford. The Flagon was dedicated in the following terms: "This Flagon is dedicated to the use of the altar in the Parish Church of Stanford in the Vale for ever, by Joseph Cox, Esq., and Catherine Sophia his wife, as an humble testimony of their unfeigned thanks to Almighty God for the recovery of their three children, Thomas, Sophia, and Charlotte, from the Small Pox, by inoculation 1752."

Since this lecture was commenced a considerable fund has been raised by public subscription, and a small church-rate, for the repair of the church path, and the church clock. The church path has been neatly paved with stone, and the clock re-faced, cleaned, and restored. A public thoroughfare through a churchyard is not perhaps in itself very desirable, and probably in former times no such right of way existed. Still such a thoroughfare is not without advantages.

Anciently, we know the approach to the imperial City of Rome was by a street of tombs. The praetors and proconsuls, hastening to their provinces along the Appian Way, passed for miles through a road crowded on either side with lofty tombs, and votive edifices to the dead. By these they were continually reminded of the passing nature of human greatness; and how much more should Christians be reminded of death and resurrection, by passing by the graves of the departed. For how different is the teaching of our humble graves from the lofty tombs of the departed heathen. The tombs along the Roman highways contained the ashes of the great, and sometimes of their faithful and favoured freedmen; but what became of the mass of the vulgar dead, the poor, the slaves? They were cast into vast pits, dug in different parts of the outskirts of the city, the largest and most famous on the Esquiline Hill. There they were fed upon by foul birds of prey. When we pass through our churchyard we are reminded, not of the rich only, but specially of the poor who have a common hope of the resurrection of the body. Because we so believe—even that the grave will one day give up her dead—we treat the body as a holy thing, and treasure up not only the ashes of the rich, as the heathen did in sepulchral urns, but the bodies of the poor, each in his own peaceful resting-place.

Many superstitions grew up in mediaeval times in con-nexion with churchyards. We hear of persons being afraid of going through them at night, an apprehension derived from the heathen belief that departed spirits came out of the tombs, and wandered about the place where the body lay. Another superstition, supposed to be derived from the Druids, is that the ghost of the person last buried wanders round the church-yard till another is interred. Such notions are entirely unwor-thy of Christian people, who need only fear the workings of an evil conscience. The oldest tombstones in our churchyard are prismatic in form, of which there are several. One, stone coffin-shaped, on which is rudely carved a cross, is connected with a foolish tale of a gipsy and a frying pan. It is, probably, one of the most ancient in the churchyard.

Some of the tombstones in Stanford churchyard are beau-tifully carved. They are said to be the workmanship of a family of the name of Strong, who for many years were masons at Stanford, and who were famous in the country round. It is to be regretted that such skill as theirs was not more universally in request, for many of the grave-stones are of a very heavy and unworkmanlike appearance. Remembering how much people are affected by outward things, by objects of beauty, it would seem that reverence and affection towards the departed should make us anxious to perpetuate their memories by tasteful and beautiful memorials. There can be no religion in ugliness, and it can only serve to discourage a visit to the spot where our friends lie interred.

Former generations were at greater pains to erect suitable memorials to the departed. For instance, what can be more simple and more beautiful than the ancient brasses, of which such perfect specimens are to be seen in Hanney and Childrey churches. Or what, again, more simply affecting than the stone cross, the symbol of our salvation, and universally used by Christians in the purest times, before corruptions grew up in the Church of God. Formerly, crosses were placed at the entrances of all churches in order to inspire recollection and reverence amongst those about to enter. The remains of one, we all know, may still be seen at the entrance of Goosey Chapel. Crosses were formerly erected in many places, and wherever they were placed, they were intended to check a worldly spirit. They were erected in market-places, in order to inculcate upright intentions and fairness of dealing. They were placed by the side of highways to restrain robberies, and to call the thoughts of the passenger to a sense of religion. The cross certainly seems a suitable symbol to mark that the departed looked to our Saviour's death upon the Cross, as his comfort in the hour of death.

Greater care, too, is certainly desirable in the selection of appropriate epitaphs on tombstones. Some are shocking exhibitions of bad taste and a low state of religious feeling. For instance, I have read one as follows: "Here lieth the lord of this manor, who was esteemed a fine gentleman by all who knew him." Here there is no expression of penitence or hope, but only a miserable attempt at flattery. Surely all laudatory epitaphs are entirely out of place on the tombstones of the dead. The early Christians contented themselves by simply painting or engraving on the tombs of their departed friends different unpretending symbols, which marked on what the foundation of their hopes for the departed were based. Thus in the recently opened catacombs at Rome, in which the first Christians were buried, the symbol of the fish continually appears, the initial letters in Greek of the phrase "Jesus Christ, Son of God, Saviour" forming the Greek word which signifies a fish. On others, the fish appears, together with bread and wine, on a table. On others was found painted a priest or bishop in the act of consecrating the elements, with a kneeling figure of a female, doubtless representing the Church. On the tombs of martyrs were simply cut the name, followed by "martyr." In such ways the early Christians were contented to mark the resting-places of those who needed no laudatory epitaph, whose only hopes were based on the Saviour, on the promises made to penitent communicants that they should be raised up at the last day.

Churchyards had anciently *lych-gates* or sheds at their entrance, where the corpse rested for interment until the arrival of the priest, a building which may still be seen in many old churchyards, and the convenience of which ought to lead to its general re-adoption.

The reason why tombstones are often found crowded on the south side of the church is said to be because the prayers of the congregation were in those times desired for the dead, and the entrance to the church, through which the people passed, was the south door. This is not done now, because, as we do not know for certain the final state of any, we cannot benefit individual souls by our prayers, although we pray "that we, with all those that are departed in the true faith of Christ's holy Name, may have our perfect consummation and bliss, both in body and soul, in His eternal and everlasting glory."

Sometimes a ring for a catch is found on ancient church doors, as on that at Stanford. This, it is said, was that which was laid hold of by persons flying to the church for sanctuary.

The tower of Stanford church forms one of the most distinguished objects in the Vale. It is furnished with six bells, all of which were recast early in the eighteenth century. A bell is always rung on Sunday morning at half-past seven. Three strokes upon each bell are always given on the death of a man or boy, and two for women or girls. These three strokes, it is said, are given in honour of the Trinity, one less to a woman to mark her inferiority. The bell, now improperly rung *after* a person's death, was originally intended for the person dying, not actually dead, and was called the "passing bell." It was a signal to the priest to hasten to the bed-side of the dying person, and to the people to pray for a soul passing into eternity. And now, having dwelt at some length on the old church and its appendages, I would pass to the old Manor House which adjoins the churchyard wall.

The great Manor House of Stanford was that now occupied as a farmhouse by Mr. Charles Hunter. From the will of Sir T. Fettiplace of Childrey it appears that in the reign of Henry VIII the manor of Stanford was his property. Whether by marriage or purchase, it soon afterwards passed into the possession of Sir Francis Knollys, K.G., Vice Chamberlain, and Captain of the Guard to Queen Elizabeth. His name is connected with an interesting period of English history. He was sent by the Queen to escort the unfortunate Mary, Queen of Scots, when she sought hospitality in England. He appears to have been much captivated by her manners, and not to have much relished the office he had to perform, especially as he

Manor Farm

was suffered to bear much of the expense himself. He was the father of a numerous family. One of his sons was created the first Earl of Banbury. One of his daughters was still more famous, for she was the notorious Lettice Knollys, who married the first time Walter, Earl of Essex, and on his death, as was reported by poison, she married a second time the famous Robert Dudley, Earl of Leicester, the unworthy favourite of Queen Elizabeth, whose history is woven by Sir Walter Scott into the novel of "Kenilworth." At the time of this marriage, Dudley's first wife, Amy Robsart of Cumnor Hall, was dead. Sir Francis Knollys had other children more worthy of his name, in particular, Richard Knollys of Stanford, on whom alone of all his sons he is said to have bestowed his spiritual blessing.

Either by Sir Francis or his son, Stanford Manor House was built. Certainly Richard Knollys was the builder of the great barn which forms so picturesque an object as seen from Football Close. On it have been lately discovered certain letters, cut in the stone, which are the initials of himself and his children, his wife, and his wife's brother, John Higham, with the date, 1618.

The eldest son of Richard Knollys was Sir Robert Knollys, and his youngest Captain Francis Knollys, to whom there is a monument in the chancel, lately restored by Mr. Byam, who is descended from his daughter Dorothy.

Anciently this house must have been a place of considerable pretensions. Much has been pulled down in the memory of persons living, but even now it bears many traces of the wealth and position of its former owners. There is a fine old oaken staircase, the stairs and landing of which are beautifully inlaid in diamond oaken patterns. There is also remaining what was formerly a handsome stone hall, though now the principal entrance is closed up, and the hall included in a sitting-room. Some handsome bedchambers still remain; one is in panel, and another is still covered with ancient tapestry. The walls of the tapestried chamber show traces of beautiful painting. The tapestry itself is worked with figures of men, animals, and trees, and seems to represent Chinese or Indian scenery. Almost all the rooms have handsome stone chimney-pieces. There are many cupboards in this old house, and though one of them certainly contains very excellent grape and black currant wine, there was one possessing still more valuable contents in the year 1631, for Letitia Knollys left to her uncle by Will, "the contents of my closet in the house at Stanford." Many strange secrets, doubtless, could that old house unfold.

The good-natured face and bald head of its present tenant are very familiar to us, and we can only hope that the ancient lords of the manor possessed some of his good qualities. Oftentimes, from the present farm gates, there must have rolled a heavy coach and six. Oftentimes must Master Richard Knollys have come forth himself, dressed in a rich jacket, with a feathered hat, and boots with large projecting tops, a sword by his side, and a staff in his hand, for such was the costume of men in his rank of life in the beginning of the seventeenth century. Sometimes thus apparelled he may have graced the sports on the village green, and like another Sir Roger de Coverley have danced round the Maypole, for the Stanford folk did dance round the Maypole in those times, as appears from an entry in our Churchwardens' Book in 1622, *"Receyved for the topp of the May-pole."*

Another costume common amongst the middle classes a little earlier would probably long linger at Stanford, viz. a dress not unlike that worn by the boys of Christ's Hospital in London, a long gown, over a petticoat or doublet, with a flat cap. A furred gown also was worn, as is mentioned in Mr. Fawconer's will, a representation of which is preserved in the livery gown of the City of London. Costumes were brighter in those days; other colours than black being worn, such as scarlet and blue. The ladies of this period invented a kind of doublet, with high wings and puffed sleeves. They also wore fardingales, that is, immense hooped petticoats. Other costumes were long bodices, with or without skirts or close-bodied gowns over them, with petticoats. They also wore ruffs and tippets. Some ladies indulged themselves in enormous head-dresses; others wore flat caps like the men, with feathers at the side.

The widow of Richard Knollys married a son or grandson of the famous Jack of Newbury. His maidens are described as arrayed while they spin:—

> *"In petticoats of stamel red,*
> *And milk-white kerchers on their head;*
> *Their smock sleeves like to winter snow.*
> *That on the western mountains flow,*
> *And each sleeve with a silken band*
> *Was fairly tied at the hand."*

The Manor House at Stanford was, as I have said, evidently a considerable place, but another still more important was the great house at Wadley. Wadley House lies about three miles from Stanford, within a small park which contains a few noble trees. An annual fair is held on Old Lady Day, by ancient charter, within the precincts of the park. The word "Wadley" is derived, it is supposed, from Wade, the name of one of the Saxon gods, the reputed father of "Weland the Smythe." He is connected in some way with water. Wadley once belonged to Stanley Abbey, in Wiltshire, but in the reign of Henry VI it passed into the hands of Oriel College, Oxford.

The house at Wadley, at the time of the Reformation, was inhabited by Sir Thomas Unton, and it continued to be the family residence of the Untons until the beginning of the seventeenth century. The family of the Untons connect this neighbourhood with much that is interesting in the history of the time. In the reign of Queen Mary one member of this family, viz. Sir Edward Unton, married Anne, Countess of Warwick, whose first marriage was one of the most memorable ever contracted by a subject in England. Lady Anne Seymour, by her first marriage Countess of Warwick, and afterwards the wife of Sir Edward Unton, was a daughter of the Protector, Duke of Somerset, and first cousin to the young king, Edward VI. Between her father and the Duke of Northumberland there was great rivalry, but in order to effect a truce between them this lady was given in marriage to the Earl of Warwick, the Duke of Northumberland's son. It was, in fact, a political marriage.

The rejoicings upon this marriage were soon turned into tears, for in the course of a few weeks fresh enmity sprang up between the families of her husband and her father, and a short time afterwards her father was beheaded on Tower Hill. After two years her father-in-law was likewise executed, and his four sons, including the Earl of Warwick, imprisoned. After his father's execution, her husband in his turn was tried and condemned. Whoever visits the Tower of London will be shown, in a room in the Beauchamp Tower, a very curious carving on the right hand of the fire-place, cut by the Earl of Warwick when in prison. It represents a chained bear and lion supporting between them a ragged staff, some lines in verse being carved beneath. This nobleman was delivered out of prison, but died ten days afterwards. His widowed countess then married, in Hatford church, Sir Edward Unton, the record of which marriage is to be found in the Hatford register. This marriage connected the family of Unton with many of the noblest families in the land, and even with royalty itself.

His mansion indeed seems to have been of a princely character. It may give some idea of it if I mention some of the rooms. There was a chapel, a hall, a great chamber, a parlour, a long gallery, a study, a drawing chamber. There was the gentlewoman's chamber, my lady's chamber, the chapel chamber, the new chamber, the little chamber next the new chamber, the maiden's chamber, the wainscot chamber, and many more.

There was a kitchen, a buttery, a pastry-house, a dry larder, a wet larder, a store-house, a brew-house, a bake-house, an armoury-house, and porter's lodge. It was elaborately furnished; for instance, in the parlour there was a long table and a frame, one table and a square frame, one livery cupboard, three green carpets, two green cloth chairs, one black wrought velvet chair, laid with silver and gold lace, three long cushions of red satin, laid with gold lace, thirteen green cloth stools, six leather stools, one cushion of Turkey work. In my lady's chamber there were hangings of dornex, a folding bedstead covered with green cloth and laid with watchet lace, surmounted with eight plumes of feathers, two chairs, and two little green stools. Such are specimens of the manner in which great houses were furnished in the reign of Elizabeth. Such was the great house at Wadley in 1573.

Then this neighbourhood was honoured by a visit from the Virgin Queen, Queen Elizabeth, of glorious memory. She came to Wadley in July, 1571, and no doubt on that occasion there were great rejoicings. Then, probably, all the neighbouring gentry would hasten to do her honour. The Knollys, of Stanford; the Yateses of Buckland; the Puseys, of Pusey; the Fettiplaces of Childrey; the Hydes, of Denchworth; the Ayshcombes, of Lyford; the Packers of Shellingford, would come, mounted and attended, to many a hunting and hawking party, to many a masque and pageant, in order to do honour to the Queen. In the train of Sir Francis Knollys, or his son, might very well have been found a Giles Gosling and a Mike Lambourne, for Goslings and Lambournes and Yarneys are names that have flourished in Stanford for centuries. Sir Walter Scott, in his novel of "Kenilworth," by the names which he introduces, shows his acquaintance with this part of Berkshire, and indeed he is said to have often been a guest at the house of the Rev. Dr. Hughes, Vicar of Uffington. Cumnor Hurst may be seen from the top of Stanford Church.

One amusement, we have reason to think, was provided for the Queen when she came to Wadley, viz. masquerading, for there was a picture existing not long ago representing a masque at the marriage of one of the Untons. The following description of it was given in the Gentleman's Magazine for 1786:—"Here we see the masquers march in order round the table. The chief masquer is Diana, who is preceded by Mercury. Before him stand two Cupids, the one black, the other white." On the occasion of this visit Sir Edward Unton presented the Queen with a handsome jewel, which is thus described in an official document: "First one juell of golde, garnished with dyamondes and rubyes and fyve perles, pendente, one bigger than the rest." Sir Edward had before given her Majesty "one fayre flower golde enamelled, and garnished with a chrysolite and an emeralde, and fully furnished with rubyes, dyamondes, and perles, and three perles pendante." Again, in 1580, he gave her "A payre of bracelets of golde containing sixteen pieces, in every one of them a small ruby garnished with a small perle."

Another distinguished member of this family was Sir Henry Unton, the friend and kinsman of Sir Philip Sidney. He was present with him at the siege of Zutphen, and was there knighted for his bravery. At the public funeral of Sidney, Sir Henry Unton walked among the twelve knights of his kinsmen and friends. He was sent by Queen Elizabeth as ambassador to France, and when some slighting word was spoken by the young Duke Henri de Guise against the honour of his queen, Sir Henry sent him this famous challenge: "Forasmuch as in the lodging of the Lord Dumayne, and in public elsewhere, impudently and indiscreetly and over boldly you spoke badly of my sovereign, whose sacred person I in this country represent: to maintain both by word and weapon her honour which was never called in question amongst people of honesty and virtue. I say you have most wickedly lied in speaking so badly of my sovereign; and you will do nothing but lie wherever you shall dare to tax her honour. Moreover, that her sacred person, being one of the most complete, accomplished, and virtuous princesses in the world ought not to be ill-spoken of by the malicious tongue of such a perfidious traitor to her law and country as you are; and hereupon I do defy and challenge your person to mine; with such manner of arms as you shall like or choose, be it on horseback or on foot. Nor would I have you think that there is any inequality of person between us; I being issued of as great a race and noble house, in all respects, as yourself. So assigning me an indifferent place, I will there maintain my words, and the lie which I have given, and which you should not endure, if you have any courage at all in you. If you consent not to meet me hereupon, I will hold you, and cause you to be held, for the arrantest coward, and most slanderous slave, that exists in France. I expect your answer," &c.

The late Mr. Hearn, rector of Hatford, the friend and correspondent of Dr. Arnold, a great lover of historical antiquities, and in whose church Sir Edward Unton was married to the Countess of Warwick, used to please himself by imagining that Sir Henry Unton and Sir Philip Sidney may both have played at bowls in his garden. We, too, may well imagine that Queen Elizabeth could not have left Wadley without paying a visit to Stanford, and accepting some jewel from that good knight Sir Francis Knollys, or his son, Master Richard Knollys. In the parish church of Faringdon there are several monuments of Sir Alexander, Sir Edward, Sir Thomas, and Sir Henry Unton. During this reign, the bishop of the diocese[15] was John Jewel, the famous author of "The Apology;" to him our churchwardens must have made their presentments, as the Churchwardens' Book tells us. He and Sir Francis Knollys were friends and companions in exile during Mary's reign.

He was also the friend and patron of another famous man, who profited by the good offices of Sir Francis Knollys, for when the judicious Hooker, the author of "The Ecclesiastical Polity," was turned out from his fellowship at Corpus Christi College, Oxford, it was to Sir Francis Knollys application was made for his restoration[16]. Some may take pleasure in remembering Hooker's visit to Jewel, when at the Bishop's parting with him he "gave him good counsel and his benediction, but forgot to give him money, which, when the Bishop had con-

---

15   Until a comparatively recent date this part of Berkshire was in the diocese of Salisbury.
16   Walton's Life of Hooker. Wordsworth's Eccl. Biog.

sidered, he sent a servant in all haste to call Richard back to him. And at Richard's return, the Bishop said to him, 'Richard, I sent for you back to lend you a horse, which hath carried me many a mile, and I thank God with much ease,' and presently delivered into his hand a walking-staff, with which he professed he had travelled through many parts of Germany. And he said, 'Richard, I do not give, but lend you my horse; be sure you be honest, and bring my horse back to me at your return this way to Oxford. And I do now give you ten groats to bear your charges to Exeter; and here is ten groats more which I charge you to deliver to your mother, and tell her I send a Bishop's benediction with it, and beg the continuance of her prayers for me. And if you bring my horse back to me I will give you ten groats more to carry you on foot to the college, and so God bless you, good Richard.'" This is the incident which gave rise to one of the ecclesiastical sonnets of the late Poet Laureate.

> "*Methinks that I could trip o'er heaviest soil,*
> *Light as a buoyant bark from wave to wave,*
> *Were mine the trusty staff that Jewel gave*
> *To youthful Hooker; in familiar style*
> *The gift exalting, and with playful smile.*
> *For thus equipp'd, and bearing on his head,*
> *The donor's farewell blessing, can he dread*
> *Tempest, or length of way, or weight of toil?*
> *More sweet than odours caught by him who sails*
> *Near spicy shores of Araby the blest.*
> *A thousand times more exquisitely sweet,*
> *The freight of holy feeling which we meet,*
> *In thoughtful moments, wafted by the gales,*
> *From fields where good men walk,*
> *or bowers wherein they rest."*

Those silver coins called groats, some of which Jewel gave to Hooker, must have been familiar enough to the people of Stanford, for one of them was shown to me the other day which was found in the thatch of an old barn. Hooker's friend, Sir Francis Knollys, the Lord of Stanford Manor, was buried at Rotherfield Greys, near Henley-on-Thames, in Oxfordshire, where there is a magnificent monument to him and his wife. Their effigies lie under a canopy supported by pillars of black marble. Seven sons and six daughters, with the Countess of Banbury, their daughter-in-law, are kneeling beneath, while the Countess is repeated, with her husband, William, Earl of Banbury, in the upper part, kneeling before a desk.

In the following reign Wadley was again honoured by a royal visit, for King James I came to Wadley in 1603, and stayed there two nights. Stanford Manor House was then the home of one of the officers of the royal household, for together with the Knollys there lived a relative, Mr. John Higham, who, as we learn from a black marble slab in the chancel, was Marshal of the Hall to King James and King Charles. Besides the old Manor House at Stanford, there are traces, at what is now called the Park Farm, of a considerable mansion, the history of which is entirely forgotten. There is a spot near it plainly laid out originally as a pleasure ground, called "the Island," surrounded by water, formerly, perhaps, constructed for a fishpond. Between the Park Farm and Stanford there are several enclosures laid in grass still known by the name of Meads. There is Whitfield's Mead, the Parson's Mead, Little Gentleman's Mead, Great Gentleman's Mead, &c. Not far from these are certain enclosures known as the Wick Closes, and a local tradition speaks of there having been buildings adjoining, a fact which seems to be pointed out by the name, *wick*, as has been said before, meaning a dwelling-place. In some of these the most beautiful wild flowers may be gathered in the early

Stanford Park Farm

spring, and here also may be found the gayest and the rarest butterflies. These Closes border on our little river Ock, in which large numbers of cray-fish are caught. Little boys may be seen in the summer lifting up the stones in the stream in search of these, and depositing them in their trowser pockets in lieu of a basket! At the extremity of Stanford parish, which runs up almost to Faringdon Clump, stands Stanford Place, a house erected not many years ago by George Butler, Esq., a direct descendant of Bishop Butler. The property is now sold, but only a few months back the dining-room at Stanford Place contained a half-length portrait of this famous prelate, the author of the "Analogy of Revealed Religion." His birthplace was the town of Wantage.

Besides the Manor House already mentioned, portions of others of great interest still exist in the neighbourhood. Thus at Charney there are the remains of what must have been the residence of an officer of the Monastery at Abingdon; in it may still be seen the ancient Oratory, with its oriel window and piscina. This is now used as a loft. The house adjoins the church, and has for many years been the principal house in the village. At Lyford we find in a farmhouse a part of the old residence of the Ayshcombes, and at Shellingford, in some out-buildings, a large walled garden and some plantations of yew surrounding a fish-pond, we see the remains of the old Manor House of the Packers, called Shellingford Castle. This house remained for a long time uninhabited, and its chimney-pieces were used as quarries to supply the Stanford boys with marbles! Another fine old Manor House is that of Hatford, formerly the residence of the Tyrrells. It contains a beautiful staircase, and some handsome rooms. Its situation is very picturesque, several fine trees on a small lawn compose a very pretty foreground. Not far from Hatford House, winding along the edge of a little brook—a favourite resort of the king-fisher, and where forget-me-nots may be gathered in profusion—is a footpath leading to the park at Wadley.

Shellingford Castle

Certain entries in our old Churchwardens' Book relate to the laws against Roman Catholics. Thus we read, *"For a booke of Articles against Recusants."* This reminds us of that succession of dark plots formed by Roman Catholics against the life of Queen Elizabeth, and the severe measures taken in consequence against them. The Five Mile Act forbade them to go more than five miles from their dwellings without a licence from two Justices of the Peace or with the assent in writing of the Lord-Lieutenant or Bishop. Four miles from Stanford is Buckland House, the seat of the Throckmortons, who came into the possession of this estate by marriage with the last female heir of the Yates. Here is preserved a curious relic, viz. a shift of Mary, Queen of Scots. The Throckmortons have been for some generations Roman Catholics, and there is a beautiful chapel in the Park, designed by Pugin. One of the priests attached to this chapel purchased some years ago of one of the farmers, an ancient service-book used in Stanford Church before the Reformation. Not far from Buckland is Carswell House, the ancient seat of the Southbys. This family espoused the Puritan cause during the time of the troubles in England, and there may yet be seen in the pleasant drawing-room of the mansion certain grim portraits of many who bore their part in the events of those times.

During the reign of King James, Stanford was the residence of one of the Royal household, for a slab in the chancel informs us "Mr John Higham was Marshal of the Hall to King James and King Charles." This Mr. Higham lived at the Manor House, and was the brother-in-law of Richard Knollys. He must have been the witness to the commencement of that terrible storm which soon broke upon England. Upon King Charles I seems to have fallen the punishment due to the acts of sacrilege perpetrated in former reigns. Insufficient pastoral care gave rise, doubtless, to that party to which the name of Puritan has been given. Some of those to whom this name was applied were doubtless men of irreproachable lives, but often greatly wanting in sound judgment and Christian charity towards others. They scrupled at clergymen wearing the surplice, and thought it wrong to kneel at the Holy Communion. But the clamour which they raised against the Church only served to aid the cause of Rome, for the Church of England in her doctrine and sober ritual, and especially in the ample provision which she makes for the reading of Holy Scripture, is the strongest barrier against Popery. The spread of licentiousness so much deplored by all good men was really owing to the need of better provision for the clergy. Their state was a most impoverished one, and in consequence many held several benefices, and others were so ignorant as to be unfit to teach.

This is set forth in a speech made by Sir Benjamin Rudyer in Parliament at the beginning of this reign. "I have observed," he said, "that we are always very eager and fierce against papistry, against scandalous ministers, and against things which are not within our power. I do not speak this, that I do mislike the destroying and pulling down that which is ill; but then let us be as earnest to plant and build up that which is good in the room of it, for why should we be desolate? The best and nearest way to dispel darkness, and the deeds thereof, is to let in light. We say that day breaks, but no man ever heard the voice of it. God comes in the still voice; let us quickly mend our candlesticks, and we cannot want light. I am afraid this backwardness of ours will give our adversaries occasion to say that we choose our religion because it is cheaper of the two; that we would willingly serve God with somewhat that should cost us nought. Believe me, Mr. Pym," he said, addressing the Speaker, "he that thinks to save any thing by his religion but his soul, will be a terrible loser in the end. We sow sparingly; that is the reason we reap so sparingly and have no more fruit. Methinks, whosoever hates papistry should by the same rule hate covetousness, for that is idolatry too. I never like hot professions and cold actions. Such a heat is rather the heat of distemper and disease than of life and saving health. As for scandalous ministers, let them be punished, but let us deal with them as God has dealt with us. God, before He made man, He made the world, a handsome place for him to dwell in. So let us provide competent livings, and then punish in God's name; but till then, scandalous livings can but have scandalous ministers." He ends by asking, "Why should we dwell in houses of cedar, and suffer God to dwell in skins?[17]"

Some complaints were made by the Puritans without much show of reason. Thus William Prynne published a book in which he not only condemned without reserve masques and dancing, but also hunting, public festivals, keeping Christmas, bonfires, and May-poles. Upon church music he was most severe, for he calls it "a bleating of brute beasts." "Choristers," he writes, "bellow their tenor as if they were oxen, bark a counterpoint like a kennel of dogs, roar a treble as if they were bulls, and grunt out a bass like a parcel of hogs[18]." As regards this indiscriminate condemnation of amusement, it might have been considered that men have need of some recreation. A wiser man than William Prynne, viz. Bishop Latimer, wrote: "Men of England in times past, when they would exercise themselves (for we must needs have some recreation, our bodyes cannot endure without some exercise), they were wont to goe abroad in the fields of shooting. It is a goodly arte," he adds, "a wholesome kinde of exercise, and much commended in physicke.[19]"

---

17 Collier's Eccl. Hist., vol. viii.
18 Ibid.
19 Wentworth's Eccl. Biog., vol. ii.

But an entry in our old church book points to that event which was the immediate cause of the troubles in Charles's reign. It is an entry respecting ship money, *"Given to John Nash, being collector for the ship money, having had great loss by the State."* This was that tax imposed by the King which became so unpopular, doubtless through the zeal of political agitators. John Hampden disputed the King's right to impose the tax. The case was tried in the Exchequer Chamber, and Hampden was defeated, but this decision of the judges increased the irritation of the people. John Hampden was connected by marriage with the Pye family, then living at Faringdon House, for Sir Robert Pye married his sister.

And now began the opposition of the Parliament to the

King, and soon that struggle commenced which carried civil war into all the villages of the kingdom, and especially into those of Berkshire. The neighbourhood of this parish, and the country lying between Abingdon and Oxford, was again and again the battleground of the contending parties. A melancholy record of this time may be read in the Register of Burials at Stanford in 1643. There we read the names of "Richard Figler, a Cheshire man; Francis Minshull, Gent.; Henry Stanton, John Neabor, troopers in Sir Thomas Aston's regiment;" and also of "Alexandre, a Frenchman, trooper in Prince Charles his regiment."

Faringdon House, then the residence of the Pyes, was garrisoned for the King, although its owner took the side of the Parliament. The garrison was commanded by Sir Marmaduke Rawdon, whose monument may be seen in the nave of Faringdon Church. The house was attacked by Cromwell in the month of June, 1645, at three o'clock in the morning, with six hundred men from the garrison of Abingdon, when he suffered a repulse. Another attack was made the following year, when the rebels were commanded by Sir Robert Pye, the owner of the house. In this attack, it is said, the spire of Faringdon Church and the south transept were beaten down by cannon placed on Faringdon Clump. Faringdon House was one of the last places which held out for the King, for it was not surrendered until the month of June, 1646, when the governor gave it up to the Parliament pursuant to the articles for the surrender of Oxford. Shot is still picked up in the neighbourhood: a ball which must have been fired from a piece of ordnance is in my possession, found not far from Faringdon Clump. The hill called Faringdon Clump is the chief landmark in the Vale, and commands extensive views. The group of Scotch firs on the top is said to have been planted by Pye, the Poet Laureate in the reign of George III, an act which, as

Faringdon House

some one has remarked, was perhaps the most poetical of his whole life.

King Charles I, on his way from Oxford to Farnborough, slept a night at Childrey, on the 9th April, 1644. He was entertained at the Manor House, then in the occupation of Lady Fettiplace. The bedroom in which he slept might have been seen some ten years ago. It communicated by a private staircase with a postern gate. The old manor house is now destroyed, but parts of it are built into the farmhouse which occupies the site. A visit to Childrey Church will well repay the pains of any who take an interest in antiquarian research. Childrey, moreover, ought to be dear to any who revere the Church in England, for it once was the residence of a man of whom England may well be proud, the home of an English saint. It was here that Dr. Edward Pocock lived. He was rector of Childrey during the time of the troubles in England, and a more devout, learned, and gentle spirit never lived. Dr. Pocock, many know, was a most famous Oriental scholar, and was chosen by Archbishop Laud to fill the post of lecturer in Arabic in the University of Oxford, a lecture which the Archbishop himself founded.

His biographer tells us that the whole life of Dr. Pocock was one continued sermon, powerfully recommending to all who were acquainted with him the several duties of Christianity. Though deeply versed in languages he carefully avoided "the shows and ostentations of learning," so much so that when one of his Oxford friends travelling through Childrey inquired for his diversion of some of his parishioners who was their minister and how they liked him? he received for an answer; "Our parson is one Mr. Pocock, a plain, honest man; but, master, he is no Latiner."

During these unhappy times we are told that with great courage he preached against the sins of the day, warning those under his charge, not only against all profane and immoral practices, but also against those schisms and divisions which were then breaking in upon the Church. Dr. Pocock was cited to appear before the triers at Abingdon, that is, before certain commissioners appointed by Cromwell for the purpose of ejecting from their benefices "ignorant, scandalous, insufficient, and negligent ministers," a wide commission, inviting all who were discontented to invent accusations. Dr. Pocock was accused of using the Book of Common Prayer, of praying for the King, of railing at professors, of denying to some godly men the liberty of preaching in his pulpit, one of these being the author of a book called "Arrows against Babylon."

To these accusations Dr. Pocock made answer, but fresh complaints were fabricated, and at last he had to appear a second time before the triers, then sitting at Wantage, and had it not been for the testimony of his friends he would have been ejected from his benefice as an ignorant minister. But his friends, many of whom, such as Dr. Owen, belonged themselves to the Puritan party, represented that to do this would be strangely foolish and unjust, seeing that Dr. Pocock was celebrated through Europe for his learning. One feature in Dr. Pocock's work at Childrey was his custom of catechizing, a custom which seems long to have been continued in the neighbouring parishes, for old people in Stanford remember when it was practised instead of a sermon every Sunday afternoon. This primitive custom has now for many years been revived in our parish, in accordance with the Rubric in the Prayer Book.

Some idea of the great insecurity of the time of the civil war may be understood, when we remember that about three years ago, a number of silver coins of the reign of King Charles were discovered hidden in the thatch of an old building at Stanford, belonging to Mr. Henry Penstone. There is a tradition to the same effect about the old Manor House at Lyford. Near the house there stands an old pigeon-house where, it is said, the money and plate belonging to the Ayshcombes was secreted in the civil war; which place of concealment being discovered by some soldiers of the rebel army, they carried off valuables to the amount of a cartload.

During the time of the troubles, the old Churchwardens' Book, from which we have often quoted, exhibits a hiatus. There are no entries between 1643 and 1652. During this time the Common Prayer Book was not permitted to be used. It was not only interdicted in churches but even in private houses. As Lord Macaulay relates, "It was a crime in a child to read by the bedside of a sick parent one of those beautiful Collects which had soothed the griefs of forty generations of Christians." The keeping of Christmas was prohibited, and the Long Parliament gave orders in 1644 that Christmas Day should be strictly observed as a fast. Marriages were made, not before God's minister, according to the practice of Christ's Church from the earliest times, but before a Justice of the Peace. Evidence of this is contained in the Church registers. Thus we have entries of marriages, that is, legal contracts, made before Sir Robert Pye at Faringdon, and also before the Mayor of Abingdon, not celebrated by God's minister at God's altar, and without any sweet peal of Stanford bells, making known across the Vale that man and wife had become one in the sight of God.

Again, baptisms were not permitted to take place with sponsors. Thus we find Mr. Cox, a gentleman of this parish, delaying the baptism of his children until the time of the Restoration, when we have entries which show that they were all brought to church and baptized with sponsors according to the Book of Common Prayer. Mr. Cox, we may suppose, shared the feelings of the poet when he wrote:—

> *"Father! to God Himself we cannot give*
> *A holier name! then lightly do not bear*
> *Both names conjoined, but of thy spiritual care*
> *He duly mindful: .still more sensitive*
> *Do thou, in truth a second mother, strive*
> *Against disheartening custom, that by thee*
> *Watched, and with love and pious industry*
> *Tended at need, the adopted plant may thrive*
> *For everlasting bloom. Benign and pure*
> *This ordinance, whether loss it would supply,*
> *Prevent omission, help deficiency,*
> *Or seek to make assurance doubly sure.*
> *Shame if the consecrated vow be found*
> *An idle form, the word an empty sound.[20]"*

---

20 Wordsworth's Eccl. Sonnets.

This Thomas Cox was no doubt the builder of the large old house, called Cox's at the present day, which stands at the entrance of Stanford village, and is now the property of Mrs. Avery Whitfield. The house was probably built at the time mentioned on an old sundial, on which is written the date 1690. It is a large house with a fore-court, built something like an old French chateau, the bedrooms opening out of a long gallery. There is a handsome stone hall which has been somewhat docked of its proportions to build another room. There are some handsome sitting rooms, panelled, full of delightful old cupboards. In one of the bedrooms there is ancient tapestry, in which the foliage represented is very beautifully worked.

The Coxes, it would appear, were of a very ancient family. In one of the wills of the Unton family, "my cousin Thomas Cox" occurs, and it is highly probable that the Coxes of Stanford were relations of the Untons. The name occurs as that of owners of property in the parish early in the seventeenth century. In the year 1738 John Cox of Stanford served the office of high sheriff. Some twenty years ago, a clergyman of the name of Cox, a fellow of Pembroke College, Oxford, purchased from the then owner an old portrait of the last owner, a certain General Cox, whom he stated to be his grandfather. This gentleman asserted that his family had been allied to Royalty, which certainly would have been the case had the Coxes been related to the Untons.

A further record of the civil war appears in an entry in the Churchwardens' Book of money paid *"For blotting out the King's armes, and for setting up the State's armes."* Before this was done, the King had been put to death. He was judged by a revolutionary tribunal and condemned to death, although he refused to plead before a court unknown to the law. King Charles behaved with great dignity in this trying hour. "No demagogue," writes Lord Macaulay, "ever produced such an impression on the public mind as the captive king, who, retaining in that extremity all his regal dignity, confronted death with dauntless courage, showing the high spirit of a gallant gentleman, the patience and meekness of a penitent Christian.[21]"

A further entry in the Churchwardens' Book brings us to the era of the Restoration. There is an entry on the 21st April, 1661, of money paid *"For the setting up the King's armes"* and other entries occur about the same time of money paid to the ringers. At this time, it would seem, as a thank-offering to God, the tower of the parish church, which is a very conspicuous object in the Vale, was raised to its present height, and the roof of the church was adorned with the present battlements. Beyond the period of the Restoration I feel unable to carry our parish history, and with some few observations I must bring it to a close.

It is remarkable what a change seems to have been effected in Christian names by the Rebellion. Whereas before children were christened with pretty simple names taken from the Gospel history, or from the early saints, such as Mary, Martha, Elizabeth, Anna, Margaret, Agnes, Bridget, Dorothy, Cicely, Katharine, Agatha, now nothing would content the Stanford people but Old Testament names—such as Susanna, Abigail, Deborah, Sarah, Rebekah, Rachel; whereas boys before were called John, James, Peter, Andrew, Stephen, Richard, Alfred, Christopher, Gregory, Augustine, now nothing would content their mothers but that they should be called Enos, Noah, Abraham, Moses, Abiah, Jeremiah, Amos. As to surnames, whilst those of the gentry have for the most part disappeared, we have preserved some amongst the yeomen and labourers for centuries. At the beginning of the seventeenth century, three gentlemen, described as of Stanford, were in the Commission

21　Macaulay's History of England.

of the Peace, viz., Francis Pigott, Esq., Richard Knollys, Esq., John Higham, Esq. All these names have passed away. Fuller complains that the gentry of Berkshire, sown thick in former, come up thin in latter ages.

Few families indeed have possessed estates in Berkshire for many generations. Among the oldest Stanford surnames are Whitehorn, Wiblin, Penstone, Collins, Spinage, Falconer, Pusey, Cowderoy, Cox, Wiltshire, Franklin, Lambourne, Gosling, Yarney. One opulent family has still a remote representative. Sir Walter Tyrrell held the manors of Hatford and Stanford at the commencement of the eighteenth century. He was high sheriff in 1723. His son is buried in Stanford churchyard, and a sum of money is lodged in the hands of trustees to be applied to the keeping up his tomb, the residue to go to the parochial school. A descendant of the Tyrrells married a Penstone, afterwards Mrs. Belcher, the mother of Mrs. Cowderoy, who possesses a silver seal engraven with the Tyrrell arms.

Another family formerly of position in this parish was that of Hatt. Captain Hatt is buried in Stanford churchyard. He fought at Culloden, and appears to have been high sheriff in 1782. A descendant of his, Miss Hatt, married a Whitfield. Mr. John Whitfield, of Sheepcroft Hill, has in his possession two swords, once the property of Captain Hatt; and not many years ago an old man in the village possessed a hat worn by him on the field of Culloden. Another relic of this gentleman is a small teapot of antique shape, in the possession of Mrs. Avery Whitfield. Many families now in the rank of labourers were once in the position of yeomen, as the Spinages, the Falconers, the Franklins, the Strattons.

Stanford—there is every reason to think—was very much cut off from the rest of the world before the formation of the Great Western Railway. For fifty or sixty years before that event, it seems to have had no resident gentry. General Cox was probably the last proprietor who resided in the village. This isolation has been the means of preserving traces of ancient manners and customs, but these are fast wearing out. The old games are still remembered, but there has been no backsword play at Stanford for more than forty years. Old people still tell of the stages which were erected at the time of Stanford feast, to give men the opportunity of breaking one another's heads. It was customary for Stanford men to pit themselves at backsword play and wrestling against the inhabitants of the Hanneys, i.e. the villages of East and West Hanney, near Wantage. Football was formerly much in vogue, as indeed may be inferred from the meadow near the church called Football Close; but not only in that field, but in others still pointed out, the game was played. The game of fives was also practised, and a wall opposite the churchyard gate is shown as the spot where many contests took place. Another game remembered is that of hockey, which still lingers amongst the Stanford boys. Other sports less manly in character were much prac-tised, such as cock fighting; and pugilistic encounters between the Stanford and Charney men were very common. Playing at marbles and chuck-farthing it is said was the usual Sunday amusement of all classes, who thus whiled away the time till the bells ceased to chime for church, some not even stopping then.

On the whole there does not seem much reason to regret the changes which have taken place. No doubt a revival of football or hockey would promote health and good fellow-ship, in the same way as is done by cricket; but I venture to think that cockfighting, boxing, Sunday marbles, and chuck-farthing are treated as they deserve in being neglected. Nay, although backsword play has found an eloquent advocate, it too, perhaps, is better honoured in the breach than in the observance. Games have probably fallen into disuse through

the gentry making London their residence so much more than formerly, as well as through the operation of other causes. But still there is no lack of thew and sinew in the Vale. Cricket is at present at low ebb, it is true, in Stanford, but it seems reviving; and some among the Stanford boys give promise of future excellence.

There is much sliding and some skating practised by both sexes in the winter, and few can be found to compete with the Vicar of Stanford in the latter exercise. There is hardly a young farmer who does not hunt for at least a few days in the season. The other day the Old Berkshire killed their fox at Stanford, and a very singular death it was. The whole field of scarlet-

coated horsemen, with the dogs, were completely at fault, when the fox was discovered on a cottage roof. Being driven from his retreat, Reynard made his way down the chimney, astonishing the owner, Betty Andrews, by appearing before her in a sooty dress. The love of field sports has not departed, nor is there any want of manly vigour. It was only a few days ago that the son of the good Rector of Shellingford taught the Londoners what those bred in the Vale can do, by carrying off the prize of a golden goblet at the athletic sports of Westminster School. No doubt it is to be desired that the labouring classes might have a few national holidays, in which some of the ancient games might take root again; but this will never be the case, I fear, until those old red-letter days, the saints' days of the English Church, the non-observance of which Charles Lamb regretted, are again revived.

The abandonment of a peculiar costume in the Vale is a real subject for regret. The sameness and ugliness of black hats, black coats, and trousers all must allow. It is this which makes a modern English crowd so sad and sombre as compared with a continental one. But black coats and Manchester shawls are a bad exchange for the clean white smock of the men, and the red cloaks of the women, once almost universal in the Vale. The white smock is still retained during the week by the older Stanford farmers, but a red cloak is seldom to be seen. Formerly red cloaks were heirlooms, and old Widow Falconer has one in her possession which has served four generations. The elder generation of farmers' wives make sad complaints against the dress of the present day—the long sleeves and long dresses, and flimsy materials of which it is composed. Formerly a material made of linen and woollen was that commonly worn, and a kind of short bedgown and short skirt, with a large serviceable check apron, a costume still retained in the North of England, was the prevailing fashion.

What was customary in the last generation in the way of female costume may be gathered from Mrs. Trimmer's tale of the "Two Farmers." Mrs. Simpkins, on her marriage, was presented with her wedding dress, of which the following is a description. She had a neat Quaker-colour silk and stuff, a white stuff petticoat, quilted in small diamonds. The gown was made with robings, and laced before with white satin ribbon, and it had no train. She, it should be explained, was not a topping farmer's wife, and laid no claim to gentility. Therefore, her cap was made of fine lawn, with a pretty edging and a snug crimped wire border, trimmed with white ribbon, pinned on in very exact puffs, and a bow before and behind. It had also a lappet trimmed with the same edging, which went behind the ribbon and came a little below the ears, but no ribbon streamers. She had also a clear double muslin handkerchief, with a narrow worked border, a pair of robings to match it, and a clear lawn apron. In addition, she was presented with a neat black cloak and bonnet, a pair of silver buckles, and a pair of white silk mittens.

At the time this costume was worn it was still usual to sit in the kitchen with the servants, a custom well remembered at Stanford. A farmer in those times would often teach the boys on the farm to read, or would ask them questions on husbandry, such as, which was the best method of reaping corn, tying up the sheaves, building up the shocks, making ricks, &c. Sometimes they would sing, while the farmer's wife or mother would ply her spinning wheel. The songs sung would be such as the "Berkshire Lady," "Fair Rosamond," the "Lamentations of Jane Shore," "Chevy Chace," and sometimes, perhaps, "Wadley Fair." Such a manner of spending the winter evenings was not, I am forced to admit, universal in Stanford, for on making inquiry of an aged labourer what was his former experience, he said that at Stone's farm, then occupied by Mr. Penstone, he and the wench sat in opposite corners of the chimney, and looked at one another. The farm house was the home of all the unmarried men, and whenever the master was a God-fearing man the custom must have been productive of much good, and have preserved the men from that bane of the labourer, the village beerhouse, to which resort is often had solely for the advantage of a cheerful fireside.

In these times the stocks and whipping-post, only lately removed from Church Green, were often in requisition, and many can remember seeing the stocks in use, and can tell of the whipping inflicted on John Clarke for stealing, by John Goulding, the tithing-man. In these days there was little locomotion. The farmers had no gigs, and a farmer named Tarrant is said to have been the first to adopt one. Travelling was principally practised on horseback, females riding behind the men on pillions, grasping them by the button-hole in front. A pillion cushion is still preserved by Mrs. Cowderoy. A relic of this custom is to be seen in the upping-stocks attached to many farm houses. Communication with London was made by the waggon, which took two or three days on the road. A little later, a coach ran from Wantage, through Faringdon, to London. Old people tell of the peace rejoicings after the last French war, when there was grand feasting on Church Green, and a booth erected for dancing at Goosey, when Mr. Spicer led off the dance. At this time gipsies abounded in the neighbourhood, and one of them, Gravelines Boswell, is buried in our churchyard; and from that circumstance, or because the gipsies when they came to church sat in the spot, the east end of the aisle is called "Gipsies' corner."

The poor had some kind friends in these times. The labourers still remember the soup given by Madam King, and the story is related that the late Madam Hughes, of Uffington, the grandmother, I believe, of Thomas Hughes, Esq., M.P. (Tom Brown) was accustomed to come over to Stanford, when the small-pox was threatening the country, and inoculate the people with a knitting needle, at the Red Lion, or as they stood in a row by the Jockey Inn. At this time ladies were called Madam and Dame, farmers and their wives Gaffer and Gammer.

Another kind friend to the labouring class, at a more recent date, was the late Philip Pusey, Esq., of Pusey. He was the first to let out land in allotments, and to encourage the planting of potatoes and other vegetables, a plan which has largely contributed to the labourers' comfort. The labourers, it is true, often suffer now from hard times, and sometimes from that which is hardest to bear, want of employment, but in a great many ways their lot is improved. Bad as are some of the cottages in Stanford, they have been worse, and that in times when no coal was to be obtained, but only wood or furze. A hundred years ago no labourer could obtain any tea or white bread, or potatoes. Now coal clubs and clothing clubs put it into the power of all who are thrifty to make provision against

Pusey House

hard times. In speaking on this subject I ought not to omit a tribute of thankfulness to the present inmate of Stanford Rectory, whose skill in medicine and thoughtful Christian charity has for a long period alleviated the sorrows of many in our village. Nay, I rejoice to say that a spirit of kindness is not confined to any class, but that whenever sickness or trouble happens, the attention of the poor one to another is most touching, putting many times the aid of the higher classes to rebuke.

Before bringing this village history to a close, it is worthy of mention that the village of Stanford was well represented at the Exhibition of 1851, when all the labourers renting allotments of Mr. Pusey were sent by him to London, clothed in white smocks, free of expense. They were marshalled in Hyde Park, and introduced by the Squire to the Queen, in a speech to which she graciously responded. The late war in the Crimea will long be remembered in Stanford, for to that war Stanford contributed a noble volunteer, the Rev. G. H. Proctor, who met his death ministering to the sick and dying. A tablet to his memory has been placed in the parish church.

Whoever reads this little work will probably connect our village with another name not unknown in England—one whom we have learned to love and venerate. He needs no eulogy of mine, and his work will have a more enduring memorial than I can give. May he long be spared to minister:—

"Where a few villagers on bended knees,
Find solace which a busy world disdains."

In conclusion, may I express a hope that if any have taken an interest in the incidents I have collected about our parish, they will strive on their part to render their own village what every village should be. We shall do this if we strive to live together as good neighbours, the strong bearing with the infirmities of the weak, and the weak with the strong.

APPENDIX.

Extract from the Original Book of the Churchwardens' Accounts of the Parish of Stanford in the Vale, Berks; containing an Inventory of the Church Goods, taken about May 11th, 1553 (7th of Edward VI): also a statement of the disposal of them by the King's Commissioners, and a record of the articles renewed in the reign of Queen Mary.

Imprimis a cope of redd velvett & a pyllow

It.   a cope and shutte [? suit] of vestments for the Prest and Subdeacon of blew satten with ther albes

It.   a cope of bawdekyns with a sute of vestments for the Prest, Dyacon, and Subdiacon of the same with the albes

It.   one old vestment of many cullers of nedull-worke with th appurtenance. Note—ii of the albes were stolne

It.   ii olde chcsabubuls of dornyx without albes

It.   i old chysabull of resid [i.e. raised] worke of grene and redde velvet the grownde golde wyer with the appurtynaunce

It.   i frunt for an alter of the same worke

Itm.   a frunt for an alter of paynttyd cavas—*stolne*

Itm.   i olde cope of hlew sarcenet

Itm. i olde vestment of syleke

Itm. i olde vestment white fustyan—with i albe—*solde*

Itm. ii crosses of copper and gylte—i other of lede florysshid one withe golde foyle—*this the Commissioners had*

Itm. viij banner clothis and i stremer of canvas paynttid—*the banners solde*

Itm. vij olde altar clothis ii towells

Itm. iij corporas clothis with casis—*this the Commissioners had*

Itm. a pece of bawdkyn for the Sepulture—*stolne*

Itm. a vayle & iij clothis for Lent—ye vale gevon T. Myller

Itm. ij olde coverletts of carpet worke

Itm. vij surpleses of all sorts—*one stolne*

Itm. iiij bells, a sance [i.e. sanctus] bell & sacryng bell

Itm. ij chalysis of sylver parcell gylte—*the Commissioners the one & the paten of the other*

Itm. ij pyxces—i copper another of brass

Itm. a canape of lynet worke

Itm.   ii cruetts of pewtter a crysmatory of pcwtter

Itm. a holywatter pot of brasse a payre of sencers of bras

These parcclls aforesayd be in the Kynge's inventory of the wich the Kyng had all (save the bells in the stepull, the alter clothis towells surpleses and albes) delyvyred to Mr. Yong Mr. J Wynchecomb ye yonger, the xi day of May a° 11 R R Edv. vj^te 7   All so ye dd [i e. they delivered] backe agayne a challes with owte a kever [i. e. cover] or paten—Mem that J Fawkener, Vicar bought all the stuffe that the Kyng's Comm^rs above namyd did receyve owt of Stanford, except plate bells brasse pewtter & the canape of Lynet & copper & gylte—the corporas caysses & ther clothis surpleses alter clothis keverletts albes & a kevering for the tabull of sylcke & payd therefore

Sma ^vii. xvi^s. ii^d.

Thes be the parcclls of goods that was lafte in the Church, & not put into the Kynge's inventori.

Imprimis a challes with a kever parcell gylt

Itm.   a payr of grayt candllstycks callyd standorts of bras

Itm.   a payre of small Candullstycks of brasse to set one the altar

Itm.   a crosse of copper and gylt

Itm.   iiij sylver sponis

Itm.   a bell for the belman & a sacryng bell

Itm.   ij here clothis for the altar

Itm.   a basson of latten (This bason was changed for a pewter bason hav more money lede to yt. as. appeareth in Thomus Collens & J. Whaye's account)

Itm.   a lanthorne
           grayt lentten clothe
           ij pecys of lawnde towell brayde with roys [i. e. rows]
           of red and yallow sylcke

Itm.   a brod sylcke cloth with roys of blew and red sylcke
           with golde wyer

Itm.   a myter of white satten with borders of red velvet

Itm.   a front for an alter of blew satten with byrds of golde
           & traylls of golde with grene and white sylcke

Itm.   an albe with a stole and fana

Itm.   a front for an alter of grene say with helmet & sheld
           trayled with gold wyer

Itm.   another front for an alter the grownde whyte sylcke
           with a trayle of grene sylcke & golde wyer

Itm.   v towells of the whiche ij be bothe brod & long

Itm.   a curten of bockeram with ryngs

Itm.   a fyne lynen cloth with a hole in the myddest that
           keveryd the pyx

Itm.   a lytull bagge of red taffeta

Itm.   a pyllobere with worke of red & blacke crule

Itm.   a dyadem for the pyx

Itm.   iij chests ij with lydels & one without a 1yd & a long
           coffer that did put in torchis

Itm.   a chest cawlyd the pore man's box

Itm.   a bybull—the paraphrasis of Erasmus ij bokes of
           comon prayer—a salter—all this in Englysh

Itm.   a baner pole with a plate of yron rownde about hit

Itm.   ij baners

Itm.   a tabull with a frame—*hit was solde*

    Thes parcels following Mr. John Fawckener Vicar bowght of the Kyng's Commissioners & solde the same unto John Whistler & Roger Churche to the use of the Churche of

Stanford for the sum of v^{li} xvi^{s} viij^{d} the wich was levyed of the Church Stockes & payde to the sayde Vicar the xxi day of December in the first yere of the reyene of the most Xtian lady Queyne Marye

Imprimis a cope of red velvett & a pyllo of the same
Itm.   a cope & sute of vestments for the Prest, Dyacon & Subdyacon of blew satten
Itm.   a cope and sute of vestments for ye Prest, Dyacon & Subdyacon of bawdkyn
Itm.   one old vestment of many cullers of nedullwork
Itm.   ij olde chesabulls of dornyx
Itm.   i olde chesabull of resyd worke of grene and red velvet the grownde golde wyer
Itm.   a frunte for an altar of ye same worke
Itm.   one olde cope of blew sarcenet
Itm.   one olde vestment of sylcke

The parcells above wrytten were delyverd to John Whistler and Roger Churche in the precens of Richard Rawlins and John Hawkyns Church Wardens and others of the paryshe.

The parcells following the Kyng's Commyssioners delyvered backe sum to the uze of the Churche sum to be gyven to pore people.

Imprimis ij old keverletts
Itm.   a stremer
Itm.   vij olde alter clothis & ij towells
Itm.   iij clothis for lent
Itm.   vij surplisis of the wich one was stolne
Itm.   a challes of sylver parcell gylt withowt a paten
Itm.   vij the others were stolne or lost

Thes parcells followyng renewed syns the begynning of Queyn Maryes regne

Imprimis Dorethe Phetyplase Voys hathe made of the Churche Stuffe ii coporas casss [? cases] one of purpull velvet with the image of Chryst Mary & John and another of Sylcke nedull worke

Itm.   the sayd Dorethe hathe made a payre of curtens for the hygh altar of the Churche Stuffe

Itm.   the sayd Mistress Dorethe hathe gevyn to ye Churche a pyx to put in the most blessed Sacrament of ye altar of clothe of tyssu

Itm.   the sayd Dorethe hathe gyven a pax

Itm.   the sayd Dorethe hathe gyven a fyne corporys clothe

Itm.   the sayd Dorethe hathe made a Sacrament clothe to be over the pyx of the Churche stuffe

Itm.   Elyzabeth Phetyplace Voys gave a pece of bawdyr to make a pawlle for to lay over the herse or a canape to carry over the Sacrament of the altar conteyning…yards…in brayd &…yards in lengeth

Itm.   J. Whayre & T. Colens the Churchwardens bought of T. Poye…olde baners and payde for them as appeareth

Itm.   ye sayde Whayre & Collens bought in this yere ij hallfe portuisis a proccssionall a manuell a payre of cruetts of pewter a chrismatory of pewter a payre of saynces [i. e. censers] a holy water stocke of brasse

Itm.   Thomas Whitehorne of Goze [i. e. Goosey Chapelry in the Parish of Stanford] gave to ye Churche of Stanford ye xx[th] day of Apryll A.D. 1556 a vestment for a Prest to see [i. e. say] Masse in of yellow sarcenett & an albe & a amyse stolle and fana [i. e. fanon] new

LIST OF VICARS.

SUBJOINED is a list of some who have had the cure of souls in the parish of Stanford in the Vale:—

Roger Campedene, Rector..................................... died 1398
John Fawconer, Vicar.. died 1586
Hugo Goodman, Vicar... died 1625
Giles Bingley, Vicar .... first appears 1641
Laurence Pocock, Vicar .... first appears 1667
John Frewen, Vicar .... first appears 1700
John Hutton, Vicar..................................... first appears 1711
James Ayscough, Vicar .... first appears 1715
——— Cranke, Vicar of Stanford
    and Hatford
Thomas Home, Vicar.................................. first appears 1757
George Turner, Vicar.................................. first appears 1768
Robert Wetherell, Vicar............................. first appears 1793
Thomas Sanders, Vicar .... first appears 1834

Christopher Wordsworth, Vicar................ first appears 1850

Part Two

THE SCOURING OF THE WHITE HORSE

A NOVEL

BY

THOMAS HUGHES

AUTHOR OF "TOM BROWN'S SCHOOL DAYS"

Illustrated by Richard Doyle

]

Thomas Hughes
1822–1896

OLD AND NEW.

See how the Autumn leaves float by, decaying,
    Down the red whirls of yon rain-swollen stream;
So fleet the works of men, back to their earth again
    Ancient and holy things fade like a dream.

Nay! see the Spring blossoms steal forth a-maying,
    Clothing with tender buds orchard and glen;
So, though old forms go by, ne'er can their spirit die,
    Look! England's bare boughs show green leaf again.

KINGSLEY.

INTRODUCTION.

 GREEMENT was reasonably broad amongst 19th-century antiquarians that the great chalk figure of a white horse on the Berkshire Downs at Uffington was carved to celebrate the victory of King Ethelred and his brother Alfred the Great over the Danes at the battle of Ashdown in 871. Working only by reference to ancient documents and local folk-memory, this was perhaps not an unreasonable assumption before the advent of the scientific dating methods from which historians benefit today. Thomas Hughes' novel recording the traditional ceremony of the Scouring of the White Horse in 1857 and its accompanying revelry, the "Pastime", reflects this conviction—and this may be why the book has fallen into neglect.

Modern scientific analysis now dates the creation of the figure to the Iron or even Bronze Age. While a prehistoric date for the creation of the White Horse does not necessarily preclude the area as the *site* of the battle of Ashdown, it does mean it cannot be regarded as a memorial *of* the battle. Retaining lengthy discussion of the topography of White Horse Hill in relation to the battle could therefore give a misleading emphasis to a connection with Alfred which at present remains legendary. This is why I have omitted the chapter on the battle of Ashdown which appeared in Hughes' original text.

This, plus the removal of one or two references of a racial

nature that were not intended to be offensive at the time but might very likely be considered so today, means that this is not a verbatim version of Hughes' book. I hope that such changes cannot be said to have diluted the flavour of the original. Indeed, in a way, they have perhaps restored its disarming inno-cence. Retention of Hughes' archaic spelling and punctuation emphasises that his writing speaks of a bygone age.

While the main characters of Richard Easy, the Hursts of Elm Close Farm and their friend Parson Warton are fictional, there are numerous references to genuine Vale residents which will be invaluable to researchers of family history. Hughes sometimes gives us brief character sketches and hints at personal appearance and particular talents ("one of the best mowers in the Vale"; "five feet eight high, with a bullet head, and light blue eye; high-couraged, cool, and with an absolutely imperturbable temper") that could never be gleaned from other sources such as parish registers or census records.

Cross-referencing with parish registers and newspaper reports reveals slight discrepancies in the spelling of some of the names of peope still living at the time of publication. This might perhaps be tactful obfuscation on Hughes' part to conceal the identities of his subjects, or it may simply be a result of his phonetic transcription of his own shorthand notes. My own explanatory footnotes in these instances, as opposed to the footnotes in the original novel, appear in italics.

Julie Ann Godson
2017

PREFACE.

HE GREAT SUCCESS of the festival (or "Pastime," as it is called in the neighbourhood) which was held on White Horse Hill on the 17th and 18th of September, 1857, to celebrate the "Scouring of the Horse," according to immemorial custom, led the Committee of Management to think that our fellow-county-men at least, if not our countrymen generally, would be glad to have some little printed memorial, which should comprise not only an account of the doings on the Hill on the late occasion, but should also endeavour to gather up the scattered legends and traditions of the country side, and any authentic historical notices relating to the old monument, of which we west-countrymen are all so fond and proud.

I had the good or ill luck (as the case may be) to be the only member of the Committee whose way of life had led him into the perilous paths of literature; so the task of compiling and editing our little book was laid on my shoulders.

Installed as chronicler to the White Horse, I entered with no ill will on my office, having been all my life possessed, as is the case with so many Englishmen, by intense local attachment, love for every stone and turf of the country where I was born and bred. But it is one thing to have zeal, and another to have discretion; and when I came to consider my materials, I found that the latter quality would be greatly needed. For, what were they? One short bright gleam of history from the writings of old monks a thousand years ago; traditions and dim legends, which I and most Berkshire men have always faithfully believed from our youth up, and shall go on believing to our dying day, but which we could hardly put before general readers in serious narrative; a dry notice here and there by some old antiquary of the seventeenth or eighteenth century; stories floating in the memories of old men still living; small broad-sheets from country town presses, with lists of the competitors for prizes at rustic games, newspaper articles, remarks by Committee-men and umpires, scraps of antiquarian lore, abuse of the Great Western Railway for not allowing the trains to stop, bits of vernacular dialogue, and odd rhymes. What could be done with them all? How out of the mass could a shapely book be called out, fit to be laid before a fastidious British public, not born in Berkshire?

Not exactly seeing how this was to be done, the only honest course which remained, was to follow the example of a good housewife in the composition of that excellent food called "stir-about"—throw them all together into the pot, stir them round and round with a great spoon, and trust that "the look of the few great raisins, and the flavour of the allspice, may leaven the mass, and make it pleasing to the eye and palate; and so, though the stir-about will never stand up in a china dish by itself, it may, we hope, make a savoury and pleasant side dish, in a common soup tureen.

The raisins, and those of the best quality, have been furnished by the great artist[1] who has kindly undertaken to give us pictures; the allspice has been contributed by the Committee and other kind friends, and I have done the milk and meal, and the stirring. The responsibility therefore rests with me, though the credit, whatever it may be, rests with others.

1   Doyle.

But let me insist here, at once, that if there be any failure in the dish, it is the fault of the dresser and not of the subject-matter. For, suppose an intelligent Englishman to be travelling in France, and to find the whole population in the neighbourhood of Tours turning out in their best clothes for a two days' holiday on a high hill, upon which the rude figure of a huge hammer is roughly sculptured. On inquiry, he finds that the figure has been there long before the memory of the oldest man living, but that it has always been carefully preserved and kept fresh; and although there is no printed history of how it came there, yet that all neighbouring men, of whatever degree, associate it with the name of Charles Martel and his great victory over the Saracens, and are ready one and all to rejoice over it, and to work and pay that it may go down to their children looking as it does now.

Or, to come to much later times, let our traveller find an eagle cut out on a hill in Hungary, similarly honoured, and associated with the name of Eugene, and the memory of the day

> "When, the old black eagle flying,
> All the Paynim powers defying,
> On we marched, and stormed Belgrade."

Should we not all thank him for giving us the best account he could of the figure, the festival, and all traditions connected with them; and think he had fallen on a very noteworthy matter, and well worth the telling when he got back to England?

Well, here we have the same thing at our own doors; a rude colossal figure cut out in the turf, and giving the name to a whole district; legends connecting it with the name of our greatest king, and with his great victory over the Pagans, and a festival which has been held at very short intervals ever since the ninth century. Rich as our land is in historical monuments, there is none more remarkable than the White Horse; and in this belief we put forth this little book in his honour, hoping that it may perhaps fix upon him, and the other antiquities which surround him, the attention of some one who can bring science and knowledge to bear upon the task to which we can only bring good will.

For, alas! let me confess at once, that in these qualities our book is like to be sadly deficient. But while we do not pretend to be antiquaries, or historians, or learned men, we do claim to be honest average Englishmen, and will yield to no man in our love for our own quiet corner of the land of our birth. We do think, that whatever deeply interests us cannot fail in a degree to interest our countrymen. We are sure that reverence for all great Englishmen, and a loving remembrance of the great deeds done by them in old times, will help to bring to life in us the feeling that we are a family, bound together to work out God's purposes in this little island, and in the uttermost parts of the earth; to make clear to us the noble inheritance which we have in common; and to sink into their proper place the miserable trifles, and odds and ends, over which we are so apt to wrangle.

We do hope that our example will lead Englishmen of other counties to cherish every legend and story which hangs round any nook of their neighbourhood, connecting it with the times and the men who have gone before; to let no old custom, which has a meaning, however rude, die out, if it can be kept alive; and not to keep either legend or custom to themselves, but (like us) to put them in the best shape they can, and publish them for the benefit of their countrymen; we of the White Horse Committee, at any rate, hereby pledging ourselves to read all such publications.

I must here take the opportunity of specially thanking three of my fellow Committee-men, and two other friends, for the trouble they have taken in various ways to lighten my work. If this book at all fulfils the objects for which it has been written, the thanks of my readers, as well as my own, will be due to

E. M. ATKINS, Esq., of Kingstone Lisle.
MR. WILLIAM WHITFIELD, of Uffington.
MR. HEBER HUMFREY, of Kingstone Farm[2]; and to
JOHN Y. AKERMAN, Esq., Secretary of the Society of Antiquaries; and
MR. LUKE LONSLEY, of Hampsted Norris, Berks.

And now, without further preface, we commend our "stir-about" to Englishmen in general, and west-countrymen in particular.

Thomas Hughes
1859

---

2 *Secretary of the British Berkshire Society, Heber Humfrey (1833–1904) was a consistent winner of prizes at agricultural shows for his Berkshire boars and sows.*

CHAPTER I.

ICHARD," said our governor, as I entered his room at five o'clock on the afternoon of the 31st of August, 1857, running his pen down the columns of the salary-book, "your quarter-day to-day I think? Let me see; you were raised to £ a-year in February last,—so much for quarter's salary, and so much for extra work. I am glad to see that you have been working so steadily; you'll deserve your holiday, and enjoy it all the more. You'll find that all right I think;" and he pushed a small paper across the table towards me, on which my account was stated in our cashier's hand, and looked at me over his spectacles.

My heart jumped at the mention of my holiday; I just ran my eye down the figures, and was glad to find the total a pound or two higher than I had expected. For I had lately learnt shorthand, and had been taking notes for our firm, for which I found they allowed me extra pay.

"Quite right, Sir," I said; "and I'm sure I'm much obliged to you, Sir, for letting me do the extra work, because—"

"Well, never mind that," said he, with a little laugh; "I shouldn't give you the extra work, Richard, if it didn't suit me, or if I could get it better done anywhere else; so the account's all square on that point. There's your money."

And he pushed over to me a very nice sum of money. I dare say you would like to know what it was, reader. Now, I'm not going to tell you. Why should you know just what my income is? I don't owe you or any one else five shillings, and have a very tidy account at the savings' bank, besides having paid for all the furniture and books in my room, not very far from Lambsconduit Street, which I reckon to be worth fifty pounds of any man's money; so you see my income is enough to keep me before the world, and I wish more of you could say as much.

"I'm very much obliged, Sir," said I again, as I wrote a receipt over a stamp which I took out of my pocket-book, and stuck on to the bottom of the account.

"No, you're not," said our governor, quite short; "it's your own money, fairly earned. You're not obliged to any man for giving you what's your own." He is such an odd fellow about these things. But mind you, I think he's quite right too; for after all, no doubt each of us earns a good penny for him over and above what he pays us, else why should he keep us on? but somehow, one can't help thanking any one who pays one money; at least, I can't.

"Now, as to your holiday," went on our governor. "There's Jobson went for his fortnight on the 30th; he'll be back on the 14th of September at latest. You can take any time you like, after that."

"Then, Sir," said I directly, "I should like it as soon as possible."

"Very well," said he; "Tuesday the 15th to Tuesday the 29th of September, both inclusive;" and he made a note in another book which lay on his desk. "Good evening, Richard."

"Good evening, Sir," said I; and away I went down to our room in as good spirits as any young fellow in our quarter of London.

Of course all the other clerks began shouting out at once to know how much money I'd got, and when I was going to have my holiday. Well, I didn't tell them what money I had, any more than I've told you, because I like to keep my own counsel about such matters. Besides, there are several of our clerks whose ways I don't at all like; so I don't do anything I can help which might look as if I liked them. No! hands off, is my motto with these sort of chaps.

I'm sure there's no pride about me, though. My name's Easy, and always was; and I like every fellow, whatever his coat is, who isn't always thinking about the cut of it, or what he has in the pocket of it. But, goodness knows, I can't stand a fellow who gives himself airs, and thinks himself a chalk above everybody who can't dress and do just as he can. Those chaps, I always see, are just the ones to do lickspittle to those that they think have more in their pockets than themselves.

But I must get on with my story, for you don't all want to know my opinions about the clerks in our office, I dare say.

Well, when I got down, as I said before, we were all just on the move (business hours being from nine till six in our office), taking down coats and hats, and clearing desks for the night, so I just sidled up to Jem Fisher, and little Neddy Baily, who are the two I like best, and told them to come up to my room to supper at eight o'clock, which they of course were very glad to promise to do, and then I went off to get ready for them.

Jem Fisher and I are both very fond of a dish which I believe very few of you ever heard of. One Sunday in May, a year or two back, he and I had been down beyond Notting Hill, listening to the nightingales; and coming back we walked through Kensington Gardens, and came out at the gate into the Notting Hill Road close to Hyde Park. We were late, for us, so we hailed a 'bus, and got on the box. The driver was full of talk about all the fine people he had been seeing walking in the gardens that afternoon, and seemed to think it hard he couldn't enjoy himself just as they did. "However, gentlemen," said he at last, "there's some things as the haristocracy ain't alive to. Did you ever eat cow-heel?" Perhaps Jem, who had all his best clothes on, didn't mind being taken for one of the aristocracy; at least just for a minute, for he's too good a fellow to like being taken for anybody but himself when he comes to think of it; at any rate, he and I took to eating cow-heel from that time. So the first thing I did, after going home and locking up most of my money, and speaking to my landlady, who is the best old soul alive if you take her in her own way, was, to set off to Clare Market[3], and buy some cow-heel and sausages; and on my way back through the Turnstile, I thought, as it was so hot, I would have some fruit too; so I bought a pottle of plums and a piece of a pine-apple, and got home.

They came in sharp to time, and I and my landlady had everything ready, and two foaming pewter pots full of bitter beer and porter. So we had a capital supper, and then cleared it all away, and sat down to eat the fruit and have a quiet pipe by the time it began to get dark.

"And so," said little Neddy (he is only just eighteen, and hasn't been in our office a year yet; but he's such a clever, industrious little chap, that he has gone over the heads of half a dozen of our youngsters, and hasn't stopped yet by a long way), "you're off on the 15th! wish I was. Well, here's luck any how," said he, nodding to me, and taking a bite out of a slice of pine-apple.

"Gentle Shepherd, tell me where?" said Jem Fisher. (Jem is very fond of quoting poetry; not that I think half that he quotes is real poetry, only how is one to find him out? Jem is a tall, good-looking fellow, as old as I am, and that's twenty-one last birthday; we came into the office together years ago, and

---

3   A maze of narrow, interconnecting streets lined by butchers' shops and greengrocers. Redeveloped in the early 20th century to create Aldwych and Kingsway.

have been very thick ever since, which I sometimes wonder at, for Jem is a bit of a swell—Gentleman Jem they call him in the office). "Now, Dick, where are you bound for?"

"Well, that's more than I know myself," said I.

"Then," said he, taking his pipe out of his pocket and filling it, "I vote we settle for him, eh, Neddy?"

"Aye, aye, Sir," said Neddy, stretching over for the pottle; "but, I say, Jem, you haven't finished all those plums?" and he poked about in the leaves with his fingers.

"Every mother's son of them," said Jem, lighting a lucifer; "if you come to that, Master Ned, hand me over some of that pine-apple. But now, about the tour; how much money are you going to spend on it, Dick?"

"Well, I haven't quite settled," said I; "but I shouldn't mind, now, going as high as four or five pounds, if I can suit myself."

"You may go pretty near to Jericho for that now-a-days," said Neddy. "As I came along Holborn to-night, I saw a great placard outside the George and Blue Boar, with 'to Llangollen and back 15s.' on it. What do you think of that? You'll be turned out at the station there with £4 5s. in your pocket."

"Where's Llangollen?" said I.

"Not half-way to Jericho," shouted Jem, with a laugh. "Where's Llangollen? Why didn't you ever hear the song of Kitty Morgan, the maid of Llangollen? You're a pretty fellow to go touring."

"Yes, fifty times," said I; "only the song don't tell you where the place is—where is it now?"

"In Wales, of course," said he, thinking he had me.

"Yes, I know that; but whereabouts in Wales," said I, "for Wales is a biggish place. Is it near anything one reads about in books, and ought to go and see?"

"Hanged if I know exactly," said Jem, puffing away; "only of course Wales is worth seeing."

"So is France," struck in Neddy; "why, you may go to Paris and stay a fortnight for I don't know how little."

"Aye, or to Edinburgh or the Lakes," said Jem.

"I want to have the particulars though," said I; "I'm not going to start off to some foreign place, and find myself with no money to spend and enjoy myself with, when I get there."

"I'll tell you what," said Neddy, jumping up, "I'll just run round to the Working Men's College, and borrow a Bradshaw from the secretary. We shall find all the cheap excursions there;" and away he went before we could say a word.

"I say," said Jem to me, "how fond he is of bringing up that place; he's always at me to go and enter there."

"So he is at me," said I, "and I think I shall, for he seems to pick up a lot of things there. How sharp he is at figures! and he knows more history and geography ten to one than I do. I'll bet he knew what county Llangollen is in, and something about it too. Let's ask him when he comes back."

"Catch me!" said Jem; "he'll look it out on the map on his way back, or ask one of the lecturers."

"Here you are! look here!" said Neddy, tumbling in with two Bradshaws and a great atlas under his arm; "'unprecedented attraction, pleasure excursions,' let me see—'Return tickets for Ireland, available for a fortnight. Waterford, 1*l.* 16*s.*; Cork, 2*l.*'"

"Nonsense!" cried Jem, who had got the other Bradshaw; "listen here: 'Channel Islands (remarkable as being the only remaining Norman possessions of the British crown), second class and fore cabin, 21*s.*'"

"'London to Dieppe, return tickets available for fourteen days, second class, 21*s.*,'" sung out Ned, from the other Bradshaw. And away they went, with Brussels, and Bangor, and the Manchester Exhibition, and Plymouth and Glasgow, and the Isle of Man, and Margate and Ramsgate, and the Isle of

Wight; and then to Gibraltar and Malta and New York, and all over the world. I sat and smoked my pipe, for 'twas no use trying to settle anything; but presently, when they got tired, we set to work and began to put down the figures. However, that wasn't much better, for there were such a lot of tours to go; and one was a bit too short, and the other too long, and this cost too much, and that too little; so all the beer was gone, and we were no nearer settling anything when eleven o'clock struck.

"Well," said Jem, getting up and knocking the ashes out of his third pipe, "I declare it's almost as good as going a tour oneself, settling it for Dick here."

"I just wish you *had* settled it," said I; "I'm more puzzled than when we began."

"Heigh-ho, fellows never know when they're well off," said Neddy; "now I never get a chance. In my holiday I just go down to the old folk at Romford, and there I stick."

"They don't indeed," said I; "I wonder to hear you talk like that, Ned. Some folks would give all they're worth to have old folk to go to."

"Well, I didn't mean it," said he, looking hurt. And I don't believe he did, for a kinder hearted fellow don't live; and I was half sorry I had said what I did say.

"Further deliberation will be necessary," said Jem, lighting his fourth pipe; "we'll come again to-morrow night; your bacchy's nearly out, Dick; lay in some bird's eye for to-morrow; real Bristol, do you hear?"

"Time to go, I suppose," said Ned, getting up and gathering the Bradshaws and atlas together; "are we to come again to-morrow, Dick?"

"To-morrow, didst thou say? methought I heard Horatio say to-morrow. Go to; it is a thing of nought," and Jem clapped on his hat and began ranting in his way; so I broke in—

"I wish you'd hold that noise, and talk sense," said I.

"Shakespere!" said Jem, stopping short, and pulling up his collar.

"Gammon!" said Neddy, bursting out laughing.

"That's right, Neddy," said I; "he's always going off with some of his nonsense, and calling it poetry."

"I didn't say it was poetry, did I?" said Jem.

"What is it then?" said I.

"Blank verse," said he.

"What's the difference?" said I. "Tumble out with you; it's time for steady folks to turn in."

So I turned them out and held the candle, while they floundered down stairs, that wretch, Jem, singing, "There's some 'un in de house wid Dinah," loud enough to be heard at the Foundling. I was glad to hear my landlady catch him at the bottom of the stairs, and give it him well about "a respectable house," and "what she was used to with her gents," while she opened the door; only I don't see what right she had to give it me all over again next morning at breakfast, and call Jem Fisher a wild young man, and bad company, because that's just what he isn't, only a little noisy sometimes. And as if I'm not to have who I please up to my room without her interfering! I pay my rent regular every month, I know.

However, I didn't mind much what she said at breakfast time, because I had got a letter from the country. I don't get a letter once a month, and it's very odd this one should have come on this very morning, when I was puzzling where to go for my holiday; and I dare say you'll think so too, when I tell you what it was about. Let's see—here it is in my pocket, so you shall have it whole:—

"Elm Close Farm, Berks, August 31, 1857.

"DEAR DICK,—You know you owe me a visit, for you've never been down here, often as I've asked you, since we was at school together—and I have been up to you four or five times. Now, why I particularly want you to come this month is, because we've got some sport to show you down in these quiet parts, which don't happen every day.

"You see there's an old White Horse cut out in the side of the highest hill hereabouts (a regular break-neck place it is, and there aint three men in the country as'll ride along the hill side under the Horse), and many folks sets a good deal of store by it, and seems to think the world'd come to an end if the horse wasn't kept all straight. May be I'm a bit of that mind myself—anyhow you'll see by the paper inside what's going on; and being a scholar, may be you'll know about the White Horse, and like to come down to a scouring. And I can tell you it will be good fun; for I remember the last, when I was quite a little chap, before I went to school, and I've never seen such games since.

"You've only got to write and say what train you'll come by, and I'll meet you at the Farringdon-road station in my trap. So, as I aint much of a penman, excuse mistakes, and remember me to Fisher and the others I met at your place; and no more at present from yours truly.

"JOSEPH HURST.

"P.S.—You must stay as long as you can, and I'll mount you on my young bay colt to see a cub killed."

I shouldn't print Joe's letter whole (and as it is I've put a good deal of the spelling right), only I'm quite sure he'll never read this book, and I hope it may serve as a warning to young fellows to keep up their learning when they go and settle down in the country. For when Joe left the Commercial Academy at Brentford, he could write just as good English as I, and if he had put "many folks seems to think," or "you've only got to write," in a theme, old Hopkins would have given him a good caning. But nothing wears out learning so quick as living in the country and farming, and Joe came into his farm when he was nineteen, and has been at it ever since. And after all, perhaps, it doesn't much signify, because nobody makes himself better understood than Joe, in one way or another; and if he wasn't a little behindhand in his grammar he wouldn't think much of me perhaps—and one don't mind being taken for a scholar even by those who are not the best judges in the world.

Well, thinks I to myself, as I finished my breakfast, this seems like business. If I go down to Joe's, and stay there all my holiday, the fares will be only seventeen shillings; and, say a pound for expenses down there; one pound seventeen shillings, say two pounds in all. I shall put three pounds into my pocket, and please an old friend, which will be much better than anything Jem Fisher and little Neddy Baily will hit out for me in a week from the end of Bradshaw. Besides, it will look well to be able to talk of going to a friend in Berkshire. I'll write to Joe, and say I'll be with him in good time on the 15th.

So I went down to the office and told Jem Fisher and little Neddy, that I had made up my mind to go and see my old friend Joe, in Berkshire, before they had had time to get their office coats on.

"What! that jolly fellow with the brown face and red whiskers," said Jem, "who came up and slept in your room last Christmas cattle-show, and wanted to fight the cabman for a gallon of beer, who charged him half-a-crown from Baker Street to Gray's Inn Lane?"

"Yes," said I, "that's the man."

"I remember him well," said Neddy; "and I'm sure you'll have a good time of it if you go to see him. But, I say, how about supper to-night? You won't want us and the Bradshaws any more, eh?"

"Oh, he isn't going to get out of it like that," said Jem, as he settled to his desk, and got his work out. "I say, Dick, you're not going to be off now, are you? I know better."

"I never was *on* that I know of," said I; "however, I don't mind standing supper at the Cheshire Cheese; but I won't have you fellows up in my room again to-night, kicking up a row on the stairs. No! just catch me at it!"

So I gave them a supper that night, and another the night after I came back from my holiday.

They seemed just the same, but how different I felt. Only two short weeks had passed, but I was as much changed as if it had been ten years. I had found something which I never could get rid of, day or night, and which kept me always in a fret and a struggle. What a life I led with it! Sometimes it cast me down and made me ready to hang myself; and then, again, it would lift me up, and seem to fill me with warmth and sunshine. But, somehow, even when I was at the worst, if an enchanter had come and offered to wipe it all out, and to put me back just where I was the night before my holiday, I should have said "No;" and at all other times I felt that it was the most precious part of my life. What was it? Ah, what was it? Some of you will smile, and some of you will sneer, when you find out, as you will (if you don't skip) before you get to the end of my story. And I can't see the least reason why I should help you to it a minute sooner.

CHAPTER II.

OW I DO PITY all the lords and great gentlefolk with nothing in the world to do except to find out how to make things pleasant, and new places to go to, and new ways of spending their money; at least, I always pity them at the beginning of my holiday, though perhaps when one first comes back to eleven months' hard grind in town the feeling isn't quite so strong. At any rate, I wouldn't have changed places with the greatest lord in the land on Tuesday morning, September 15th.

I was up as soon as it was light, and saw the sun rise over the Gray's Inn Lane chimney-pots; and I declare they looked quite beautiful. I didn't know at all before what a fine outline they make when the rays come flat along the roofs; and mean often to get up in time to see them by sunrise next summer; but just now it's very cold of mornings, and I dare say they don't look so well. When I put my head out of the window it was quite clear and fresh, and I thought I could smell the country.

I hadn't much to do, for I had packed my bag over night; but I went over all my things again, and changed the places of some of them in my old bureau (which belonged to my father, who was clerk for forty years in one of the oldest houses in Clement's Inn), and locked up all the drawers; and then I set to work to lay breakfast for three, for I had asked my two friends to come and see me off, and they had made it all up with my landlady. So about six o'clock they came in, and we had a capital breakfast; and then we started off to walk up to the Paddington station, carrying my bag between us. I had settled to go by the 7.30 train, because if I hadn't they couldn't have come with me; besides, it is the first train which stops at Farringdon-road; and I was very glad when we got into the bustle of the station, for they were rather low, and I felt almost ashamed of being so jolly, though certainly they had had their holiday earlier in the year. But when I saw their faces out of the window of the second-class carriage, just as the starting-bell rang, I should like to have paid their fares out of my own pocket, if they could have gone with me.

However, by the time we got past Wormwood Scrubbs (which looked so fresh and breezy with the gossamer lying all over it), I could think of nothing else but the country and my holiday. How I did enjoy the pretty hill with the church at top and the stream at the bottom by Hanwell, and the great old trees about half a mile off on the right before you get to Slough, and the view of Windsor castle, and crossing the Thames at Maidenhead, with its splendid weeping willows, and the old Bath-road bridge, and the reach beyond with the woods coming down to the bank, and the great lords' houses up above. And then all the corn-fields, though by this time most of them were only stubble, and Reading town, and the great lasher at Pangbourn, where the water was rushing and dancing through in the sunlight to welcome me into Berkshire; and the great stretches of open land about Wallingford-road and Didcot. And after that came great green pasture-fields, and orchards, and grey-stone farm-houses, and before I could turn round we were at Farringdon-road station, and it was a quarter past eleven. As I got out and gave up my ticket, I couldn't help thinking of the two lines Jem Fisher would go on saying when we went out walking in Combe Wood and Richmond Park one Sunday this last May—

How beautiful the country do appear
At this time of the year.

I know he was laughing, and made them out of his own head, though he declared they were in Chaucer; but they are just as true for all that, whether Jem Fisher or Chaucer made them, though the English isn't as good as the sense.

There I found Joe waiting for me, with his trap, as he called it, at the door, and the inn ostler standing by the head of the horse, which was a bright chestnut and looked very fine. I own I very much enjoyed going off in that dark-green high-wheeled carriage.

"In with you, Dick," cried out Joe, as he took hold of the reins, and patted the horse on the neck. "There, shoot your bag in behind; look alive, she don't stand well. That'll do," he shouted to the ostler, who jumped back and touched his hat just as if Joe owned half the parish. If the horse couldn't stand well, at any rate she could step out, and away we whirled down the white road; Joe red in the face with holding on, his feet well out to the splashboard, his chest thrown forward and his elbows down at his side, hauling the chestnut's head right back, till her nose nearly touched the collar. But for all that, away went her legs right straight out in front, shooting along so fast that I began to feel queer, not being used to horses, and took tight hold of the seat with my left hand, so that Joe shouldn't see; for the cart jumped sometimes enough to pitch you out.

"Gently there, gently, my beauty," said Joe, as the chestnut dropped into a little quieter pace. "There now, ain't she a pictur'?" said he to me;—"ever see a mare lay down to her work like that? Gently, my beauty! if it wasn't for the blaze in her face, and the white feet, the Squir'd give me one hundred pounds for her to-morrow. And I won't sell her under. It's a mortal shame to drive her. Her mouth's like a kitten's." How Joe could talk so, when he was pulling fit to burst himself at the reins, I don't know; I thought once or twice where we should go to if one broke, but I didn't say anything. I found out afterwards that Joe meant a great white mark, when he talked of the blaze in her face. I suppose men can't see any faults in their own horses, any more than they can in their children.

After a bit, the pace got quite steady, and then I began to enjoy myself, and could look at the famous rich fields, and the high hedges full of great heavy masses of clematis, and sniff up all the country smells, as we whirled along, and listen to Joe, who was going grinding on about, 'how badly the parish roads were kept up; and that he had set his mind to have them well mended with flints instead of chalk, and to have all the thistles at the side kept down, which were sowing the whole country round, because their vestry was so stingy they wouldn't put any men on the road to set it right,' and I could see that Joe was in the middle of a good quarrel with all the other farmers about it.

When he had done his story, I asked him about the White Horse, and he pointed me out the highest of the hills which ran along on our left hand a mile or two away. There, sure enough, I saw the figure quite plain; but he didn't know much about it. Only, he said, he had always heard tell that it was cut out by King Alfred the Great, who lived in those parts; and 'there was a main sight of strange old things up there on the hill, besides the White Horse; and though he didn't know much about how they got there, he was sort of proud of them, and was glad to pay his pound or two, or double that if it was wanted, to keep them as they should be;' "for, you see," said Joe, "we've lived about here, father and son, pretty nigh ever since King Alfred's time, which I reckon is a smartish time ago, though I forget how long." And though I think Joe, and parties in the counties generally, set too much store by such things, and hold their noses much higher than they've any need to do, because their families have never cared to move about, and push on in the world, and so they know where their great-grandfathers were born, I couldn't help feeling there was something in it after all.

And the more I thought of this strange old White Horse, the more it took hold of me, and I resolved, if I could, while I was down in the country to learn all about it. I knew, you see, that if I could only get people to tell me about it, I should be able to carry it all away; because, besides having a very good memory, I can take down everything that is said as fast as most people can speak it, and that's what gives me such an advantage over Jem Fisher and Neddy, who spent all the time it took me to learn short-hand in reading poetry and other rubbish, which will never help to get them on in the world, or do them a bit of good that I can see.

Presently we came in sight of a house with farm buildings behind, which stood some way back from the road; and Joe pulled up opposite a gate which led into the field before the house.

"Here we are, then," said he; "just jump out, and open the gate, Dick; I'd do it, only I can't trust you with the ribbons."

It was a beautiful great green pasture-field which we drove into, with a score of fat sleek cows feeding in it, or lying about chewing the cud; and Joe was very proud of them, and walked the chestnut along slowly while he pointed out his favourites to me, especially one short-horn, whose back he said was like a kitchen-table, though why she should be any the handsomer for that I can't say. The house was an old brick building, with tall chimneys and latticed windows; in front of it was a nice little flower-garden, with a tall, clipped holly hedge running round it, so thick that you couldn't see through; and beyond that, a kitchen-garden and an orchard. Outside the inclosure stood four such elms as I never saw before, and a walnut-tree nearly as big as they, with queer great branches drooping close to the ground, on which some turkeys were sitting. There was only a little wicket-gate in the holly hedge, and a gravel foot-path up to the front door, so we drove into the farm-yard at the back; and while Joe and his man took care of the chestnut, I had time to look about, and think what a snug berth Joe seemed to have fallen upon.

The yard must be sixty yards across, and was full of straw where the pigs were lying with nothing but their snouts out; lots of poultry were scratching and pecking about before the barn doors, and pigeons were fluttering down amongst them, and then up again to the tops of the barns and stables, which ran all round the yard. The rick-yard, full of long stacks of hay, and round stacks of corn, was beyond. A terrier and spaniel were sleeping in sunny corners, and a greyhound was stalking about and looking at the pigs; and everything looked sleepy and happy, and as if life went easily along at Elm Close Farm.

Presently Joe came out of the stable, carrying his whip, and took me into the house, calling into the kitchen as we passed to send in dinner directly. There was nobody in the parlour at first, but I saw that the table was laid for three; and, before I could look round at the prints and samplers on the wall, Joe's mother and the dinner came in. She was a good-looking old lady, dressed in black, with a very white lawn cap and collar, and was very kind and civil, but a little deaf. Joe bustled about, and got out I don't know how many bottles of home-made wine, clary, and raisin, and ginger; all of which he made me drink, besides beer, for he said that no one in the Vale had such receipts for wine as his mother. And what with the dairy-fed pork, and black puddings, and a chicken almost as big as a turkey, and the cheesecakes and tarts afterwards, and the hearty welcome and good example which Joe gave me, I don't remember when I have made so good a dinner.

The old lady went off directly after dinner, and I could see that Joe wanted to go and see after his men; so I told him not to mind me, for I should enjoy loitering about the place better than anything. And so I did; first I went into the flower-garden, and watched and listened to the bees working away so busy in the mignonette, and the swallows darting up into their nests under the eaves, and then diving out again, and skimming away over the great pasture; and then round the kitchen-garden, and into the orchard, where the trees were all loaded with apples and pears, and so out into a stubble-field at the back, where there were a lot of young pigs feeding and playing queer tricks, and back through the farm-yard into the great pasture, where I lay down on the grass, under one of the elms, and lighted my pipe; and thought of our hot clerks' room, and how Jem Fisher and little Neddy were working away there; and watched a flock of little shiny starlings hopping up on to the backs of some old south-down wethers who were feeding near me, and flying backwards and forwards into the old elms and walnut-trees, talking to one another all the while.

And so the time wore on, till a stout lass in a blue cotton print came out, and called the cows in to milking; and they all went trooping slowly by into the farm-yard, some of them just stopping to stare at me with their mild eyes, and smelling so sweet, that I hadn't the heart to go on smoking, and let my pipe out. And after a bit I followed into the line of sheds where they were being milked by the lass and a man, who balanced himself on two legs of the milking-stool, and drove his head into the cow's side; and I thought I had never heard a sweeter sound than the tinkling sound which the milk made in the bright tin pails.

I soon got into a talk with the lass, who was very pleasant and free spoken; and presently, when her pail was full, I lifted it out for her, all frothing up, and looking not a bit like our London sky-blue; and I told her I didn't think I had ever tasted real new milk; so she got me a long straw, and while she went on milking, I went down on my knees, and began to suck away through the straw. But I had hardly begun, when I heard a noise behind, and looking round, there stood Joe, laughing all over; and by his side a young woman in a broad straw hat and a grey jacket; and though, for good manners, she didn't laugh out like Joe, I could see it was all she could do to keep from going off too.

Why was I ashamed of being caught? I don't know, but I was ashamed; and as I stuck there on my knees in the deep straw with the pail before me looking at them, the blood rushed up to my head and made my ears sing, so that I couldn't hear a word that Joe said. But I could see he did say something, and then went off into another great roar of laughter; and the lass and the man left off milking and began laughing too, till I thought they would have dropped off the stools.

Then the young woman who was with Joe said something to him, and I thought I heard the words "What a shame!" and "your oldest friend;" and then she caught up a straw, and came and knelt on the opposite side of the milk-pail, and began to suck away herself without looking at me. In another moment Joe plumped down too, clapping me on the back.

"I say," said he, "start fair! Here, make room for me; you and Lucy ain't going to have it all to yourselves," and he began sucking away too; and then I recovered myself, and we all went on for a minute, when Joe took his straw out of his mouth, and said, "This is my sister Lucy, Dick; there, shake hands over the pail, and then let's go in to tea."

So she looked up, and blushed, and gave me her hand, her merry blue eyes twinkling with mirth, though she tried to keep grave. But I was all right now, and went off myself, and Joe followed, and then she, with the clearest, brightest laugh you ever heard; and then the man and the lass, and by the time we had done, I felt as if I had known them all for years. But as for Miss Lucy, as we walked away to the house to tea, I felt as if I could have given her my skin, if she would only have had a pair of shoes made out of it for her dear little feet.

The old lady was sitting at the tea-table in great force, with plates of buttered toast and cake, and pots of blackberry and redcurrant jam, and the great loaf all set out ready; and after tea we three walked out again till the sun set, and then came in to supper, at which I was surprised to find myself eating away just as if I had had nothing all day; country air does give one such an appetite.

After supper the old lady sat in her chair knitting and telling stories, till she nodded off and the spectacles fell on to the end of her nose, and her hands into her lap, but still holding the needles; and every now and then giving a catch with her head, and making belief to go on for a stitch or two. And Miss

Lucy sat stitching at a patch-work coverlet, fitting in all sorts of scraps of silk in the prettiest patterns in the world, and we on the other side of the table watching her, and talking quite low not to disturb the old lady. But what made it so pleasant was, that I had pretty near all the talking, for they seemed never tired of hearing about London, and how people lived there, and what they thought; especially Miss Lucy, who had never been out of Berkshire in her life. I thought Joe a great fidget, when soon after nine he began to walk about and waked his mother, and got the servants in to prayers and bustled them off to bed; but I believe it was all because he wanted to have his pipe, which he wouldn't smoke in the parlour. So we went into the kitchen and finished the day there, under half a score of great brown sides of bacon, and tufts of sweet herbs which hung drying from the corners of the rack, and opposite to the dresser with its rows of pewter plates as bright as silver, till I went to bed in sheets smelling of lavender, and dreamt of Miss Lucy.

I dare say that, though I should never be tired of telling about everything that happened to me at Elm Close, some people may get tired of reading about it. So I shall only begin my story of the next day after breakfast, when Joe had the trap out again, and carried me off to see what was doing up on White Horse Hill.

We had a very pleasant drive through the Vale to Uffington, which lies at the foot of the hill, and here Joe put up the trap, at the Swan, and we set off on foot to walk up. It was very hot, and the white road glared as we tramped along it, but very soon we came to broad strips of turf on each side, and then it was pleasant enough; so we plodded up a gentle rise called Sour Hill, and crossed the Iceldon or Iggleton way, which I've found out since was an old Roman road; and then the ascent became quite steep, and everything was clear hill and down before us, not a fence to be seen, and a fresh breeze came sweeping over the hill.

The road now became very bad, with ruts in the chalk like water-courses. On our left hand there was a deep narrow valley like a little bay running up into the hill, on the opposite side of which valley a large wood hung along the steepest part of the hillside, which Joe informed me was Uffington wood, a well-known meet for the hounds; it made me giddy to look at the places which he declared the huntsman, and any one who wanted to be sure of a good place when the hounds broke cover, had to ride along.

And now the great green hill seemed to be hanging right over us, as we came to a curious round mound on our right hand, up which Joe scrambled, and I after him, till we both pulled up out of breath on the flat top some fifty yards across.

"This is Dragon's Hill," said Joe, pulling off his hat and mopping his face with his handkerchief, "where St. George killed the Dragon in the old times. Leastways so they says about here, only they calls him King George instead of Saint George. And this bare place is where his blood ran out, and nothing'll grow on it since, not so much as a thistle."

Of course I knew better than to believe that, but it is a beautiful place; for just below it another little deep valley, like the one on the left, only narrower and steeper at the sides, runs right up into the hill-side. The road we had left winds round the head of this gorge, for any one to drive along who isn't particular about breaking his neck, for the hill is like a wall up above, and down below, with nothing but a little bank between you and the descent.

"Those are the giants' seats opposite," said Joe, pointing across the valley to a set of beautiful great green slopes, like huge ridges and furrows, which went sweeping down into the valley one after another as far as I could see; "and this is the

Manger, this great hole in the hill-side, because it lies right under the old Horse's nose. Come along, let's get up to him; there he is, you see, right above us."

So we scrambled down the side of Dragon's Hill, crossed the road, and then started up a row of steps cut in the turf. I'm sure it must be twice as steep as the hill in Greenwich Park, and I don't mind confessing that I shouldn't have liked to look round just at first, and wouldn't have minded giving myself a help with my hands if I hadn't been afraid of Joe's seeing me and laughing. I should think we must have gone up two hundred steps, when all of a sudden Joe stopped just above me, and called out, "Here we are;" and in about four steps I came to a trench cut into the chalk about two feet deep, which ran up the hill-side right ahead of us. The chalk in the trench was all hard and flat, and seemed to have been scraped and brushed up quite lately.

"This is his tail," said Joe. "Come on; look, they're scouring him up above; we're in luck—I thought they'd have done before this; and there's the Squire too with 'em."

So I looked up; and there, some way above, I saw a lot of men with shovels, and besoms, and barrows, cleaning away at the trench, which, now that I began to look at it, certainly came out more and more like a horse galloping; and there amongst them, working away as hard as any one, was a person in yellow leather gaiters, who I saw at once must be the Squire[4], though I had never seen a squire before. I own I had a great prejudice against a country squire when I went down into Berkshire; which was natural enough, you see, because I had never been farther from town than Twickenham (except by boat to Margate), and had belonged to a debating society near Farringdon-market ever since I left school, where we take in three liberal papers, and once a week have as good speaking as they get in the House of Commons. I haven't been to the debates much lately, myself; but when I was an active member, we used to have a regular go in about once a quarter at the un-paid magistracy. How we did give it them! They were bloated aristocrats, who by the time they were thirty had drunk out all the little brains they ever had, and spent their time in preserving and killing game and foxes at the expense of the farm-ers, and sending every good man in their villages either to the Bastile (as we called the workhouse) as a pauper, or to the county gaol as a poacher.

Joe and I very nearly quarrelled over one of those debates to which I took him, like a great gaby as I was, when he came up to see me at the time of a cattle-show. He would get up to speak, all I could do to stop him; and began, all red in the face, pitching into one of our best speakers who had just finished, calling him a cockney, and asking him what right he had to jaw about squires when he talked about a fox's ears and tail, and didn't know mangold-wurzel from swedes. And then all our fellows began to shout and hiss, and Joe began to swear,

4   *Mr Edwin Martin Atkins of Kingston Lisle Park. See page 284.*

and wanted to take his coat off, and fight all who had spoken; "one down, and t'other come on," as he said. I got him out and took him home; but his blood was up, and he would go on at our Society, and call us a set of quill-driving jackanapes. And I couldn't stand that, so I began at the landed interest, and said all the bad of them I could think of, about the Poor-laws, game preserving, and the Corn-laws. Joe was very near going off in a huff, but we shook hands over it at last, and agreed that we neither of us knew much about the sort of life the other led, and so had better not talk about it as if we did.

Well, this was the first squire I had ever seen, so I looked at him with all my eyes; and if all squires were like him, I don't wonder at Joe's getting in a passion at our talk in Farringdon-market. I should think he must be about forty-five years old, and stands not far short of six feet high; for when he came to stand by Joe, I could see he was the taller of the two; but he didn't look so tall quite when he stood by himself—I suppose because his figure was so good. For you never saw such a clean

made man; he was for all the world like a well-rounded wedge from his shoulders down, and his neck and head put on like a statue. He looked just as if he could have jumped the highest five-barred gate in the Vale, and then have carried it off on his shoulders, and run up the hill with it. And his face, which was well browned, was so manly and frank, and his voice so cheery, and he looked you so straight in the face, that you felt he wasn't ashamed of anything, or afraid of anybody; and so you looked him back and spoke out, and were twice as good a man at once yourself while you were talking to him.

Well, when the Squire saw Joe, he stopped working away with his shovel, and called out to him; and so Joe went up and shook hands with him, and began talking to him, and in another minute the Squire called for his coat—a grey tweed shooting jacket it was—and put it on, and took up his riding-whip, and told the men to look alive and get their job done, and then to send up to the Castle for some beer and bread and cheese which he would order for them.

Then Joe and the Squire walked away along the hill-side talking, and I went and sat down on a little mound, just above the Horse's ears, and watched the men working, and looked at the view. How I did enjoy myself! The turf was as soft as a feather bed, and as springy as horse-hair; and it was all covered with thistle-down, which came drifting along like snow with the south wind; and all down below the country looked so rich and peaceful, stretching out for miles and miles at my feet in the hazy sunshine, and the larks right up overhead sang so sweetly, that I didn't know whether to laugh or cry. I should have liked to have had a turn at the besoms and shovels with the men, who seemed very good-tempered, only I was too shy, and I couldn't make out half they said. So I took out my pipe and lighted it, and sat looking on at the work, and thinking of nothing.

Presently a gentleman whom I hadn't noticed, but who was poking about the place, came and sat down near me. He was dressed in dark clothes, very quiet; I suppose he was a parson from some of the villages near. And we began talking about the weather, and what chance there was of having fine days for the Pastime. He was a very grave, elderly man, but easy and pleasant, and had a keen look in his grey eyes, and a sort of twinkle about his mouth, which made me put my best leg foremost, and take care what I said.

Well, when we had done about the weather, thinks I, "This is just the sort of gentleman to tell me what I want to know about the White Horse and all the rest of it," and you'll see as you go on that I never made a better guess in my life. So I got my note-book out quietly, so that he shouldn't take much notice of what I was about, and began, "I suppose, Sir," said I, "that it's all right about Alfred, and that he really did cut out this figure after winning a great battle up here?"

"Yes," said he, "the battle of Ashdown in the year 871. I think so myself, because there has always been a tradition in the country side that this was so. And where antiquaries differ, a tradition of this sort may always be pretty safely believed. Country folk hold on to such stories, and hand them down in a very curious manner; but you know, I dare say, that it is claimed by some as a Druidical, or at any rate a British monument, which would make it several hundred years older at least."[5]

I didn't know anything about it, but why should I tell him so.

"Don't you think it very curious, Sir, that the figure should have lasted all this time?" said I; "because you see, Sir, if you or I were to cut a trench, two feet or so deep, up here, on the side of the hill, and stamp down the chalk ever so hard, it would be all filled up and grown over in a few years."

"You are not the first person who has made that remark," said he. "In the year 1738, an antiquary of the name of Francis Wise, who lived at Oxford, visited the hill, and wrote a letter on the subject to Dr. Mead, the most learned antiquary of that day. First he speaks of the figure of the horse as 'being described in so masterly a manner that it may defy the painter's skill to give a more exact description of the animal.'"

"How could he talk like that, Sir?" said I; "why the figure isn't a bit like—"

"You are as bad as Camden," said he, "who talks of 'I know not what shape of a horse fancied on the side of a whitish hill;' but the truth is, it is a copy of the Saxon standard, which, of course, was a rude affair. However, Wise, whom I was telling you of, goes on:—

"When I saw it, the head had suffered a little and wanted reparation; and the extremities of his hinder legs, from their

5   *The figure is now believed to be of the Iron or Bronze Age.*

unavoidable situation, have by the fall of rains been filled up in some measure with the washings from the upper parts; so that, in the nearest view of him, the tail, which does not suffer the same inconvenience, and has continued entire from the beginning, seems longer than his legs. The supplies which nature is continually affording, occasion the turf to crumble and fall off into the white trench, which in many years' time produces small specks of turf, and not a little obscures the brightness of the Horse; though there is no danger from hence of the whole figure being obliterated, for the inhabitants have a custom of 'scouring the Horse,' as they call it; at which time a solemn festival is celebrated, and manlike games with prizes exhibited, which no doubt had their original in Saxon times in memory of the victory."[6]

"Scouring the Horse! yes, of course," said I, "that is what they are doing now, and the games are to come off to-morrow."

"Exactly so," said he, "but you will like to hear how Wise goes on:—

"If ever the genius of King Alfred exerted itself (and it never failed him in his greatest exigencies), it did remarkably so upon account of this trophy. The situation of his affairs would not permit him to expend much time, nor his circumstances much cost, in effecting one," (truly, for he had six more pitched battles to fight between April and November). "His troops, though victorious, were harassed and diminished by continual duty; nor did the country afford, to any man's thinking, materials proper for a work of this kind. Though he had not therefore the opportunity of raising, like other conquerors, a stupendous monument of brass or marble, yet he has shown an admirable contrivance, in erecting one magnificent enough, though simple in its design—executed, too, with little labour

6   Wise's Letter to Dr. Mead, "concerning some Antiquities in
     Berkshire," ed. 1, pp. 25, 26.

and no expense—that may hereafter vie with the Pyramids in duration, and perhaps exist when those shall be no more."

"But, dear me, Sir," said I, "how can the White "Horse vie with the Pyramids in duration? Why, the Pyramids were built—"

"Never mind when they were built," said he; "don't you see the old antiquary is an enthusiast? I had hoped you were one also."

"Indeed, Sir, I am very anxious to hear all you can tell me," said I, "and I won't interrupt again."

"Well, as to the scouring, Wise says:—

"The ceremony of scouring the Horse, from time immemorial, has been solemnized by a numerous concourse of people from all the villages round about. I am informed, though the Horse stands in the parish of Uffington, yet other towns claim, by ancient custom, a share of the duty upon this occasion.

"Since, therefore, this noble antiquity is now explained, and consequently the reason of the festival, it were to be wished that, in order to prevent for the future its falling into oblivion, some care was taken of the regulation of the games, and that they were restored to their ancient splendour, of which, without question, they are fallen much short. I know that these rites are cavilled at and maligned by the more supercilious part of mankind; but the dislike to them seems to be founded merely upon the abuse of them to riot and debauchery, which I intend by no means to justify or excuse.

"The practice of the best and wisest states, whose maxims we approve and profess to follow, is sufficient authority for their use. The liberty we so justly boast, and which ought to be a common blessing to all, pleads loudly for them. The common people, from their daily labour, stands at least in as much need of proper intervals of recreation as their superiors, who are exempt from it, and therefore in all free states have been indulged in sports most suited to their genius and capacity. And if manlike games contribute anything towards the support of the natural bravery of these, who are to be our bulwark and defence in times of danger, they cannot be more seasonably revived than at this juncture, when, through the general luxury and dissoluteness of the age, there was never more likelihood of its being extinguished."

I didn't say a word now, though he seemed to have finished.

"Well," said he, after a minute, "have you nothing to say? You're very glad that it's over, I suppose?"

"No, Sir, indeed I am not," said I; "but I am very much obliged to you for your kindness in telling me all that you have."

"You are a very intelligent young man, Sir," said he; "most young fellows of your age would have been bored to death, even if they hadn't managed to run off altogether, and so they would have lost a good lesson in English history—not that they would have cared much for that though. But now, I dare say you are getting hungry. Let us go up and see what they are doing in the Castle, and I shall be very glad if you will do me the honour of lunching with me."

"Well," thought I, as we got up from the turf, "there are not many better things for getting a man on than being a good listener. Here is a very learned old gentleman who doesn't know my name, and I have got the length of his foot, and he has asked me to luncheon, just because I have been listening to his old stories. I wonder where the lunch is to be though? he spoke of a Castle, perhaps he lives in it—who knows?"

So we strolled away together up over the brow of the hill.

CHAPTER III.

"WELL, HERE'S the Castle, you see," said he, when we had walked a few hundred yards, and were come quite to the top of the hill.

"Where, Sir?" said I, staring about. I had half expected to see an old stone building with a moat, and round towers and battlements, and a great flag flying; and that the old gentleman would have walked across the drawbridge, and cried out, "What ho! warder!" and that we should have been waited upon at lunch by an old white-headed man in black velvet, with a silver chain, and keys round his waist.

"I can't make up my mind about this Castle," he went on, without noticing me; "on two sides it looks like a regular Roman castrum, and Roman remains are found scattered about; but then the other sides are clearly not Roman. The best antiquaries who have noticed it call it Danish.[7] On the whole, I think it must have been seized and occupied in succession by the lords of the country for the time being; and each successive occupier has left his mark more or less plainly. But, at any rate, you see it is a magnificent work."

"Yes, Sir," said I, "no doubt;" though I own I was a good deal disappointed. For what do you think the Castle is? Up at the very top of the hill, above the White Horse, there is a great flat space, about as big as Lincoln's Inn Fields, only not the same shape, because it is only square on two sides. All round this space there is a bank of earth, eight or ten feet high in some places, but lower at others. Then, outside, there is a great, broad, deep ditch; it must be twenty-five feet from the top of

7   *It is now thought to be early Iron Age.*

the inner bank to the bottom of the ditch; and outside that again, is another large bank of earth, from the foot of which the downs slope away on every side. But the banks and ditch are all grown over with turf, just like the rest of the downs, and there isn't even a single stone, much less a tower, to be seen. There are three entrances cut through the double banks, one on the west, one on the southeast, and the third at the northeast side, which was the one through which we entered.

But if there were no warders and seneschals and drawbridges, there was plenty of life in the Castle. The whole place seemed full of men and women, and booths and beasts, and carts and long poles; and amongst them all were the Squire and Joe, and two or three farmers, who I afterwards found out were Committee-men, trying to get things into some sort of order. And a troublesome job they were having of it. All the ground was parcelled out for different purposes by the Committee, and such parts as were not wanted for the sports were let at small rents to any one who wanted them. But nobody seemed to be satisfied with his lot.

Here a big gypsy, who wouldn't pay any rent at all, was settling his cart and family, and swinging his kettle, on a bit of ground, which the man who owned the pink-eyed lady had paid for. There a cheap-Jack was hustling a toyman from Wantage, and getting all his frontage towards the streets (as they called the broad spaces which were to be kept clear for the people to walk along). In another place, a licensed publican was taking the lot of a travelling showman into his skittle-alley. Then there were old women who had lost their donkeys and carts, and their tins of nuts and sacks of apples; and donkeys who had lost their old women, standing obstinately in the middle of the streets, and getting in everybody's way; and all round, saws and axes and hammers were going, and booths and stalls were rising up.

I shouldn't have liked to have had much to do with setting them all straight, and so I told Joe, when he came up to us, after we had been looking on at all the confusion for a minute or two. For most of the men were very rough-looking customers, like the costermongers about Covent Garden and Clare Market, and I know that those huckstering, loafing blades are mostly terrible fellows to fight; and there wasn't a single policeman to look like keeping order. But Joe made light enough of it—he was always such a resolute boy, and that's what made me admire him so—and said, "For the matter of that, if they were ten times as rough a lot and twice as many, the Squire and the farmers and their men would tackle them pretty quick, without any blue-coated chaps to help! Aye, and nobody knows it better than they, and you'll see they'll be all in nice order before sundown, without a blow struck; except amongst themselves, perhaps, and that's no matter, and what they're used to. But now, you come in," said Joe, turning towards one of the large publicans' booths, which was already finished, "the Committee have got a table here, and we must dine, for we shan't be home these four hours yet, I can see."

"Sir," said my new friend to Joe, drawing himself up a bit, but very politely; "this gentleman is my guest. He has done me the honour of accepting my invitation to luncheon."

"Oh! beg pardon, Sir, I'm sure," said Joe; staring; "I didn't know that Dick had any acquaintance down in these parts. Then," said he to me, "I shall take my snack with the rest presently; you'll see me about somewhere, when it's time to get back." Joe went back into the crowd, and I followed the old gentleman.

We went into the booth, which was a very big one, made of strong double sail-cloth, stretched over three rows of fir poles, the middle row being, I should say, sixteen or eighteen feet high. Just on our right, as we entered from the street, was the bar, which was made with a double row of eighteen-gallon casks, full of ale, along the top of which boards were laid, so as to make a counter.

Behind the bar the landlord and landlady, and a barmaid, were working away and getting everything into order. There were more rows of large casks, marked XX and XXX, ranged upon one another against the side of the booth, and small casks of spirits hooped with bright copper, and cigar boxes, and a table covered with great joints of beef and pork, and crockery and knives and forks, and baskets full of loaves of bread, and lettuces and potatoes. It must have cost a deal of money to get it all up the hill, and set the booth up. Beyond the bar was a sort of inner room, partly screened from the rest of the booth by a piece of sail-cloth, where a long table was laid out for luncheon, or "nunching," as the boots, who was doing waiter for the occasion, called it. The rest of the booth, except a space before the bar which was kept clear for casual customers to stand about in, was set about with rough tables and forms.

We got a capital dinner; for the landlord knew my entertainer, and was very civil, and brought us our ale himself and poured it out, making an apology because it hadn't had quite time to fine down, but it would be as clear as a diamond, he said, if we would please to call in to-morrow. After we had done we went round behind the booth, where some rough planking had been put up to serve for stalls, and the boots, in his waiter's jacket, brought out the old gentleman's cob.

"Peter," said he, when he had mounted, "here is sixpence for you; and now mind what you are at, and don't get drunk and disgrace yourself up on the hill."

Peter, who seemed to be very much afraid of the old gentleman, kept pulling away at his forelock, and hunching up his shoulders, till we turned the corner of the booth.

"Now I must be riding home," said my friend. "If you have time to walk down to that little clump of trees over there, you will find an old Druidical cromlech well worth examining. It is called Wayland Smith's cave. Walter Scott, who should have known better, says that the Danish king killed at Ashdown was buried there. He was no more buried there than in Westminster Abbey.[8] Good-bye."

And so he put his cob into a canter, and went off along the Ridgeway[9]. When he was gone I walked down to the clump of trees and went into the cave; and then sat down on the great flat stone which covers it over; and thought what odd people a man finds about the world, and how many things there are which one never heard of that other folk are spending their lives over. Then I went up to the camp again to find Joe, for the afternoon was getting on.

True enough, as he had said, when I got back there I found it all getting into order. All along the north side were the theatres and peep-shows, and acrobats, and the pink-eyed lady, and the other shows.

On the west side were the publicans' booths, some of them all ready, and others half up, but all with their places settled; and the great street of huxters' stalls and cheap-Jacks was all set out along the south side, and as more and more of them came up they went off to the end of the line and pitched regularly.

The gypsies and people with no regular business were all got away into a corner, behind the stalls. On the west side the county police were pitching their large tent close away by the bank, out of the way of everybody; and, some way in front of them, Lord Craven's[10] people had put up two military-looking

---

8   *Wayland's Smithy is now thought to date to the Neolithic.*
9   *See page 295.*
10   *See page 287.*

tents which I heard had belonged to the 42d Regiment, with a great flagstaff close by them. About the middle of the camp stood a large stage about six feet high, roped round for the backswording and wrestling. There was plenty of room now, and all the people who were not working at the booths and stalls were sitting about boiling kettles and getting their food. It was a very cheerful, pretty sight, up there out of the way of everything.

I soon found Joe amongst a group of farmers and one or two young gentlemen, some on horseback and some on foot, standing round the Squire. They were talking over the arrangements before going home; and I stood a little way off, so as not to interrupt them or to seem to be pushing myself into their company.

"Now I think we have done all we can to-day," said the Squire, gathering up his reins; "but some of us must be up early to-morrow to get the lists made, and settle everything about the games."

"About ten o'clock, Sir?"

"Yes, that will do capitally. Now I shall just go and see how they have done the Horse."

So he rode out of the camp, and we all followed over the brow of the hill till we came to a good point for seeing the figure, which looked as bright and clean as a new sixpence.

"I think he'll do very well," said the Squire.

"Listen to the scourers," said one of the young gentlemen.

They had finished their work, and were sitting in a group round a large can of beer which the Squire had sent down to them; and one of them was singing a rumbling sort of ditty, with a tol-de-rol chorus, in which the rest joined lazily.

One of these young gentlemen gave me what he said were the words they were singing, afterwards, when I came to know him (as you will hear in the next chapter); and it seems he had found out that I was collecting all I could about the Horse. But I don't quite know whether he wasn't cutting his jokes upon me, for he is "amazin' found of fun," as Joe said; and for my part, I could never quite tell, when I was with him, whether he was in jest or earnest. However, here are the words he gave me:—

BALLAD OF THE SCOURING OF THE WHITE HORSE.

I.

The owld White Harse wants zettin to rights,
And the Squire hev promised good cheer,
Zo we'll gee un a scrape to kip un in zhape,
And a'll last for many a year.

II.

A was made a lang lang time ago
Wi a good dale o' labour and pains,
By King Alferd the Great when he spwiled their consate
And caddled,[11] thay wosbirds[12] the Danes.

III.

The Bleawin Stwun in days gone by
Wur King Alfred's bugle harn,
And the tharnin tree you med plainly zee
As is called King Alferd's tharn.

IV.

There'll be backsword play, and climmin the powl,
And a race for a peg, and a cheese,
And us thenks as hisn's a dummell[13] zowl
As dwont care for zich spwoorts as theze.

---

11   "Caddle"—to worry: from cad, strife.—The Berkshire scholiast suggests, that the modern "cad," having regard to the peculiarities of the class, must be the same word.

12   "Wosbird," bird of woe, of evil omen.

13   "Dummell," dull, stupid.

When we had done looking at the Horse, some went one way and some another, and Joe and I down the hill to the Swan Inn, where we got the trap and started away for Elm Close.

"Why, Dick, how did you manage to pick up the old gentleman who was treating you at dinner?" said Joe; "I suppose he's one of your London folk."

"'Twas he who picked me up," said I, "for I never set eyes on him before. But I can tell you he is a very learned party, and very kind too. He told me ever so many more old stories."

"Sooner you than I," said Joe. "Well, I thought I knew his face. He must be the old gent as was poking about our parish last fall, and sort of walking the bounds. Though there isn't any call for that, I'm sure, for we walk the bounds ourselves every year. The men as he hired told me he was looking after some old stone, the play stone I think he called it, and would have it he knew more about the names of the fields, and why they were called so, than they as had lived there all their lives. However, he stood 'em something handsome for their trouble. I expect he isn't quite right up here," said he, touching his forehead and looking at me.

"Just as right as you," said I, "and I've no doubt he does know more about your parish than all of you put together. I think he must be some great antiquary."

"Ah! that's what the Squire said when I told him. A great angular Saxon scholar he called him."

"Anglo-Saxon, Joe," said I, "not angular."

"Well, Anglo or angular, it's no odds," said Joe; "I calls it angular—that's good English at any rate."

"But, Joe," said I, "I've taken down all he said, and should like to read it to you. I'm sure it would interest you."

"Well, after supper to-night, over a pipe, perhaps," said Joe; "I ain't much of a hand at your old-world talk, you see. Or,

I'll tell you what, you shall read it to Lu; she takes to book-learning and all that better than I."

"I shall be very glad indeed to read it to your sister," said I; "and I daresay she can tell me something more."

"May be," said Joe, drawing his whip gently over the mare's loins; and then he began telling me about the talk he had had with the Squire.

He seemed to have been telling him all about his quarrel at the vestry with the other farmers, about keeping up the parish roads; and the Squire had smoothed him down, and given him some good advice as to how to get the roads made and the fences kept up without losing his temper. Joe owned to me that he was often falling out with some of his neighbours, or his hired men, when he couldn't get things quite his own way (for that's what it came to, and Joe is a warm-tempered fellow), and that he would sooner come six miles to get the Squire to "tackle it," than go to any other justice who lived nearer; "for he knows our ways, and manages one way or another to get it out all straight without making a Sessions job of it," said Joe, as we drove up to his gate; and though I was looking out to catch a sight of Miss Lucy, and hoping she might be out in the garden, I couldn't help allowing to myself that perhaps the country mightn't get on so much better after all if the unpaid magistracy were done away with.

Joe went off to the stable to see after his precious chestnut, and seemed to pity me because I didn't go with him. But I was off round the house and into the garden, to try and find Miss Lucy. When I did find her though, I wasn't quite pleased at first, as you may fancy when you hear what she was doing.

There is a trellis-work about eight feet high between the little flower-garden and the kitchen-garden, and in it a wicket-gate, through which runs a nice green walk by which you get from one to the other. The trellis-work is so covered with roses, and jessamine, and other creepers, that you can't see through, at least not in summer time; and I heard merry voices on the other side, but they couldn't hear me on the turf. So I hurried up to the wicket-gate; and the moment I got through, there I saw Miss Lucy, and close by her side a young man in a black coat, dark grey trousers, and a white tie. He had a great ribstone-pippin apple in one hand, off the best tree in the or-chard, out of which he had taken a great bite or two, which I thought rather vulgar; and there he was, holding up his bitten apple and some of the creepers against the trellis-work, with both hands above Miss Lucy's head.

And she stood there in her pretty white-straw hat, with the ribbons dangling loose over her shoulders, tying up the creep-ers to the trellis-work close to his face. I could see, too, that she was very well dressed, for she had on a pretty embroidered collar, as white as snow, with a nice bow of fresh pink ribbon in front; and the sleeves of her gown were loose, and fell back a little as she reached up with the string to tie the creepers, and showed her nice, white, round arms, which looked very pretty, only I wished she had waited for me to hold up the creepers instead of him. At her feet lay a basket full of apples and pears, and lavender and mignonette; so they must have been going about together for some time, picking fruit and flowers.

I stopped at the gate, and felt half inclined to go back; but he said something to her, and then she turned round and called me, so I walked up feeling rather sheepish. By the time I got up to them they had finished tying up the creeper, and she introduced me to Mr. Warton, of London. He held out his hand, and said he had often heard Joseph speak of me, and was very glad to meet an old friend of his friend Hurst.

So we shook hands, and he began eating his apple again, and she picked up her basket, and we walked together towards the house; but they were so free and pleasant together, and laughed and joked so, that it made me feel rather low, and I couldn't talk easily, though I did manage to say something about the White Horse, and how well it looked, and what a wonderful place it was up on the hill, when they asked me about it.

I wasn't sorry when she went in to look after the tea, and he sat down to write a letter. So I went round to the farm-yard to look for Joe, that I might find out from him about this Mr. Warton. I found Joe with his fogger,[14] as he called him, looking at some calves, and thinking of nothing but them and the pigs. However, I stuck to him and praised all the beasts just as if I knew all about them, and so at last got him out of the yard; and then I told him there was a Mr. Warton come.

"No! is he?" said he; "I'm so glad. I was afraid he couldn't come down as he didn't answer my last letter."

"Who is he, Joe?" said I.

"Haven't I told you?" said he; "why, he's a parson up somewhere in London, and a real right sort. He was curate here for five years before he went up to town."

"He seems to know you and Miss Lucy very well," said I.

"Bless you, yes!" said Joe; "Lu was in his school, and he prepared her for confirmation. He's the best company in the world, and not a bit proud, like some parsons. When he was down here, he used to drop in of an evening two or three times a week, and take his tea, or a bit of supper, just like you might."

"He's a good bit older than we, though," said I.

"Well, four or five years, maybe," said Joe, looking rather surprised at me; "I should say he was about thirty last grass, but I never asked him; what does it matter?" and so we got to the front door, and I went up-stairs to my room to wash my hands before tea. I made myself as smart as I could, but I own

---

14   "Fogger "—quasi fodderer—he who giveth fodder to the cattle—generally used for the farmer's head man.

I didn't half like the way this Mr. Warton went on. However, I thought Miss Lucy must see he was too old for her.

As I was dressing, I turned the matter over with myself, how I was to behave down-stairs. First, I thought I would try to ride the high horse, and be silent and vexed, and make them all uncomfortable; but then, thought I, will Miss Lucy see why I do it? It may be all out of love for her, and jealousy of this Mr. Warton; and they say no young woman dislikes to see men jealous about her. But suppose she shouldn't see it in that light? Mightn't she only think, perhaps, that I was a very changeable and disagreeable sort of fellow? That would never do. Besides, after all, thought I, I'm down here at Joe's house, and I owe it to him to be as pleasant as I can. How's he to know that I am in love with his sister already? And this Mr. Warton, too; he's a clergyman, and seems a very good sort, as Joe said; and then he has known them all so well, for so long; why am I to give myself airs because he likes talking to Miss Lucy? So I settled it in my own mind to go down with a smiling face, and to do all I could to make all the rest happy; and I felt much better myself when I had made up my mind.

There never was such a tea and supper (for we had them both together that night, as it was late) in the world; and I don't think I could have stood out five minutes if I had gone down in the sulks, as I thought of doing at first. The old lady, and Joe, and Miss Lucy, were all in great spirits at getting Mr. Warton down; and he was just like a boy home for his holidays. He joked and rattled away about everything; except when they talked about any of his old parishioners or scholars, and then he was as kind and tender as a woman, and remembered all their names, and how many children there were in every family, and the sort of mistakes the boys and girls used to make in school.

And he drew Miss Lucy out about the school, and Joe

about the markets and the labourers, and the old lady about the best way of pickling cabbages, and me about London and my work, and shorthand, which he managed to find out that I could write in no time. So we were all in the best humour in the world, and pleased with one another and with him; and spent half an hour in praising him after he had gone upstairs to finish some writing which he had to do.

Then I asked them about the Pastime, and what we should see next day on the hill. Miss Lucy began directly about the stalls and the sights, and the racing and the music; and cold dinner on the hill-side, and seeing all her friends in their best dresses. Joe listened to her for a bit, and then struck in—

"That's all very well for you women," said he; "but look here, Dick. If what I hear comes true, we shall have a fine treat on the stage; for they tells me there's a lot of the best old gamesters in Somersetshire coming up, to put in for the backsword prizes."

"Then I'm sure I hope they won't be allowed to play," said Miss Lucy.

"Not let to play!" said Joe; "who put that into your head? Why, there's the printed list of the sports, and £12 prize for backswording, and £10 for wrestling."

"Well, it's a great shame, then," said Miss Lucy; "for all the respectable people for miles round will be on the hill, and I think, the gentlemen ought to stop them."

"If they do, they'll spoil the Pastime; for there won't be one man in twenty up there who'll care to see anything else. Eh, old fellow?" said Joe, turning to me.

"I agree with Miss Lucy," said I; "for I'm sure if the women are against these games, they can't be good for the men, and ought to be put down."

"Dick, you're a cockney, and know no better," said Joe, giving me a great spank on the back, which hurt a good deal and was very disagreeable, only I didn't say anything because I knew he meant it kindly; "but as for you, Lucy, you, a west-country yeoman's daughter, to talk like that! If you don't take care, you sha'n't go up the hill to the Pastime to-morrow at all; I'll leave you at home with mother," and he shook his great fist at her.

"Won't I go up though?" said she, laughing; "we'll see, Master Joe; why, I can walk up by myself, if it comes to that; besides, any of the neighbours will give me a lift—or here's Mr. Richard, or Mr. Warton. I'm sure—"

"What's that you're saying, Miss Lucy? What am I to do, eh?" and the parson walked in just as I was going to speak. I was vexed at his just coming in, and taking the word out of my mouth.

"Why I was telling Joe that you'll stop and take me up the hill, if he leaves me behind; won't you now, Mr. Warton?"

"Leave you behind, indeed! here's a pretty to do!" said he, laughing. "What in the world are you all talking about?"

"About the wrestling and backsword play," struck in Joe; "now she says—"

"Well now, I'll leave it to Mr. Warton," said Miss Lucy, interrupting him; "I know he won't say it's right for men to be fighting upon a high stage before all the country side."

"Stuff and nonsense with your fighting!" said Joe; "you know, sir, very well that they are old English games, and we sets great store by them down here, though some of our folk as ought to know better does set their faces against them now-a-days."

"Yes, you know, Joe, that three or four clergymen have been preaching against them only last Sunday," said Miss Lucy.

"Then they ain't the right sort, or they'd know better what to preach against. I don't take all for Gospel that the parsons say, mind you," said Joe.

Miss Lucy looked shocked, but Mr. Warton only laughed.

"Hullo, Joseph," said he, "speaking evil of your spiritual pastors! However, I won't say you're altogether wrong. Parsons are but men."

"But, sir," said I, quite confidently, "I'm sure no clergyman can stand up for fighting and quarrelling."

"Of course not," said he; "but what then?"

"Well, sir, these sports, as they call them, are just fighting and nothing else, and lead to all sorts of quarrels and bad blood, and so—"

"They don't lead to nothing of the kind," shouted Joe; "and you know nothing about it, Dick."

"Now, Joe, at our last feast," said Miss Lucy, "didn't Reuben Yates get his head broken, and his arms all black and blue at backsword play?"

"Yes, and didn't you and mother patch him up with yards of diachylum, and give him his supper every night for a week, to come and be doctored and lectured? Rube liked his suppers well enough, and didn't mind the plastering and lecturing much; but if he don't go in to-morrow for the young gamesters' prize, my name ain't Joe Hurst."

"Then he'll be a very ungrateful, wicked fellow," said Miss Lucy.

"And you and mother won't give him anymore suppers or diachylum," said Joe; "but I dare say he won't break his heart if you don't give him the preaching by itself. It does seem to me plaguy hard that the women won't let a man get his own head broke quietly, when he has a mind to it."

"And there was Simon Withers, too," went on Miss Lucy, "he sprained his ankle at the wrestling, and was in the house for three weeks, and his poor old mother nearly starving."

"'Twasn't at wrestling though," said Joe, "'twas at hurdle-racing. He'd much better have been at backsword; for a chap can go to work with a broken head next morning and feel all the better for it, but he can't with a sprained ankle."

"What does Mr. Warton think?" said I; for somehow he was keeping back, and seemed a little on Joe's side, and if he showed that, I thought he would lose ground with Miss Lucy.

"Oh! I'm sure Mr. Warton is on our side, ain't you, Sir? Do tell Joe how wrong it is of him to go on talking as he does."

"No, no, Miss Lucy, I'm not going to be drawn into the quarrel as your knight; you're quite able to take your own part," said Mr. Warton.

"I'm sure Mr. Warton is against us in his heart," said I to Miss Lucy; "only he's a clergyman, and doesn't like to say so."

"Come now, I can't stand that," said he to me, "and you and I must have it out; only mind, Miss Lucy, you mustn't come in; one at a time is enough for me."

"I won't say a word, Sir, if Joe won't."

"Very well," said he, "and now let's get our ground clear. Do you approve of the other sports, running matches, jumping matches, and all the rest?"

"Yes, Sir, of course I do," said I.

"And you see no harm in one man beating another in a race for a prize?"

"No, Sir, no harm at all."

"Well, but I suppose one must have activity and endurance to win in any of them?"

"Yes," said I, "and good pluck too, Sir. It takes as much heart, I'm sure, any day, to win a hard race as a bout at backsword." "Very good," said he. "Then putting everything else aside, tell me which you think the best man, he who doesn't mind having his head broken, or he who does?"

"Well, Sir," said I, beginning to fence a bit, for I thought I saw what he was driving at, "that depends on circumstances."

"No, no," said he, " I want a short answer. We've nothing to do with circumstances. Suppose there were no circumstances in the world, and only two men with heads to be broken?"

"Well then, Sir," said I, "I suppose the one who doesn't mind having his head broken must be the best man."

"Hah, hah!" laughed Joe, "that puts me in mind of old Ben Thomson last feast. When he threw up his hat on the stage he said he could get his pint of beer any day for tuppence, but it wasn't every day as he could get his pint of beer and a broken head too for the same money."

"Oh, but Mr. Warton—" broke in Miss Lucy.

"Now you were not to say a word, you know," said he.

"But Joe began, Sir."

"Joseph, hold your tongue."

"Very well, Sir," said Joe, grinning.

"Then we come to this," said he to me, "a man must have just the same qualities to win at backsword as to win a race; and something else besides, which is good in itself?"

"But, Sir," said I, "that doesn't meet the point. What I say is, that backsword is a game in which men are sure to lose their tempers and become brutal."

"But don't they sometimes lose their tempers in races?" said he.

"Yes, sometimes perhaps," said I, "but not often."

"And sometimes they don't lose them at backsword?" said he.

"Well, perhaps not, Sir."

"Then it seems that all that can be said against backsword is, that it is a harder trial of the temper than other games. Surely that's no reason for stopping it, but only for putting it under strict rules. The harder the trial the better. I'm sure that's good English sense."

I didn't quite know what to say, but Miss Lucy broke in again.

"Oh, but Mr. Warton, did you ever see any backsword play?"

"Now, Miss Lucy, that is against law," said he; "but I don't mind answering. I never did, and I dare say your champion never has."

"No, Sir," said I; "but though you may have got the best of me, I don't believe you really mean that you think us wrong."

"Would you, really, Sir, preach a sermon now in favour of backsword play and wrestling?" asked Miss Lucy, with a long face.

"What's that got to do with it, Lucy?" broke in Joe. "We're not talking about preaching sermons, but about what's right for country chaps to do at Pastimes."

"Now, Joseph, I'm not going to ride off on any hobby of yours —besides, your sister's test is right. Several of your clergy about here have preached against these games, as was their duty if they had considered the subject well, and thought them wrong. I have never thought much about the matter till to-night. At present I think your clergy wrong. If I hold to that belief I would preach it; for I hope I never seriously say anything in the parlour which I wouldn't say in the pulpit."

Just then, the tall clock in the passage outside gave a sort of cluck, which meant half-past nine o'clock, and Joe jumped up and opened the door for the servants, and gave Mr. Warton the prayer book. And then as soon as ever prayers were over, he bustled his mother and sister off to bed, though I could see that Miss Lucy wasn't half satisfied in her mind about the backsword play and wrestling, and wanted to stay and hear something more from Mr. Warton. But Joe is always in a hurry for his pipe when half-past nine strikes, so we all had to humour him, and Mr. Warton and I went with him into the kitchen to smoke our pipes.

CHAPTER IV.

OW WHEN we had fairly lighted up, and Joe had mixed us a glass of gin and water a piece, I felt that it was a very good time for me to have a talk about the White Horse and the scourings. I wasn't quite satisfied in my mind with all that the old gentleman had told me on the hill; and, as I felt sure that Mr. Warton was a scholar, and would find out directly if there was anything wrong in what I had taken down, I took out my note-book, and reminded Joe that he had promised to listen to it over his pipe. Joe didn't half like it, and wanted to put the reading off, but Mr. Warton was very good-natured about it, and said he should like to hear it—so it was agreed that I should go on, and so I began. Joe soon was dozing, and every now and then woke up with a jerk, and pretended he had been listening, and made some remark in broad Berkshire. He always talks much broader when he is excited, or half asleep, than when he is cool and has all his wits about him. But I kept on steadily till I had got through it all, and then Mr. Warton said he had been very much interested, and believed that all I had taken down was quite correct.

""What put it into your head," said he, "to take so much interest in the Horse?"

"I don't know, Sir," said I, "but somehow I can't think of anything else now I have been up there and heard about the battle." This wasn't quite true, for I thought more of Miss Lucy, but I couldn't tell him that.

"When I was curate down here," said he, "I was bitten with the same maggot. Nothing would serve me but to find out all I could about the Horse. Now, Joe, here, who's fast asleep—"

"No, he beant," said Joe starting, and giving a pull at his pipe, which had gone out.

"Well, then, Joe here, who is wide awake, and the rest, who were born within sight of him, and whose fathers fought at Ashdown, and have helped to scour him ever since, don't care half so much for him as we strangers do."

"Oh! I dwon't allow that, mind you," said Joe; "I dwon't know as I cares about your long-tailed words and that; but for keeping the Horse in trim, and as should be, why, I be ready to pay—"

"Never mind how much, Joseph."

Joe grinned, and put his pipe in his mouth again. I think he liked being interrupted by the Parson.

"As I was saying, I found out all I could about the Horse, though it was little enough, and I shall be very glad to tell you all I know."

"Then, Sir," said I, "may I ask you any questions I have a mind to ask you about it?"

"Certainly," said he; "but you mustn't expect to get much out of me."

"Thank you, Sir," said I. "A thousand years seems a long time, Sir, doesn't it? Now, how do we know that the Horse has been there all that time?"

"At any rate," said he, "we know that the Hill has been called, 'White Horse Hill,' and the Vale, the 'Vale of White Horse,' ever since the time of Henry the First; for there are cartularies of the Abbey of Abingdon in the British Museum which prove it. So, I think, we may assume that they were called after the figure, and that the figure was there before that time."

"I'm very glad to hear that, Sir," said I. "And then about the scourings and the Pastime? They must have been going on ever since the Horse was cut out?"

"Yes, I think so," said he. "You have got quotations there from Wise's letter, written in 1736. He says that the scouring was an old custom in his time. Well, take his authority for the fact up to that time, and I think I can put you in the way of finding out something, though not much, about most of the Scourings which have been held since."

And he was as good as his word; for he took me about after the Pastime to some old men in the neighbouring parishes, from whom I found out a good deal that I have put down in this chapter. And the Squire, too, when Joe told him what I was about, helped me. Now I can't say that I have found out all the Scourings which have been held since 1736, but I did my best to make a correct list, and this seems to be the proper place to set it all down.

Well, the first Scouring, which I could find out anything about, was held in 1755, and all the sports then seem to have been pretty much the same as those of the present day. But there was one thing which happened which could not very well have happened now. A fine dashing fellow, dressed like a gentleman, got on to the stage, held his own against all the old gamesters, and in the end won the chief prize for backsword-play, or cudgelplay, as they used to call it.

While the play was going on there was plenty of talk as to who this man could be, and some people thought they knew his face. As soon as he had got the prize he jumped on his horse, and rode off. Presently, first one, and then another, said it was Tim Gibbons, of Lambourn, who had not been seen for some years, though strange stories had been afloat about him.

It was the Squire who told me the story about Tim Gibbons; but he took me to see an old man who was a descendant of Tim's, and so I think I had better give his own account of his ancestor and his doings. We found the old gentleman, a hale, sturdy old fellow, working away in a field at Woolstone, and, as near as I could get it, this was what he had to say about the Scouring of 1755:—

Squire. "Good morning, Thomas. How about the weather? Did the White Horse smoke his pipe this morning?"

Thos. "Mornin', Sir. I didn't zee as 'a did. I allus notices he doos it when the wind blaws moor to th' east'ard. I d'wont bode no rain to day, Sir."

Squire. "How old are you, Thomas?"

Thos. "Seventy year old this Christmas, Sir. I wur barn at Woolstone, in the hard winter, when I've heard tell as volks had to bwile their kettles wi' the snaw."

Squire. "I want to know something about your family, Thomas."

Thos. "Well, Sir, I beant no ways ashamed of my family, I can assure 'ee. I've a got two zons, and vour daaters. One on 'em, that's my oldest bwoy, Sir, wur all droo' the Crimee wars, and never got a scratch. In the Granadier guards, Sir, he be. A uncommon sprack[15] chap, Sir, though I says it, and as bowld as a lion; only while he wur about our village wi' t'other young chaps, he must allus be a fighting. But not a bad-tempered chap, Sir, I assure 'ee. Then, Sir—"

Squire. "But, Thomas, I want to know about those that came before you. What relation was Timothy Gibbons, whom I've heard folks talk about, to you?"

Thos. "I suppose as you means my great-grandvather, Sir."

Squire. "Perhaps so, Thomas. Where did he live, and what trade did he follow?"

Thoms. "I'll tell 'ee, Sir, all as I knows; but somehow, vather and mother didn't seem to like to talk to we bwoys about 'un."

15   "Sprack,"—sprightly.

Squire. "Thank 'ee, Thomas. Mind, if he went wrong it's all the more credit to you, who have gone straight; for there isn't a more honest man in the next five parishes."

Thos. "I knows your meanings good, and thank 'ee kindly, Sir, tho' I be no schollard. Well, Timothy Gibbons, my great grandvather, you see, Sir, foller'd blacksmithing at Lambourn, till he took to highway robbin', but I can't give 'ee no account o' when or wher'.

"Arter he'd been out, may be dree or vour year, he and two companions cum to Baydon; and whilst hiding theirselves and baiting their hosses in a barn, the constables got ropes round the barn-yard and lined 'em in. Then all dree drawed cuts[16] who was to go out fust and face the constables. It fell to Tim's two companions to go fust, but their hearts failed 'em, and they wouldn't go. So Tim cried out as 'he'd shew 'em what a Englishman could do,' and mounted his hos and drawed his cutlash, and cut their lines a-two, and galloped off clean away; but I understood as t'other two was took.

"Arter that, may be a year or two, he cum down to a Pastime on White Hos Hill, and won the prize at backswording; and when he took his money, fearing lest he should be knowed, he jumped on his hos under the stage, and galloped right off, and I don't know as he ever cum again to these parts. Then I've understood as things throve wi' 'un, as urn will at times, Sir, wi' thay sort o' chaps, and he and his companions built the Inn called 'the Magpies,' on Hounslow Heath; but I dwon't know as ever he kep' the house hisself, except it med ha' been for a short while.

"Howsomever, at last he was took drinking at a public-house, someweres up Hounslow way, wi' a companion who played a cross wi' 'un, and I b'live 'a, was hanged at Newgate. But I never understood as he killed anybody, Sir, and a'd used

16 "Draw cuts,"—to draw lots.

to gie some o' the money as he took to the poor, if he knowed they was in want."

Squire. "Thank'ee, Thomas. What a pity he didn't go soldiering; he might have made a fine fellow then!"

Thos. "Well, Sir, so t'wur, I thinks. Our fam'ly be given to that sort o' thing. I wur a good hand at elbow and collar wrastling myself, afore I got married; but then I gied up all that, and ha' stuck to work ever sence."

Squire. "Well, Thomas, you've given me the story I wanted to hear, so it's fair I should give you a Sunday dinner."

Thos. "Lord love 'ee, Sir, I never meant nothin' o' that sort; our fam'ly—"

We were half-way across the field, when I looked round, and saw old Thomas still looking after us and holding the Squire's silver in his hand, evidently not comfortable in his mind at having failed in telling us all he had to say about *his fam'ly*, of which he seemed as proud as any duke can be of his, and I dare say has more reason for his pride than many of them. At last, however, as we got over the stile, he pocketed the affront and went on with his work.

I could find out nothing whatever about the next Scouring; but I was lucky enough to get the printed hand-bill which was published before the one in 1776, which I made out to be the next but one after that at which Tim Gibbons played. This hand-bill was kindly given me by H. Godwin, Esq., of Newbury.

When I showed this old hand-bill to the Parson he was very much tickled. He took up the one which the Committee put out this last time, and looked at them together for a minute, and then tossed them across to me.

"What a queer contrast," said he, "between those two bills."

"How do you mean, Sir?" said I; "why the games seem to be nearly the same."

"So they are," said he; "but look at the prizes. Our great grandfathers you'll see gave no money prizes; we scarcely any others. The gold-laced hat and buckskin breeches have gone, and current coin of the realm reigns supreme. Then look at the happy-go-lucky way in which the old bill is put out. No date given, no name signed! who was responsible for the breeches, or the shoe-buckles? And then, what grammar! The modern bill, you see, is in the shape of resolutions passed at a meeting, the chairman's name being appended as security for the prizes."

"That seems much better and more business-like," said I.

"Then you see the horse race for a silver cup has disappeared," he went on. "Epsom and Ascot have swallowed up the little country races, just as big manufacturers swallow up little ones, and big shops whole streets of little shops, and nothing but monsters nourish in this age of unlimited competition and general enlightenment. Not that I regret the small country town-races, though."

"And I see, Sir, that 'smocks to be run for by ladies' is left out in the modern bill."

"A move in the right direction there, at any rate," said he, "the bills ought to be published side by side." So I took his advice, and here they are:—

"WHITE HORSE HILL, BERKS, 1776.

"The scowering and cleansing of the White Horse is fixed for Monday the 27th day of May; on which day a Silver Cup will be run for near White Horse Hill by any horse, &c. that never run for any thing, carrying 11 stone, the best of 3 two-mile heats, to start at ten o'clock.

"Between the heats will be run

PASTIME.

To be held on the occasion of the Scouring of the White Horse, September 17th and 18th, 1857.

"At a meeting held at the Craven Arms, Uffington, on the 20th day of August, 1857, the following resolutions (amongst others) were passed unanimously:—

First. That a Pastime be held on the White Horse Hill, on Thurs for by Poneys, a Saddle, Bridle and Whip; the best of 3 two-mile heats, the winner of 2 heats will be entitled to the Saddle, the second best the Bridle, and the third the Whip.

"The same time a Thill harness will be run for by Cart-horses, &c. in their harness and bells, the carters to ride in smock frocks without saddles, crossing and jostling, but no whipping allowed.

"A flitch of Bacon to be run for by asses.

"A good Hat to be run for by men in sacks, every man to bring his own sack.

"A Waistcoat, 10s. 6d. value, to be given to the person who shall take a bullet out of a tub of flour with his mouth in the shortest time.

"A Cheese to be run for down the White Horse Manger.

"Smocks to be run for by ladies, the second best of each prize to be entitled to a Silk Hat.

"*Cudgel-playing for a gold-laced Hat* and a pair of buckskin Breeches, and *Wrestling* for a pair of silver Buckles and a pair of pumps.

"The horses to be on the White Horse Hill by nine o'clock.

"No less than four horses, &c. or asses to start for any of the above prizes."

day and Friday, the 17th and 18th of September, in accordance with the old custom at the time of "The Scouring of the Horse."

2ndly. That E. Martin Atkins, Esq. of Kingston Lisle, be appointed Treasurer.

3rdly. That prizes be awarded for the following games and sports, That is to say—

Backsword Play. Old gamesters, £8. Young gamesters, £1.

Wrestling. Old gamesters, £5. Young gamesters, £4.

A jingling match.

Foot races.

Hurdle races.

Race of cart-horses in Thill harness (for a new set of harness).

Donkey race (for a flitch of bacon).

Climbing pole (for a leg of mutton).

Races down "the Manger" (for cheeses).

A pig will be turned out on the down, to be the prize of the man who catches him (under certain regulations); and further prizes will be awarded for other games and sports as the funds will allow.

4thly. That no person be allowed to put up or use a stall or booth on the ground, without the previous sanction of Mr. Spackman, of Bridgecombe Farm [the occupier], who is hereby authorized to make terms with any person wishing to put up a stall or booth.

Signed, E. MARTIN ATKINS, Chairman.

Then came a Scouring on Whit-Monday, May 15th, 1780, and of the doings on that occasion there is the following notice in the *Reading Mercury* of May 22d, 1780:—

"The ceremony of scowering and cleansing that noble monument of Saxon antiquity, the White Horse, was celebrated on Whit-Monday, with great joyous festivity. Besides the customary diversions of horse-racing, foot-races, &c. many uncommon rural diversions and feats of activity were exhibited to a greater number of spectators than ever assembled on any former occasion. Upwards of thirty thousand persons were present, and amongst them most of the nobility and gentry of this and the neighbouring counties; and the whole was concluded without any material accident. The origin of this remarkable piece of antiquity is variously related; but most authors describe it as a monument to perpetuate some signal victory, gained near the spot, by some of our most ancient Saxon princes. The space occupied by this figure is more than an acre of ground."

I also managed to get a list of the games, which is just the same as the one of 1776, except that in addition there was, "a jingling match by eleven blindfolded men, and one unmasked and hung with bells, for a pair of buckskin breeches."

The Parson found an old man, William Townsend by name, a carpenter at Woolstone, whose father, one Warman Townsend, had run down the manger after the fore-wheel of a wagon, and won the cheese at this Scouring. He told us the story as his father had told it to him, how that "eleven on 'em started, and amongst 'em a sweep chimley and a milord; and the milord tripped up the sweep chimley and made the zoot flee a good 'un;" and how "the wheel ran pretty nigh down to the springs that time," which last statement the Parson seemed to think couldn't be true. But old Townsend knew nothing about the other sports.

Then the next Scouring was held in 1785, and the Parson found several old men who could remember it when they were very little. The one who was most communicative was old William Ayres of Uffington, a very dry old gentleman, about eighty-four years old:—

"When I wur a bwoy about ten years old," said he, "I remembers I went up White Hoss Hill wi' my vather to a Pastime. Vather'd brewed a barrel o' beer to sell on the Hill—a deal better times then than now, Sir!"

"Why, William?" said the Parson.

"Augh! bless'ee, Sir, a man medn't brew and sell his own beer now; and oftentimes he can't get nothin' fit to drink at thaay little beer-houses as is licensed, nor at some o' the public-houses too for that matter. But 'twur not only for that as the times wur better then, you see, Sir—"

"But about the sports, William?"

"Ees Sir, I wur gandering sure enough," said the old man; "well now, there wur Varmer Mifflin's mare run for and won a new cart-saddle and thill-tugs—the mare's name wur *Duke*. As many as a dozen or moor horses run, and they started from Idle's Bush, which wur a vine owld tharnin'-tree in thay days—a very nice bush. They started from Idle's Bush, as I tell 'ee, Sir, and raced up to the Rudge-waay; and Varmer Mifflin's mare had it all one way, and beat all the t'other on 'um holler. The Pastime then wur a good 'un—a wunderful sight o' volk of all sorts, rich and poor. John Morse of Uffington, a queerish sort of a man, grinned agin another chap droo' hos collars, but John got beaat—a fine bit of spwoort to be shure, Sir, and made the folks laaf. Another geaam wur to bowl a cheese down the Mainger, and the first as could catch 'un had 'un. The cheese was a tough 'un and held together."

"Nonsense, William, that's impossible," broke in the Parson.

173

"Augh Sir, but a did though, I assure 'ee," persisted William Ayres, "but thaay as tasted 'un said a warn't very capital arter all."

"I daresay," said the Parson, "for he couldn't have been made of anything less tough than ash pole."

"Hah, hah, hah," chuckled the old man, and went on.

"There wur running for a peg too, and they as could ketch 'un and hang 'un up by the tayl had 'un. The girls, too, run races for smocks—a deal of Pastime, to be sure, Sir. There wur climmin' a grasy pole for a leg of mutton, too; and backsoordin', and wrastlin', and all that, ye knows, Sir. A man by the name of Blackford, from the low countries, Zummersetshire, or that waay some weres, he won the prize, and wur counted the best hand for years arter, and no man couldn't break his yead; but at last, nigh about twenty years arter, I'll warn[17] 'twur—at Shrin'um Revel, Harry Stanley, the landlord of the Blawin' Stwun, broke his yead, and the low-country men seemed afeard o' Harry round about here for long arter that.

"Varmer Small-bwones of Sparsholt, a mazin' stout man, and one as scarce no wun go where 'a would could drow down, beaat all the low-country chaps at wrastlin', and none could stan' agean 'un. And so he got the neam o' Varmer Greaat Bwones. 'Twur only when he got a drap o' beer a leetle too zoon, as he wur ever drowed at wrastlin', but they never drowed 'un twice, and he had the best men come agean 'un for miles. This wur the first Pastime as I well remembers, but there med ha' been some afore, for all as I knows. I ha' got a good memorandum, Sir, and minds things well when I wur a bwoy, that I does. I ha' helped to dress the White Hoss myself, and a deal o' work 'tis to do't as should be, I can asshure 'ee, Sir. About Claay Hill, 'twixt Fairford and Ziziter, I've many a time looked back at 'un, and 'a looks as nat'ral as a pictur, Sir."

Between 1785 and 1803 there must have been at least two

---

17   "Warn,"—contraction of the word " warrant."

Scourings, but somehow none of the old men could remember the exact years, and they seemed to confuse them with those that came later on, and though I looked for them in old county papers, I could not find any notice of them

At the Scouring of 1803, Beckingham of Baydon won the prize at wrestling; Flowers and Ellis from Somersetshire won the prize at backsword play; the waiter at the Bell Inn, Farringdon, won the cheese race, and at jumping in sacks; and Thomas Street, of Niton, won the prize for grinning through horse collars, "but," as my informant told me, "a man from Woodlands would ha' beaat, only he'd got no teeth. This geaam made the congregation laaf 'mazinly."

Then came a Scouring in 1808, at which the Hanney men came down in a strong body and made sure of winning the prize for wrestling. But all the other gamesters leagued against them, and at List their champion, Belcher, was thrown by Fowler of Baydon;—both these men are still living. Two men, "with very shiny topboots, quite gentlemen, from London," won the prize for backsword play, one of which gentlemen was Shaw, the life-guardsman, a Wiltshire man himself as I was told, who afterwards died at Waterloo after killing so many cuirassiers.[18] A new prize was given at this Pastime and a very blackguard one, viz: a gallon of gin or half a guinea for the woman who would smoke most tobacco in an hour. Only two gypsy women entered, and it seems to have been a very abominable business, but it is the only instance of the sort that I could hear of at any Scouring.

The old men disagree as to the date of the next Scouring, which was either in 1812 or 1813; but I think in the latter year, because the clerk of Kingstone Lisle, an old Peninsula man, says that he was at home on leave in this year, and that there was to be a Scouring. And all the people were talking about

18   *Corporal John Shaw was actually from Nottinghamshire. See page 288.*

it when he had to go back to the wars. At this Scouring there was a prize of a loaf made out of a bushel of flour, for running up the manger, which was won by Philip New, of Kingstone-in-the-Hole; who cut the great loaf into pieces at the top, and sold the pieces for a penny a piece. I am sure he must have deserved a great many pennies for running up that place, if he really ever did it; for I would just as soon undertake to run up the front of the houses in Holborn. The low country men won the first backsword prize, and one Ford, of Ashbury, the second; and the Baydon men, headed by Beckingham, Fowler, and Breakspear, won the prize for wrestling. One Henry Giles (of Hanney, I think they said) had wrestled for the prize, and I suppose took too much beer afterwards; at any rate, he fell into the canal on his way home, and was drowned. So the jury found, "Killed at wrastlin';" "though," as my informant said, "'twur a strange thing for a old geamster as knew all about the stage, to be gettin' into the water for a bout. Hows'mever, Sir, I hears as they found it as I tells 'ee, and you med see it any day as you've a mind to look in the parish register."

Then I couldn't find that there had been another Scouring till 1825, but the one which took place in that year seems by all accounts to have been the largest gathering that there has ever been. The games were held at the Seven Barrows, which are distant two miles in a south-easterly direction from the White Horse, instead of in Uffington Castle; but I could not make out why. These seven barrows, I heard the Squire say, are probably the burial-places of the principal men who were killed at Ashdown, and near them are other long irregular mounds, all full of bones huddled together anyhow, which are very likely the graves of the rank and file.

After this there was no Scouring till 1838, when, on the 19th and 20th of September, the old custom was revived, under the patronage of Lord Craven. The *Reading Mercury* congratulates its readers on the fact, and adds that no more auspicious year could have been chosen for the revival, "than that in which our youthful and beloved Queen first wore the British crown, and in which an heir was born to the ancient and noble house of Craven, whom God preserve." I asked the Parson if he knew why it was that such a long time had been let to pass between the 1825 Scouring and the next one.

"You see it was a transition time," said he; "old things were passing away. What with Catholic Emancipation, and Reform, and the new Poor Law, even the quiet folk in the Vale had no time or heart to think about Pastimes; and machine-breaking and rick-burning took the place of wrestling and backsword play."

"But then, Sir," said I, "this last fourteen years we haven't had any Reform Bill (worse luck) and yet there was no Scouring between 1843 and 1857." "Why can't you be satisfied with my reason?" said he; "now you must find one out for yourself."

The last Scouring, in September, 1843, Joe had been at himself, and told me a long story about, which I should be very glad to repeat, only I think it would rather interfere with my own story of what I saw myself. The Berkshire and Wiltshire men, under Joe Giles of Shrivenham, got the better of the Somersetshire men, led by Simon Stone, at backsword play; and there were two men who came down from London, who won the wrestling prize away from the countrymen.

"What I remember best, however," said Joe, "was all the to-do to get the elephant's caravan up the hill, for Wombwell's menagerie came down on purpose for the Scouring. I should think they put-to a matter of four-and-twenty horses, and then stuck fast four or five times. I was a little chap then, but I sat and laughed at 'em a good one; and I don't know that I've seen so foolish a job since."

"I don't see why, Joe," said I.

"You don't?" said he, "well, that's good, too. Why didn't they turn the elephant out and make him pull his own caravan up? He would have been glad to do it, poor old chap, to get a breath of fresh air, and a look across the Vale."[19]

But now that I have finished all that I have to tell about the old Scourings (at least all that I expect anybody will read), I must go back again to the kitchen on the night of the 16th of September, 1857. Joe, who, as I said, was half asleep while I was reading, soon waked up afterwards, though it was past eleven o'clock, and began to settle how we were to go up the hill the next morning.

"Now I shall ride the chestnut up early," said he, "'cause, I may be wanted to help the Squire and the rest, but it don't matter for the rest of you. I'll have a saddle put on my old brown horse, and he'll be quiet enough, for he has been at harvest work, and the four-wheel must come up with Lu somehow. Will you ride or drive, Sir?" said he, turning to the Parson.

"Oh, I don't mind; whichever is most convenient," said Mr. Warton.

"Did'st ever drive in thy life, Dick?" said Joe to me.

I was very near saying "yes," for I felt ashamed of not being able to do what they could; however, I told the truth, and said "no;" and next minute I was very glad I had, for, besides the shame of telling a lie, how much worse it would have been to be found out by Miss Lucy in the morning, or to have had an upset or some accident.

So it was settled that Mr. Warton should drive the four-wheel, and that I should ride the old horse. I didn't think it necessary to say that I had never ridden anything but the donkeys on Hampstead Heath, and the elephant in the Zoological Gardens. And so, when all was settled, we went to bed.

---

19   *Joe is quite right about the horses. See illustration on page 194.*

CHAPTER V.

NEXT MORNING I got up early, for I wasn't quite easy in my mind about riding Joe's old horse, and so I thought I would just go round and look at him, and ask the fogger something about his ways. It was a splendid morning, not a cloud to be seen. I found the fogger strapping away at the horses. Everybody had been up and about since daylight, to get their day's work done, so that they might get away early to the Pastime. All the cows had been milked and turned out again, and Joe was away in the fields, looking after his men.

I stood beating about the bush for some time, for I didn't want to let the man see what I was thinking of if I could help it. However, when he brought out the old brown horse to clean him down, I went up and patted him, and asked whether he was a good saddle horse.

"Ees, there warn't much fault to find wi' un," said the fogger, stopping his hissing and rubbing for a moment, "leastways for them as didn't mind a high goer."

I didn't quite know what he meant by a high goer, so I asked him if the brown was up to my weight.

"Lor' bless 'ee, ees. He'd make no account o' vivteen stun. Be you to ride un up the hill, Sir, make so bold?" said he.

"Yes, at least I think so," said I.

"Hev 'ee got arra loose tooth, Sir?" said he, grinning.

"No," said I, "why?"

"'Cause he'll be as likely as not to shake un out for 'ee, Sir, if you lets un hev his head up on the downs."

I didn't like this account of the brown horse, for as I hadn't ridden much, he might take his head perhaps whether I let him have it or not. So I made up my mind not to ride. I thought I would go behind in the four-wheel, for I didn't like to leave Miss Lucy all alone with the Parson for so long; but then I found out that one of the carter-boys was to go behind to look after the horses, and I didn't choose to be put up side by side with him, to look ridiculous. There was a big wagon going up, too, full of the farm servants, but that didn't seem to suit me any better, so I settled with myself that I would just start and walk up.

Joe, luckily for me, thought he had settled everything, and so at breakfast said nothing more about the old horse; though I was afraid he would every minute, and then I should have had to pretend I was going to ride, or they might have found out that I didn't quite like the notion. I was very glad when I saw him fairly off after breakfast, cantering away on the chestnut; and, very soon afterwards, I took a good stout stick of Joe's in my hand, put my note-book in my pocket, and started off quietly by myself.

At first as I walked along I didn't enjoy myself much for thinking of the four-wheel, and I was almost getting jealous of the Parson again. But I soon got over it, when I remembered how kind he had been the night before. And I felt, too, that if he really was making up to her there was very little chance for me, so I had better make up my mind anyhow to see and enjoy everything I could. I don't think I was very much in love at the time; if it had been a week later I should have found it much harder perhaps. I kept along the shady side of the road, for it was getting hot already, and crossed the canal, and kept making up towards the hills. I wasn't sure of the way, but I knew that if once I got up the hill I should find the Ridgeway, and could follow it all the way up to the Castle. After a bit I fell in with groups of people, all going the same way; and so, following on with them, after about an hour's walk, I came to the

foot of the hills; and found a pretty little inn, standing back from the road, nestled into a plantation, where everybody else seemed to be stopping; and so I stopped too, and sat down on the bench before the door to have a glass of beer before facing the pull up to the top.

In front of the door was an oak tree, and under the tree a big stone with some curious holes in it, into which pieces of wood were fitted, secured by a padlock and chain. I was wondering what it could be, when the landlord came out with some of his guests, and pulling out a key unlocked the padlock, and took the pieces of wood out of the holes. Then there was some talk between the young men and their sweethearts, and first one and then another stooped down and blew into the hole at the top, and the stone made a dull moaning sound, unlike anything I had ever heard. The landlord told me that when it was well blown on a still day, it could be heard for four or five miles, and I should think it could; for I left them blowing away when I started again, and heard the sound every now and then until I was close up to the Castle, though the wind blew from the south, and down the hill.[20]

---

20   *See page 290.*

I should think a dozen parties, in all sorts of odd go-carts and other vehicles, or on foot, must have passed the Blowing-stone in the ten minutes which I spent on the bench. So I got quite eager to be up at the Castle, and paid for my beer and started again. It is a very long stiff pull up Blowing-stone Hill, and the road is not a very good one; so I soon began to pass the gigs and carts, most of which had to stop every hundred yards or so, to let the horses and donkeys get their wind. Half way up, in the worst part of the hill, I found an old huckstering woman and a boy in great trouble. They had a little cart laden with poles and boards for a stall, and two great sacks of nuts and sweetstuff; and only one donkey in the shafts, who had got one wheel of the cart into a deep chalk rut, and stood there like a post. The woman and boy were quite beat with dragging at his head, and trying to lift the wheel out of the rut, and as I came up she was "fairly giving out."

"Lawk-a-massy! how ever be I to scawt[21] up? Do'ee lend a help, there's a good soul," said she to me.

Well, I couldn't go by and leave her there, though I didn't half like having to stop; so I helped to lift the wheel out, and then we pushed the cart up a few yards, and the old donkey tried to sidle it into another rut, and we had another fight with him. My blood got up at his obstinacy; I don't believe there ever was another such a donkey in the world; so the more he backed and sidled, the more I and the old woman and the boy fought. And then the people that passed us began to laugh and joke at us, and I got very angry at them, and the old woman, and everybody; but I set my teeth, and made up my mind to get him up to the top if I stayed there all day.

I should think we must have been nearly half-an-hour at work, and had got on about three hundred yards or so, when a fine dogcart on high wheels came up. I heard the gentlemen in it talking and laughing as they came near us; but I didn't look up, and kept working away at the donkey, for I was afraid they would only joke at us.

"Oh deary me, deary me, Master Gaarge, be that you?" I heard the old woman call out; "now do'ee stop some o' the chaps, and tell 'em to help. I be nigh caddled to death wi' this drattled old jack-ass—oh dear, oh dear!"

"Why, Betty! what in the world are you after?" said a merry voice, which I thought I had heard before; and, looking up, I saw the young gentleman who had promised me the song.

"Oh, you see, Master Gaarge, I thought as I might turn a honest penny if I could only win up to the Pastime wi' some nuts and brandy-balls. So I loaned neighbour Tharne's cart as he fetches coals from the canal wi', and his ass—and if 'twas Balaam's ass hisself he couldn't be no wus—and here I be; and if it hadn't a been for this kind gentleman—"

---

21 "Scawt"—to get up.

"Well, stop your talk, Betty, and take hold of his head," said he, jumping out of his dog-cart and giving the reins to the one who was beside him. "Ah, good morning," nodding to me, as he came to the back of the cart, "now then, with a will! shove away!"

So we shoved the cart hard against the donkey's legs. "Don't pull, Betty, let him have his head; just keep hold of the reins. Look out, boy; stop him making for the ditch;" and away went Master Neddy scrambling up hill, for he found that the cart was coming over his back if he didn't move on. Master George was as strong as a ballast heaver, and the donkey seemed to find it out quick enough, for we were up the hill in no time.

"Bless your kind heart, Master Gaarge!" almost sobbed the old woman; "I be all straight now. Do'ee hev summat to suck now, or some nuts, and this kind gentleman too; you allus wur fond o'suck;" and she began untying the neck of one of her sacks.

"Oh, Betty, you wicked old lone woman!" said he, "haven't you made me ill often enough with your nastinesses fifteen years ago?"

"Dwont'ee, now, call 'em names, Master Gaarge."

"Good-bye, Betty, and make haste up to the Castle before all the small boys are poisoned. I can give you a lift, Sir," said he to me, "if you'll jump up behind."

I thanked him, and got up behind, by the side of one of the other young gentlemen, who I thought didn't seem much to like having me there; and I felt very pleased, as we bowled along the Ridgeway, passing all the people who had been laughing at me and the donkey, that they should see that I was in such good company, and should be up at the Castle before any of them.

The whole Ridgeway was alive with holiday folk, some walking with their coats and bonnets off, some in great wagons, some in all sorts of strange vehicles, such as I had never seen before (many of which Master George declared had been impressed by Alfred's commissariat and hospital staff, in his wars against the Danes, when they were strong young traps); but from one and all there rose up a hum of broad Berkshire, and merry laughter, as we shot by them. Sometimes a yeoman in his gig, or on his stout hackney, would try to keep up with us, or to stop us from passing him, but Master George was a reckless driver, and somehow or another, galloping or trotting, on the right side or the wrong, he *would* pass; so in about ten minutes we had got over the two miles of downs, and were close up to the Castle.

Here the first thing I saw was Joe, with two other farmers, carrying a lot of little white and pink flags, and measuring ground. "Please put me down, Sir," said I, "there's my friend."

"Ah, yes," said Master George, pulling up, "I see—you're staying with Farmer Hurst. Well, I'm much obliged to you for helping poor old Betty—she's a good struggling old widow body in our village; I've known her ever since I could walk and suck. Good morning, Mr. Hurst; likely to be a good muster to-day."

"Mornin', Sir," said Joe, touching his hat, "I think so—there's a smart lot of folk in the Castle already."

"Well, I hope we may meet again," said Master George to me, "I won't forget the song for you,"—and away he drove towards the Castle.

"Why, Dick man, where's the old horse?" said Joe, looking as if I had come from the moon.

"Oh, I walked," said I, "I prefer it, when I have time."

"Come own it, Dick," said he, "thou wast ashamed of the old horse's long rough coat—I didn't think thou hadst been such a dandy."

"Upon my honour it was nothing of the sort," said I, glad enough that he wasn't on the right scent.

"And how did you get along with one of our young squires?" said he.

"Oh, he offered me a lift," said I; and then I told him my story.

"Well, you always seem to fall on your legs," said he; "who are they with him?"

"Oxford scholars, I think," said I, "from their talk; but I didn't get on much with them, they're not so free spoken as he is. But what are you about here, Joe?"

"Oh, helping the umpires to measure out the course for the cart-horse race," said he; "look, there are the flags right along for half a mile, and the finish is to be up there by the side of the Castle, for all the folk to see. But come along, for I must be after the umpires; I see they want me."

"I think," said I, "I should like to go and see what's going on in the Castle."

"Very good," said he, "then I'll look after you when we've done this job;" and away he went.

I wouldn't take time to go round by either of the entrances, but made straight across to the nearest point of the great earthworks, and scrambled over the outer bank, and down into the deep ditch, and up the inner bank, and stood there on the top, looking down on all the fun of the fair; for fair it was already, though it was very little past eleven o'clock in the morning.

There was the double line of booths and stalls which I had seen putting up the day before, making a long and broad street, and all decked out with nuts and apples, and gingerbread, and all sorts of sucks and food, and children's toys, and cheap ribbons, knives, braces, straps, and all manner of gaudy-looking articles. Opposite, on the north side, all the shows had got their great pictures up of the wonders which were to be seen inside, and the performers were strutting about on the stages outside, and before one of them an acrobat was swinging backwards and forwards on the slack rope, and turning head over heels at the end of each swing. And every show had its own music, if it were only a drum and pan pipes, and all the musicians were playing, as loud as they could play, different tunes. Then, on the east side, were the great booths of the publicans, all decked out now with flowers and cheap flags, with their skittle-grounds behind; and lots of gypsies, and other tramps, with their "three sticks a penny," and other games. The west side was only occupied, as I said before, by the great white tent of the County Police, where the Committee were sitting, and Lord Craven's tents some way in front; but these looked pretty and gay now, for they had hoisted some good flags; and there in the middle stood the great ugly stage, and the greasy pole. The whole space was filled with all sorts of people, from ladies looking as if they had just come from Kensington Gardens, down to the ragged little gypsy children, with brown faces and brick-coloured hair, all moving about, and looking very much as if they were enjoying themselves. So after looking a minute, I got down into the crowd, and set to work to see everything I could.

I hadn't been pushing about amongst the rest above five minutes, when two men stopped close by me, one (who was the Wantage crier, I found out afterwards) with his hand full of papers, and the other carrying a gong, which he began to beat loud enough to deafen one. When the crowd had come round him, the crier began, and I should think he might have been heard at Elm Close:—

"Oh yes! oh yes! by order of the Committee, all persons who mean to play for prizes must enter their names on the umpires' lists. Oh yes! oh yes! the umpires' lists are open in the tent, and names may be entered from now till half-past twelve. Oh yes! a list of the umpires for the different games and sports may be seen on the board outside the tent-door. God save the Queen!"

As soon as he had done, he and the man with the gong went off to another part of the Castle, but I could see some of the men and boys, who had been standing round, sidling off towards the great tent to enter for some the games, as I guessed. So I followed across the Castle to the space in front of the tent.

I could see, through the entrance, two or three of the Committee sitting at a table, with paper and pens and ink before them; and every now and then, from the little groups which were standing about, some man would make a plunge in, and go up to the table; and, after a word or two with them, would enter his name on one or more of the lists, and then come out, sometimes grinning, but generally looking as if he were half ashamed of himself. I remarked more and more through the day what a shy, shamefaced fellow the real countryman was, while the gypsies and racing boys and tramps, who entered for the races, but not for the backsword or wrestling prizes, were all as bold as brass, and stood chattering away to the Committee-men till they were almost ordered out of the tent.

I sat down on the turf outside the tent to watch; for I felt very much interested in the games, and liked to see the sort of men who came to enter. There were not many very stout or tall men amongst them; I should say they averaged about eleven stone in weight, and five feet eight inches in height; but they looked a very tough race; and I could quite believe, while looking at them, what Joe told me one day—"Though there's plenty of quicker men, and here and there stronger ones, scarce any man that ever comes down our way—either at navigator's work, or loafing about, like the gypsies and tramps—can ever come up to our chaps in *last*, whether at fighting or working."

There was one man amongst them who struck me particularly, I suppose because he wore a Crimean medal with four clasps, and went quite lame on a crutch. I found out his history. Old Mattingly, the blacksmith of Uffington, had three sons when the Russian war broke out. They all went for soldiers. The first was shot through the hand, as that grey deadly dawn broke over Inkermann, on the 5th of November, 1854. Had he gone to the rear he would probably have lived. He fought till the last Russian vanished along the distant road, and over the bridge heaped with slain, like a gallant Berkshire lad—and then went to hospital and died of his wounds within a week. The second lies before Sebastopol in the advanced trenches of the right attack. The third, the young artilleryman, went through the whole war, and after escaping bayonet and shot and shell, was kicked by the horse of a wounded officer, and probably lamed for life. According to the rules of the service, my informant seemed to think, he was not entitled to a pension for life, "but they had given him one for eighteen months after his discharge, so that he had almost a year of it to run; and perhaps he might learn blacksmith-work in that time, if he could stand at all, for that was mostly armwork."

I didn't know what the regulations as to pensions were, or how long young Mattingly would take to learn blacksmith work, but I did feel rather ashamed that England couldn't afford to do a little more for such as he; and should be glad for my part to pay something towards it, if the Chancellor of the Exchequer, or somebody, would find out a way to set this right. Or perhaps if this should ever meet the eye of the Commander in-chief, or of any of the gentlemen, who were made K.C.B.'s in the war-time, or of any other person who has interest in the army, they may see whether anything more can be done for young Mattingly.

Many of the younger ones I could see hadn't made up their minds whether or no they should enter, and were larking and pushing one another about; and I saw several good trials of strength, and got an idea of what the wrestling was like before the lists were closed.

"Bi'st in for young geamsters prize at wrastlin', shepherd?" asked a young carter with his hat full of ribbons, of a tight-made neatly-dressed fellow, who had already won a second prize, I heard, at his village revel.

The shepherd nodded.

"Mose, mun," went on the carter, "thee shouldst go in. Thee bi'st big enough."

Moses was an over-grown raw-boned fellow of about eighteen, in a short smock-frock and a pair of very dilapidated militia trousers. He had been turning the matter over in his own mind for some time, and now, after looking the shepherd over for a minute, pulled his great hands out of his pockets, hunched up his shoulders, and grunted out—

"'Zay! Try a file[22] wi' thee, shepherd."

The bystanders all cheered. Moses, the militiaman, was rather a joke to them. The shepherd looked scornful, but was ready to try a file; but he stipulated that Mose must borrow some shoes instead of his great iron-clouted high-lows (no man is allowed to wrestle, I found with any iron on his shoes).

This seemed likely to stop the fun. Moses pulled off his highlows, and appeared in sinkers,[23] at which everybody roared; but no shoes were to be had. Then he offered to wrestle without shoes; but at last a pair were found, and Moses advanced with his great hands stretched out towards the shepherd, who, not deigning to take one hand out of his pocket, caught Moses' elbow with the other. After one or two awkward attempts, and narrowly escaping some well-meant trips, Moses bored in; and before the shepherd could seize the militiaman's col-

---

22 "File"—a fall.
23 "Sinkers"—stockings without feet.

lar with his second hand, over he went, and Moses was proclaimed winner of a file, amid shouts of laughter. Then they buckled to again, the shepherd doing his best; but somehow Moses managed to keep his legs; and when they went down, both fell on their sides, and it was only a dogfall.

In another minute I saw the militiaman in the tent before the table.

"Plaze, Sur, put down Moses Tilling—young geamster—wrastlin'."

After watching the tent till the lists were just closing, I started off to see if I could find Miss Lucy, who ought to have been up by this time, and to get something to eat before the sports began. The luncheon I managed easily enough, for I went over to the great booth in which I had dined the day before, and sat down at the long table, where Peter welcomed me, and soon gave me as much as I could eat and drink. But when I had finished, and went out to look for my friends, I found it a very difficult business, and no wonder, for there were more than 20,000 people up on the Hill.

First I went to the outside of the Castle, where all the carriages were drawn up in long rows, to see if I could find the four-wheel amongst them. As I was poking about, I came close to a fine open carriage, and hearing a shout of merry laughter, looked up. There were a party at lunch; two ladies and some quite young girls inside, some boys on the box, and several gentlemen standing round, holding bottles and sandwiches; and they were all eating and drinking, and laughing at an old gypsy woman, who was telling the fortune of one of the ladies.

"Love'll never break your heart, my pretty lady," said the old woman; "let the Norwood gypsy see your hand, my pretty lady."

The lady held out her right hand, and the little girls glanced at the lady, and one another, brimming with fun.

"It's the other hand the gypsy ought to see. Ah, well then, never mind," she went on, as the lady looked quietly in her face, without moving a muscle, "the old Norwood gypsy can read it all in your eyes. There's a dark gentleman, and a light gentleman, who'll both be coming before long; there'll be sore hearts over it, but the richest will win before a year's out—" Here the girls clapped their hands, and burst into shouts, and the lady showed her other hand with a wedding-ring on, and went on quietly with her lunch.

"Ah! I never said she wasn't married!" said the gypsy to the girls, who only laughed the more. I had got quite close up to the carriage, and at this moment caught the eye of the lady, who was laughing too; then I felt awkward all at once, and as if I was where I had no right to be. But she didn't look the least annoyed, and I was passing on, when I saw that Mr. Warton was amongst the gentlemen on the other side of the carriage. "Ah," thought I, "I wonder if he'll know me now he's with his fine friends?" But the next minute I was ashamed of myself for doubting, for I heard him wish them good-bye, and before I was ten yards from the carriage, he put his arm in mine.

"Well, you never rode after all," he began.

"No, Sir," said I. "But where are they? I haven't seen Joe this two hours."

"Oh, not far off," said he; "feeding, like the rest of us."

And further down the line we found Joe, and Miss Lucy, and several friends of theirs, lunching on the turf by the four-wheel. So we sat down with them, but I didn't half like the way in which Miss Lucy was running on with two young farmers, one on each side of her. She told me afterwards that she had known them ever since they were children together, but some-how that didn't seem to me to mend the matter much. And then again, when Joe got up, and said it was time to move, for the sports would be just beginning, nothing would serve her but to walk off to Wayland Smith's cave. I wonder whether she did it a little bit to provoke me; for she knew that I had been to see it the day before, and that I wanted particularly to see all the sports. But I don't think it could have been that after all, for when I said I should stay with Joe, she was just as pleasant as ever, and didn't seem to mind a bit whether I or any one else went with her or not.

I am afraid I shall make a very poor hand at telling about the sports, because I couldn't be in five or six places at once; and so I was kept running about, from the stage in the middle of the Castle out on to the downs to see the cart-horse race, and then back again into the Castle for the jingling match, and then out on the other side to the manger for the cheese races, and so on backwards and forwards; seeing the beginning of one sport, and the end of another, and the middle of a third. I wish the Committee would let the sports begin earlier, and then one might be able to see them all. However I must do the best I can, and just put down what I saw myself.

The first move for the sports was made a little before one, just as I got back into the Castle, after seeing Miss Lucy start for Wayland Smith's cave. The Committee came out of their tent in a body, each man carrying the lists of the entries for the sports over which he was to preside. But instead of going different ways, each to his own business, they walked across in a body to the stage, and stopped just underneath it, in the middle of a great crowd of men and boys; and then they shouted for silence, and the chairman spoke:—

"We wish to say a few words, my men, to those who are going to play with the sticks or wrestle to-day. There has been a good deal of talk about these sports, as you all know; and many persons think they shouldn't be allowed at all now-a-days—that the time for them has gone by. They say, that men always lose their tempers and get brutal at these sports. We have settled, however, to give the old-fashioned games a fair trial; and it will rest with yourselves whether we shall ever be able to offer prizes for them again. For, depend upon it, if there is any savage work to-day, if you lose your tempers, and strike or kick one another unfairly, you will never see any more wrestling or backsword on White Horse Hill. But we are sure we can trust you, and that there won't be anything to find fault with. Only remember again, you are on your trial, and the stage will be cleared at once, and no prizes given, if anything objectionable happens. And now, you can put to as soon as you like."

The Committee then marched off, leaving a very large crowd round the stage, all eager for the play to begin.

The two umpires got up on to the stage, and walked round, calling out, "Two old gamesters at backsword, and two old gamesters at wrastlin', wanted to put to." But I suppose the chairman's speech had rather taken the men by surprise, for no one came forward, though there was a crowd twenty deep round the stage.

"Who are the old gamesters?" I asked of the man next me.

"Them as has won or shared a first prize at any revel," answered he, without looking round.

After a minute the chairman's brother, who didn't seem to have much scruple about these sports, jumped up on the stage, and blew an old French hunting-horn, till the young ones began to laugh; and then told the men not to be afraid to come up, for if they didn't begin at once there wouldn't be light to play out the ties.

At last there was a stir amongst the knot of Somersetshire men, who stood together at one corner of the stage; and one of them, stepping up, pitched on to it his stumpy black hat, and then climbed up after it himself, spoke a word to the umpires, and began handling the sticks, to choose one which balanced to his mind, while the umpires proclaimed, "An old gamester wanted, to play with John Bunn of Wedmore."

"There he stands, you see," said Master George, who was close by me, though I hadn't seen him before, "the only remaining representative of the old challenger at tourneys, ready to meet all comers. He ought to have a herald to spout out his challenge in verse. Why not?"

"I don't know what he could say more than the umpire has, Sir," said I.

"He might blow his own trumpet at any rate," said he; "somehow thus;" and he repeated, after a false start or two—

THE ZONG OF THE ZUMMERZETSHIRE OWLD GEAMSTER.

I.

"Cham[24] a Zummerzetshire mun
    Coom here to hev a bit o'vun.
Oo'lt[25] try a bout? I be'ant aveard
    Ov any man or mother's zun.

II.

"Cham a geamster owld and tough,
    Well knowed droo all the country zide,
And many a lusty Barkshire man
    To break my yead hev often tried.

III.

"Who's vor a bout of vriendly plaay,
    As never should to anger move?
Zich spwoorts wur only meaned vor thaay
    As likes their mazzards broke for love."

---

24 "Cham"—"I am," a form still used in parts of Somersetshire.
25 "Oo'lt"—wilt thou.

John Bunn[26] looked by no means a safe man to play with. He stood about five feet eleven, with spare long muscular limbs, a sallow complexion, and thick shock head of black hair,—a good defence in itself against any common blow of a stick. But now that the ice was broken, his challenge was soon answered; and George Gregory of Stratton, one of the best mowers in the Vale, appeared to uphold the honour of Berks and Wilts. He stood half a head shorter than his opponent, but was, probably, the stronger man of the two, and had a sturdy and confident look, which promised well, and was fair-haired, and, like David, ruddy to look upon.

While they were taking off coats and waistcoats, and choosing sticks, two wrestlers got up on the stage, and showed the shoes in which they were going to wrestle to the umpires, for approval; and stood at the ropes, ready to begin as soon as the first bout at backsword was over. The crowd drew a long breath, while Bunn and Gregory came forward, shook hands; and then throwing up their guards, met in the middle of the stage.

26 *James Bunn, according to* Jackson's Oxford Journal, *26th September 1857.*

At the first rattle of the sticks, the crowd began cheering again, and pressed in closer to the stage; and I with them, for it was very exciting, *that* I felt at once. The coolness and resolution in the faces of the two men, as they struck and parried with those heavy sticks, trying all the points of each other's play in a dozen rapid exchanges; the skill and power which every turn of the wrist showed; and the absolute indifference with which they treated any chance blow which fell on arm or shoulder, made it really a grand sight; and with all my prejudices I couldn't help greatly admiring the players. "Bout," cried Bunn, after a minute or so, and down came their guards, and they walked to the side of the stage to collect coppers from the crowd below in the baskets of their sticks, while the two first wrestlers put to in the middle

I suppose there are more unsettled points in wrestling, or it is harder to see whether the men are playing fair, for the crowd was much more excited now than at the backsword play, a hundred voices shouting to the umpires every moment to stop this or that practice. Besides, the kicking, which is allowed at elbow and collar wrestling, makes it look brutal very often; and so I didn't like it so much as the backsword play, though the men were fine, good-tempered fellows, and, when most excited, only seemed to want what they called "fair doos."

I stopped by the stage until Gregory had lost his head. How it happened I couldn't see, but suddenly the umpires cried out "Blood!" The men stopped; Gregory put up his hand to his hair, found that the blood was really coming, and then dropped his stick and got down, quite as much surprised as I was. And two more old gamesters were called up, the first head being to Somersetshire. But now I heard that the cart-horse race was just coming off, and so, following the crowd, made my way across to the east of the Castle.

I scrambled up to the highest part of the bank, and so got

a capital view of the scene below. The course was marked out all the way down to the starting-post by rows of little pink and white flags, and the Committee-men were riding slowly up and down, trying to get the people to keep back behind the flags. The line was, on the whole, pretty well kept; but as the crowd got thicker every minute, every now and then a woman with two or three children would wander out to escape the pressure from behind; or a young couple keeping company would run across, hoping to better their position; or a lot of uproarious boys would start out for a lark, to try the tempers, and very possibly the whips, of the Committee.

Joe presently rode by the place where I was standing, and called out to me to come down and see the mounting. So I slipped out of the crowd, and ran down the back of the line to the starting place. There I found the Squire and the umpires, passing the men and horses. Five or six were all ready; the great horses in their thill harness, which jingled and rattled with every movement; and the carters perched up in the middle of the wood and leather and brass, in their white smock-frocks, with the brims of their break-of-days turned up in front, and a bunch of ribbons fluttering from the side, and armed with the regular long cart-whip. Just as I came up, Mr. Avery Whitfield's bay horse, *King of the Isle*, was passed, and took his place with the others. He was one of the three favourites, I heard people say.

"Call the next horse."

"Mr. Davenport's grey mare, *Dairymaid*," shouts the umpire. Here she comes, with old Joe Humphries[27], the jockey and horse breaker, on her back. He is in full jockey costume—cap, jacket, and tops, with a racing whip and spurs. The umpires look doubtfully at him, and consult the Squire. At first they seem inclined not to let Joe ride at all, but as the owners of the

27   *"Old" Joe Humphries was around 42 and served in the Squire's household.*

other horses don't object, they only insist on his taking off his spurs and changing his whip for a common long carter's whip. Then *Dairymaid* is passed, and then one other horse; eight in all. Two of the Committee gallop down in front to clear the course for the last time; the word "Off" is given; and away go the great steeds in furious plunging gallop, making the whole hill shake beneath them, and looking (as I heard one of the Oxford scholars remark) like a charge of German knights in some old etching. Close after them came the umpires, the Committee-men, and all the mounted farmers, cheering and shouting pieces of advice to the riders; and the crowd, as they pass, shout and wave their hats, and then rush after the horses. How everybody isn't killed, and how those men can sit those great beasts in the middle of that rattling mass of harness, were my puzzles, as I scrambled along after the rest.

Meantime, in the race, *Dairymaid* shoots at once some yards ahead, and improves her lead at every stride; for she is a famous mare, and old Joe Humphries understands the tricks of the course, and can push her and lift her in ways unknown to the honest carters and foggers, who come lumbering behind him—Joe even has time for a contemptuous glance over his shoulder at his pursuers. But the race is not always to the swift, at least not to those who are swiftest at starting. Half-way up the course, *Dairymaid* ceases to gain; then she shows signs of distress, and scarcely answers to old Joe's persuasions. *King of the Isle* is creeping up to her—the carter shakes his bridle, and begins to ply his long cart-whip—they are crossing the Ridgeway, where stand the carter's fellow-servants, Mr. Whitfield's fogger, shepherd, ploughboys, &c. who set up a shout as he passes, which sends the bay right up abreast of the mare. No wonder they are excited, for the master has promised that the three guineas, the price of the new thill harness, shall be divided between them, if the bay wins.

In another fifty yards he is drawing ahead. All old Joe's efforts are in vain; his jockeyship has only done him harm, whereas the carter's knowledge of what his steed's real powers are, has been the making of him, and he rides in, brandishing his long cart-whip, an easy winner. *Dairymaid* is second, but only just before the ruck; and old Joe creeps away, let us hope, a humbler and a wiser man.

Of course I couldn't see all this myself, because I was behind, but Joe told me all about the race directly afterwards. When I got up there was a great crowd round *King of the Isle*, from whose back the carter was explaining something about the race. But I couldn't stay to listen, for I heard that the races for the "prime coated Berkshire fives" (as they called the cheeses), were just coming off; so I hurried away to the brow of the hill, just above the Horse, where it is steepest; for I wanted of all things to see how men could run down this place, which I couldn't get up without using both hands.

There stood Mr. William Whitfield, of Uffington, the umpire who had to start the race, in his broad brimmed beaver, his brown coat and waistcoat with brass buttons, and drab breeches and gaiters. I thought him a model yeoman to look at, but I didn't envy him his task. Two wild-looking gypsy women, with their elf-locks streaming from under their red handkerchiefs, and their black eyes flashing, were rushing about amongst the runners, trying to catch some of their relations who were going to run; and screaming out that their men should never break their limbs down that break-neck place.

The gypsies dodged about, and kept out of their reach, and the farmer remonstrated, but the wild women still persevered. Then, losing all patience, he would turn and poise the wheel, ready to push it over the brow, when a shout from the bystanders warns him to pause, and, a little way down the hill, just in the line of the race, appear two or three giggling lasses, hauled along by their sweethearts, and bent on getting a very good view. Luckily at this moment the Chairman appeared, and rode his white horse down to the front of the line of men, where there seemed to me to be footing for nothing but a goat.

Then the course was cleared for a moment, he moved out of the line, making a signal to the farmer, who pushed the wheel at once over the brow, and cried, "Off." The wheel gained the road in three bounds, cleared it in a fourth monster bound which measured forty yards, and hurried down far away to the bottom of the manger, where the other two umpires were waiting to decide who is the winner of the race

Away go the fourteen men in hot pursuit, gypsies, shepherds, and light-heeled fellows of all sorts, helter-skelter; some losing their foothold at once, and rolling or slipping down; some still keeping their footing, but tottering at every step; one or two, with their bodies well thrown back, striking their heels firmly into the turf, and keeping a good balance. They are all in the road together, but here several fall on their

faces, and others give in; the rest cross it in a moment, and are away down the manger. Here the sheep-walks, which run temptingly along the sides of the manger, but if they would look forward will take the runners very little nearer the bottom where the wheel lies, mislead many; and amongst the rest, the fleetest of the gypsies, who makes off at full speed along one of them.

Two or three men go still boldly down the steep descent, falling and picking themselves up again; and Jonathan Legg, of Childrey, is the first of these. He has now gained the flat ground at the bottom, where after a short stagger he brings himself up, and makes straight for the umpires and the wheel. The gypsy now sees his error; and turning short down the hill, comes into the flat, running some twenty yards behind Jonathan. In another hundred yards he would pass him, for he gains at every stride; but it is too late; and we, at the top of the hill, cheer loudly when we see Jonathan, the man who had gone straight all the way, touch the wheel a clear ten yards before his more active rival.

I should have liked to have seen the boys' races down the manger, but was afraid of missing some other sport, so I left farmer Whitfield at his troublesome post, shouting out the names of the boys and trying to get them into line, and went back into the Castle, where I found a crowd round the greased pole; and when I got up to it, saw a heavy-looking fellow, standing some five feet up the pole, with one foot in a noose of cord depending from a large gimlet, and the other leg hooked round the pole. He held in his right hand another large gimlet, which he was preparing to screw into the pole to support a second noose, and gazed stolidly down at a Committee-man, who was objecting "that this wasn't fair climbing—that if gimlets and nooses were to be allowed, he could get up himself." I thought he was right; but public feeling seemed to side with the climber; so the Committee-man gave in, declaring that there would be no more legs of mutton to climb for, if anything but arms and legs were to be used.

"Rather a slow bit of sport this," I said to an old grey-headed man, who was leaning on his stick at my side, and staring up at the performer.

"Ees, Zur," answered he, "I dwon't knaow but what it be."

"Do you call it fair climbing, now?"

"Auh, bless'ee, not I. I minds seein' the young chaps when I wur a buoy, climin' maypowls a deal higher nor that, dree at a time. But now-a-days 'um be lazy, and afraid o' spwiling their breeches wi' the grase."

"Are there any maypoles about here now?"

"Never a one as I knows on, Zur, for twenty mile round. The last as I remembers wur the Longcott one, and Parson Watts of Uffington had he sawed up nigh forty year ago, for fear lest there should ha' been some murder done about 'un."

"Murder about a maypole! Why, how was that?"

"Auh! you see, Zur, this here Longcott maypowl wur the last in all these parts, and a wur the envy of a zight o' villages round about. Zo, one cluttery[28] night in November, thirty of our Ashbury chaps thay started down to Longcott, and dug 'un up, and brought 'un cler away on handspikes, all the waay to the Crown'd Inn at Ashbury, and 'tis quite vour mil'd."

"On handspikes! Why, how big was he, then?"

"Auh! a fyeightish sized 'un. How big? whoy a sight bigger, bless'ee, nor that 'un, and all the bottom half on 'un solid oak. When thay cum to put 'un up afore the bar winder of the Crown'd, a reached right up auver the tops o' the housen. But zoon arter a wur put up, the Uffington chaps cum up, and tuk and carried 'un down ther'. Ther' was a smartish row or two about 'un at Uffington arter that, but they watched 'un night

28 "Cluttery "—pelting with rain.

and day; and when the Lambourn chaps cum arter 'un one night, they chucked scaldin' water right auver'm. Zo then Parson Watts, he tuk and sawed 'un up, and guv 'un to the owld women at Christmas for virewood."

I walked away from the pole, turning over in my mind whether Parson Watts was right or wrong in his summary method of restoring peace to his parish, and, somehow or other, found myself again close under the stage. Now, and throughout the day, I found no flagging there; whenever I passed there was the crowd of men standing round, and the old and young gamesters hard at work. So I began to believe what Joe had said, that the countrymen thought more about these games than anything else, and wouldn't care to go to the Pastime if they were stopped. I found that the Ashbury men were carrying it all their own way in the wrestling, and that their champion, old Richens[29] (the rat-catcher, an old gamester in his fiftieth year), would probably not even have to wrestle at all; for his own men were throwing all the gamesters of the other parishes, and of course would give up to him when it came to the last ties. The men all wrestle in sides, at least the old gamesters do; so that a man generally plays for his parish, and not for his own head, which is a better thing, I think.

As to the backsword play, the stage was strewed with splinters of sticks and pieces of broken baskets, and many a young gamester has had his first broken head in public. But, for the chief prize, matters are going hard with Berks and Wilts. The Somersetshire old gamesters have won two heads to one; and, as they have six men in, and Berks and Wilts only four, the odds are all in favour of the cider county, and against the beer drinkers. In good time up gets an old gamester, who looks like the man to do credit to the royal county. It is Harry Seeley[30],

29 *Robert Richens.*
30 *Henry Sealey, according to* Jackson's Oxford Journal. *A labourer.*

of Shrivenham, the only Berkshire man in; for there has been some difference between Berks and Wilts, and Harry's two mates haven't entered at all. So he, being one of the true bull-dog breed, is in for his own head, against all odds, and is up to play the next Somersetshire man.

Harry is a fine specimen of an Englishman. Five feet eight high, with a bullet head, and light blue eye; high-couraged, cool, and with an absolutely imperturbable temper. He plays in a blue shirt, thin from age and wear, through which you may see the play of his splendid arms and chest. His opponent is a much younger man, about the same size; but a great contrast to Harry, for he has a savage and sly look about him. They shake hands, throw themselves into position, and the bout begins. Harry is clearly the finer player, and his adversary feels this at once; and the shouts of anticipated victory, in the Berkshire tongue, rouse his temper. Now comes a turn of the savage play, which ought never to be seen on a stage. The Somerset man bends far back, and strikes upper cuts at the face and arms, and then savagely at the body. He is trying to maim and cow, and not to win by fair brave play.

The crowd soon begin to get savage too; upper-cutting is not thought fair in Berks and Wilts; a storm begins to brew, hard words are bandied, and a cry of "Foul," and "Pull him down," is heard more than once, and the Committee man, who watches from below, is on the point of stopping the bout. But nothing puts out old Harry Seeley; no upper cut can reach his face, for his head is thrown well back, and his guard is like a rock; and though the old blue shirt is cut through and through, he makes no more of the welts of the heavy stick than if it were a cat's tail. Between the bouts his face is cheery and confident, and he tells his friends to "hold their noise, and let him alone to tackle the chap," as he hands round his basket for the abounding coppers.

Now I could see well enough why the parsons don't like these games. It gave me a turn, to watch the faces round the stage getting savage, and I could see what it might soon get to if there was much of this wild work. And there were Master George, and the two Oxford scholars, at the opposite corner of the stage, shouting till they were hoarse for old Seeley, and as savage and wicked looking as any of the men round them; setting such a bad example, too, as I thought,—whereas it didn't matter for a fellow like me, who was nobody,—so I shouted, and threw my coppers to old Seeley, and felt as wild as any of them, I do believe. Three bouts, four bouts pass; Harry's stick gets in oftener and oftener. Has the fellow no blood in him? There it comes at last! In the fifth bout, Harry's stick goes flashing in again, a fair down blow from the wrist, which puts the matter beyond all question, as the Somersetshire man staggers back across the stage, the blood streaming from under his hair. Loud are the shouts which greet the fine-tempered old gamester, as he pulls on his velveteen coat, and gets down from the stage.

"Why, Harry, thou'dst broke his yead second bout, mun, surely!" shout his admirers. "No," says Harry, dogmatically, "you see, mates, there's no 'cumulation of blood belongs to thay cider-drinking chaps, as there does to we as drinks beer. Besides, thay drinks vinegar allus for a week afore playin', which dries up most o' the blood as they has got; so it takes a 'mazin' sight of cloutin' to break their yeads as should be."

After this bout all the other play seemed to be tasteless; so, promising myself to come back and see the ties played off (unless Miss Lucy turned up in the meantime, in which case I shouldn't have dared to go near the stage, and in fact I felt rather nervous already lest she should have seen or heard of me there), I marched off, and joined the crowd which was collecting round the jingling ring. That crowd was one of the pleasantest sights of the whole day. The jingling match seemed a very popular sport, especially with the women. There they were, of all ranks—for I'm certain I saw some young ladies in riding habits, and others in beautiful muslins, whom I, and Jem Fisher, and little Neddy have often seen riding with very great people in the Park, when we have managed to get down to Rotten Row on summer evenings—seated on the grass or standing round the ring, in all sorts of dresses, from fine silks down to cottons at 2*d.* a yard, and all looking pleasant and good tempered, and as if they were quite used to being mixed up like this every day—which I'm sure I wish they were, for my part, especially if the men were allowed to join in the crowd too, as we were round the jingling ring. For there were gentlemen, both parsons and others, and farmers, and plough-boys, and all manner of other men and boys.

I don't know what sort of fun a jingling match is in general, but I thought this one much the slowest game I saw. The ring must have been forty yards across, or thereabouts, and there were only eight blindfolded men running after the bell-man. To make it good fun there should have been twenty-five or thirty at least. Then the bellman, who has his hands tied behind him, ought to have the bell tied round his neck, or somewhere where he can't get at it to stop the ringing; but our bellman had the bell tied to his waistband behind, so that he could catch hold of it with his hands, and stop it when he was in danger. Then half the men could see, I'm sure, by the way they carried their heads up in the air, especially one gypsy, who, I think, won the prize at last.[31] The men who couldn't see were worth watching, for they kept catching and tumbling over one another. One time they made a rush to the rope, just where some of the young ladies were sitting, and, as nearly as could be, tumbled over among them. I thought there would

31   *"Moody Hazard, gipsy", according to* Jackson's Oxford Journal. *Aged 19.*

have been a great scrambling and screaming; not a bit of it—they never flinched an inch, or made the least cry, aud I was very proud to think they were my countrywomen. After the bellman had been caught about a minute, there was a great laugh at one of the blinded men, who made a rush, and caught a Committee-man, who was standing in the ring, in his arms. But on the whole I thought the game a poor one, and was glad when it was over.

I hurried away directly after the jingling match, and went across the Castle, and out on to the down where the cart-horse race had been run to see the foot-races, which were run over the last half of the same course, on which ten good stiff sets of hurdles at short distances apart had been set up. I found a debate going on between the umpires and some of the men as to whether they were all to start together. The regular agricultural labourers were remonstrating as to some of the candidates.

"It beant narra mossel o' use for we chaps to start along wi' thay light-heeled gentry," said one,—"Whoy, look 'ee here, zur's one, and yander's another, wi' a kind o' dancin' pumps on, and that 'un at tother end wi' a cricketin' waistcut."

"And there's two o' them little jockey chaps amongst 'em, sumweres, Zur," said another, looking about for these young gentlemen, who dodged behind some of the bigger candidates.

"How can we help that?" said the umpire.

"Auh, Zur, thay be all too nimble by half for we to be of any account to 'em," persisted the first speaker. "If twur for the sticks now, or wrastling—"

"Well, but what shall we do then?" interrupted the umpire.

"Let I pick out ten or a dozen on 'em to run by theirselves." The umpires proposed this to the rest, and, no one objecting, told Giles the protester to pick out the ten he was most afraid of. This Giles proceeded to do with a broad grin on his face, and generally seemed to make a good selection. But presently he arrived at, and after a short inspection passed over, a young fellow in his blue shirt sleeves and a cloth cap, who to the umpire's eye seemed a dangerous man.

"Why, Giles," said he, "you're never going to pass him over?"

"Auh, ees, Zur," said Giles, "let he 'bide along wi' we chaps. Dwont'ee zee, he's a tipped and naayled 'un?"

When Giles had finished his selection, the first lot were started, and made a grand race; which was won by a Hampshire man from Kingsclere[32], the second man, not two feet behind, being a young Wiltshire farmer[33], who, having never been beaten in his own neighbourhood, had come to lose his laurels honourably at the Scouring.

The running in the second race was, of course, not so good, but much more amusing. The "tipped and naayled'uns" were a rushing lot, but very bad at rising. Hurdle after hurdle went down before them with a crash, and the most wonderful summersaults were executed. The second hurdle finished poor Giles, who charged it manfully, and found himself the next moment on his broad back, gazing placidly up into the evening sky. The cloth cap[34], notwithstanding his shoes, went easily ahead, and won in a canter. I heard one of the umpires rallying Giles afterwards at his want of eyes.

"Ees, Zur," said Giles, hunching up his great shoulders, "I wur tuk in, zure enough. He wur a town chap arter all, as wouldn't ha' knowed a piece o' dumpers afore he cum across to White Hos Hill."

I left the umpires now to start the other races, and got back once again into the Castle. I was now beginning to get very tired in my legs, though not in my spirits, so I went and sat down outside the crowd, which was thicker than ever round

---

32   *William Pooke, according to* Jackson's Oxford Journal.
33   *James Buckton of Purton, according to* Jackson's Oxford Journal.
34   *James Burge, Cirencester, according to* Jackson's Oxford Journal.

the stage, for the ties were being played out. I could hear the umpires call every now and then for some gamester who was not forthcoming to play out his tie—"John Giles, if you beant on the stage in five minutes, to put to with James Higgins[35], you shall lose your head"— through all the cheers and shouts, which rose louder and louder now that every blow or trip might decide the prizes.

And while I was sitting, the donkey races were run outside, and I heard were very good fun; especially the last one, in which no man rode his own donkey, and the last donkey had the prize. I hope my friend, the old suck-woman, entered neighbour Thorne's beast, for if she did I'll be bound he carried off the prize for her. They were the only sports that I didn't manage to see something of.

It was now just five o'clock, the hour for the pig-race, which seemed to be a most popular sport, for most of the lookers-on at the stage went off to see it, leaving only a select crowd of old and young gamesters, most of whom had been playing themselves, and whom nothing could drag five yards from the posts until the ties were all played out. I was just considering whether I should move or stay where I was, when Master George came striding by and caught sight of me.

"Hullo," said he, "how is it you're not on the move? You must see the pig-race; come along." So I got up and shambled along with him.

The pig was to be started on the slope below the west entrance, where the old gentleman had stood and lectured me the day before. There was the spring cart, covered with a net, with a fine young Berkshire pig in it. When we came up, the runners, thirty in number, with their coats and waistcoats off, were just being drawn up in line inside the Castle, from which place they were to be started, and run down through the west

35   *J. Wiggins, according to* Jackson's Oxford Journal.

entrance out on to the open down, at the word "off." It was thought that this rush down between the double banks, covered thickly with the crowd, would be the finest sight of the race.

But the rush never came. Piggy was to have five minutes law, and the Committee-man who went down to turn him out put his snout towards Ashdown Park, and gave him a push in hopes that he would take straight away over the downs, and so get a good start. Of course, he turned right round and came trotting and grunting up towards the Castle, to see what all the bustle could be about.

Then the crowd began to shout at him, and to press further and further down the outer earthworks, though all the Committee were there to keep the course clear for the regular runners; and at last, before half of the five minutes were over, the whole line broke up with a great shout, and the down was covered in a moment with countless men and boys in full chase of Piggy. Then the lawful candidates could stand it no longer, and away they went too, cleaving their way through the press, the Committee riding after them as fast as was safe in such a crowd, to see fair play if possible at the finish.

In a minute or two, Piggy was mobbed, surrounded, seized first by one of the crowd, and then by a lawful runner. These tumbled over in their struggle without loosing their hold and more of their friends over them, and from the middle of the mass poor Piggy sent up the most vigorous and dismal squeals, till the Committee-men rode in, laying about with their whips; and Farmer Whitfield, springing off, seized Piggy, and in another minute was cantering away with him towards Wayland Smith's cave.

Here he was turned out again for a fair race, and was won by Charles Ebury of Fernham[36]; who, fearing the results of his racing performances, sold him at once for 10s. to the Woolston carrier. But I am happy to say that he wasn't really hurt, for I went to see him some days afterwards, and found him as hearty as pig could be.

Master George and I agreed, as we walked back to the Castle, that it is a shame to have a pig-race.

"No," said he, "let men run any risk they like of broken heads or limbs for themselves; they may play or not as they like. But Piggy has no choice, and to let him run the risk of having the legs pulled out of his body before he is wanted for pork, isn't fair."

"He didn't seem to think it was, certainly, Sir," I said.

"No," said he, laughing; "did you ever hear such a song as he made? No animal can talk like a pig. He can scold or remonstrate just as well as a Christian. Any one who knows the language can tell you just what he is saying. Well," he went on, "I see you don't believe me; now I will go and hear what he has to say about this proceeding, and give you it word for word."

This was what he gave me afterwards, with the other songs he had promised me:—

---

36   *There seems to be some doubt over the identity of the winner of the pig.*
     Jackson's Oxford Journal *lists him simply as "a party from Fernham".*

THE LAY OF THE HUNTED PIG.

"Vathers, mothers, mothers' zons!
You as loves yer little wuns!
Happy pegs among the stubble,
Listen to a tale of trouble;
Listen, pegs in yeard and stye,
How the Barkshire chaps zard I.

"I wur barn at Kingstone-Lisle,
Wher I vrolicked var a while,
As vine a peg as e'er wur zeen
(One of a litter o' thirteen)
Till zome chaps wi' cussed spite
Aimed ov I to make a zite,
And to have a 'bit o' vun,'
Took I up to Uffington.

"Up, vorights[37] the Castle mound
They did zet I on the ground;
Then a thousand chaps, or nigh,
Runned and hollered arter I—
Ther, then, I, till I wur blowed,
Runned and hollered all I knowed,
When, zo zure as pegs is pegs,
Eight chaps ketched I by the legs,

Two to each—'tis truth I tell 'ee—
Dree more clasped I round the belly!
Under all they fellers lyin'—
Pegs!—I thought as I wur dyin'.

"But the Squire (I thenks I zee un),
Varmer Whitfield ridin' wi' un,
Fot I out o' all thuck caddle,
Stretched athurt the varmer's zaddle—

---

37 "Vorights "—opposite.

MEMORIES OF THE VALE

Bless 'em, pegs in yeard and stye,
Them two vrends as stuck to I.

"Barkshire men, vrom Hill and Vale,
All as ever hears this tale,
If to spwoort you be inclined,
Plaze to bear this here in mind—
Pegs beant made no race to win,
Be zhart o' wind, and tight o' skin,
Dwont'ee hunt 'em, but instead
At backswyrd break each other's yead
Cheezes down the manger rowl—
Or try and clim the greasy powl.

"Pegs! in stubble yeard and stye,
May you be never zard like I,
Nor druv wi greasy ears and tail,
By men and bwoys drough White Horse Vale."

CHAPTER VI.

MASTER GEORGE slipped away from me somehow, after the pig race, so I strolled up into the Castle again. The sports were all over, so the theatres and shows were making a greater noise than ever, but I didn't feel inclined to go to any of them, and kept walking slowly round the bank on the opposite side, and looking down at the fair. In a minute or two I heard cheering, and saw an open carriage, with postilions, driving out of the Castle, and three or four young ladies and a gentleman or two cantering along with it. I watched them for some way across the downs, and thought how nice it must be to be able to ride well, and to have nice horses to go galloping over the springy downs, into the golden sunset, putting up the larks and beautiful little wheatears; and, besides all that, to have all the people cheering one too! So down I went into the crowd, to find out who they were.

It was Lord Craven and his party, the first man I came across told me; and then I quite understood why this carriage should be the only one to come inside the Castle, and why the people should cheer; because, you see, the White Horse, and Dragon's Hill, and the Manger, all belong to him, and he is very good-natured in letting everybody go there and do pretty much what they please. There were other carriages going off now from the row outside, and coachmen bringing up their horses to harness, and a few of the foot people who came from the longest distances, starting along the Ridgeway, or down the Uffington Road.

I was standing watching all this, and thinking how I was to find my party, and whether I should go behind in the four-wheel (which I began to feel very much inclined to do, for I was getting tired, and it would be dark), when I saw Joe bustling about amongst the crowd, and looking out for some one; so I made across to him.

"Ah, there you are," said he, as soon as he caught sight of me, "I've been hunting for you; it's all over for to-day. Lu sent me after you to come and have some tea. If you like, you can go home directly afterwards with her and Mr. Warton."

I was very pleased to hear that Miss Lucy had sent after me, but I didn't want to show it.

"What are you going to do?" said I.

"Oh," said Joe, "I shan't leave till all the Committee go; I must be at the giving away of the prizes in the tent; and then, if anything should happen afterwards—any row, you know, or that sort o' thing—I shouldn't like to be gone."

I didn't say anything more, as I thought I might just as well leave it open; so I followed him to the west side of the Castle, where the police tent stood, and it was quite quiet.

"Here they are," said Joe, "over in the ditch;" and he scrambled up the bank, and I after him, and in the ditch below sure enough was a most cozy tea-party.

Miss Lucy, with her bonnet off, was sitting cutting up a cake, and generally directing. Two other young women, nice fresh-looking girls, but not to be named with her, were setting out a few cups and saucers and plates, which they had borrowed from some of the stalls. Mr. Warton was on his knees with his hat off, blowing away till he was red in the face at a little fire made of chips and pieces of old hampers, over which the kettle, also borrowed, hung from three sticks driven into the ground so that their tops met above the fire. Two or three young farmers sat about looking on, or handing things as they were wanted, except one impudent young fellow of about eighteen, with scarcely a hair on his chin, who was almost in

Miss Lucy's pocket, and was meddling with everything she was doing.

"Well, here you are, at last," said she, looking up at us; "why, where have you been all day?"

"I am sure I have been hunting after you very often," said I, which, perhaps, was rather more than I ought to have said; "but it isn't easy for one who is a stranger to find people in such a crowd."

"I don't know that," said she, with a pretty little toss of her head; "where there's a will there's a way. If I hadn't found friends, I might have been alone all day—and there are three or four of the shows I have never seen, now."

I began to look as sorry as I could, while I thought what to answer, when the young man who was close to her tried to steal some of the cake; she turned round quickly, and rapped his fingers with the back of her knife, and he pretended to be hurt. She only laughed, and went on cutting up the cake, but she called him Jack, and seemed so intimate with him that it put me out, and I sat down on the other side of the circle, some way off.

"It's all right," said the Parson, looking up from the fire; "boils splendidly—give me the tea."

Miss Lucy handed him a little parcel of tea from her bag, and he put it into the kettle.

"I declare we have forgotten the milk," said she; "do run and fetch it, Jack—it's in a bottle under the back seat of the four-wheel."

I jumped up before Jack, who hardly moved, and ran off to fetch the milk; for which she gave me a pleasant smile when I came back, and I felt better pleased, and enjoyed the tea and cake and bread and butter, and all the talk over it, very much; except that I couldn't stand this Jack, who was forcing her to notice him every minute, by stealing her teaspoon or her cake, or making some of his foolish remarks. The sun set splendidly before we had finished, and it began to get a little chilly.

"Well," said Joe, jumping up, "I'm off to get the horse put to. You'd better be starting, Lu; you won't be down hill much before dark, now, and there's no moon—worse luck."

"Very well," said she, taking up her bonnet, and putting it on; "we shall be ready in five minutes."

"You'll go behind with them, I suppose," said Joe to me.

"I'm to have a seat, mind," struck in that odious Jack; "Lucy promised me that an hour ago." I could have given him a good kick; however, I don't think I showed that I was put out.

"How can you tell such fibs, Jack?" said she; but I didn't take any notice of that.

"Thank you, I wish to stay on the hill," said I. "Besides, the four-wheel will be full without me."

She didn't seem to hear; and began talking to one of the other girls.

"But how are you to get down?" said Joe.

"Oh, I can walk," said I, "or ride behind you."

"Very good, if you like," said he; "the chestnut would carry six, if her back was long enough;" and away he went to get the four-wheel ready. We followed; Miss Lucy sticking close to her friend, and never saying a word to any of us. I walked with Mr. Warton, who was in the highest spirits, looking over his shoulder, and raving about the green tints in the sunset.

When we got to the carriages, there was kissing and shaking of hands, and the rest went off, while the parson and Miss Lucy packed into the front seat, and Jack and Jem the carter-boy into the hind seat of the four-wheel; and away they drove, wishing us "good night." I watched them for some time, and could see Jack leaning forward close to her ear; and turned back with Joe into the Castle, more out of sorts than I had been since I left London.

Joe hurried off to the police tent, where the Committee were giving away the prizes, saying I should find him there when I wanted him; and I loitered away to see whatever was to be seen. At first nothing seemed to please me. I watched the men and boys playing at three sticks a penny, and thought I might as well have been on Primrose Hill. Then I went and looked at the shows; and there was the fellow in flesh-coloured tights, turning over and over on the slack rope, and the clari-onet and French horn and drum, played by the three men in corduroys, all out of tune, and louder than ever, as if they had only just begun, instead of having been screaming and rum-bling away all day; and the man outside the pink-eyed lady's caravan was shouting away for the hundredth time all about her, and then playing the pan-pipes, as if no other woman in the world had pink eyes.

I was determined they shouldn't have any of my money at any rate, so I strolled further down the line, and looked into a low booth where a fiddle was going. Here several couples were dancing, with their arms a-kimbo, on some planks which had been put down on the grass, and all the rest of the booth was crowded with others looking on. This pleased me better, for the dancers seemed to enjoy themselves wonderfully, and made a sort of clattering accompaniment to the music with their hob-nailed shoes, which was merry and pleasant.

When I was tired of watching them I thought I would go and find Joe; so I went over to the tent, and there I got all right, and began to enjoy myself again. In the further corner of the tent the Squire and another justice were sitting, and hear-ing a charge of pocket picking, of which there were only two during the whole day, the police told me. Opposite the door, the rest of the Committee were sitting at a table and giving away the prizes.

Joe beckoned me in, and I went round to the back of the

table and looked on. As the men came up from the group round the door, when their names were called out, the umpires said a few words to each of them and then gave them their prizes, and most of them made some sort of speech in answer; for they were much less shy than in the morning, I suppose from the sense of having earned their right to hold up their heads by winning. The owner of the successful donkey[38] was just carrying out the flitch of bacon when I arrived; after him the Somersetshire backsword players[39] were called in to take the first three prizes for that sport, they having beaten all the Wiltshire men; while old Seeley, the only Berkshire man entered, to everybody's surprise had not played out his tie, but had given his head (as they said) to his second opponent. Therefore, although entitled to the last prize for having won his first bout, he had not done all his duty in the eyes of the umpires, who gently complained, while handing him over his four half-crowns, and wondered that so gallant an old gamester, and a Vale man, should not have played out his ties for the honour of the county.

"Well, gen'l'men," said old Seeley, giving a hitch with his shoulders, "I'll just tell you how it was. You see, ther wur six Somersetshire old gamesters come up to play, and ther wur six of our side to play 'em; dree Wiltshire and dree Barkshire, if so be as we could have made a party. But the dree from Wiltshire they wouldn't go in along wi' we, and turned their backs on me and my two mates; so my two mates wouldn't go in at all, and wanted me to give out too. But you see, gen'l'men, I'd a spent a matter of a pound over getting myself a little better food, and making myself lissom; so thinks I, I must go up and have a bout, let it be how t'wool. And you saw, gen'l'men, as I played a

---

38   *John Stratford owned the victorious* Jack Sheppard.

39   *James Bunn and George Mapstone of Wedmore, Somerset, and Richard Slade of Purton, Wiltshire, according to* Jackson's Oxford Journal.

good stick. When it cum' to playing off the ties, there wur dree Somersetshire tiers, and two of our side, that's Slade and me. But when a man turns his back on me, gen'l'men, why I turns my back on him; so I guv my head to young Mapstone, and left Slade to win if he could. Though I thinks, if thay Wiltshire chaps had behaved theirselves as thay should, we might ha' had the prize, for I knows as I never played freer in my life. And I hopes, gen'l'men, as you don't think I wur afeard of any man as ever got on that stage. Bless you!" said old Seeley, warming up, "I be that fond o' thay sticks, I assure you, gen'l'men, I'd as lief meet a man as is a man for a bout wi' thay sticks, as I would—a joint of roast beef."

Old Seeley's speech carried conviction, for there could be no mistake about the tone in which he drew his last comparison, after a moment's pause to think of the thing he liked best, and he retired from the tent in high favour, as I think he deserved to be.

After watching these doings for some time I began to feel very hungry, for I had eaten hardly anything at tea, so I told Joe that he would find me over in the great booth getting some supper, and went out. It was getting quite dark, and the stage and poles looked black and melancholy as I passed by them. But the publicans' booths were all lighted up inside and looked very cheerful, and were full of holiday folk, fortifying themselves with all sorts of meat and drink before starting for the descent of the hill and the walk home in the dark.

I pushed my way through the crowd round the door, and reached the bar, where the landlord recognised me directly and handed me over to Peter, who soon landed me at the table in the recess, which was still well supplied with cold joints and bread and cheese. While he went off to get my plate and ale, I had time to look round. The booth was much gayer than the day before; every post was decked more or less with flowers and evergreens, and the flags had been brought inside. The whole place was lighted with dips and flickering oil lamps, which gave light enough to let one see all parts of the tent pretty clearly.

There were a good many tables ranged about; the one nearest to ours wasn't yet occupied, but at all the others were groups of men drinking beer, and some smoking and talking eagerly over the events of the day. Those nearest the high table seemed under some little restraint, and spoke low; but from the farther tables rose a loud hum of the broadest Berkshire, and an occasional scrap of a song. A few women were scattered here and there—mostly middle-aged, hard-working housewives—watching their good men, and anxious to carry them off in good time, and before too much of the harvest-savings had found its way to the landlord's till. About the entrance was a continually-changing crowd, and the atmosphere of the whole was somewhat close, and redolent of not very fragrant tobacco.

At the supper-table where I was were seven or eight men. The one just opposite me was a strong-built, middle-aged man, in a pepper-and-salt riding-coat and waistcoat, with an open, weather-beaten face, and keen, deep-set, grey eyes, who seemed bent on making a good supper. Next above him were the two Oxford scholars, but they didn't take the least notice of me, which I thought they might have done, after our morning's ride together. They had finished supper, and were smoking cigars, and chatting with one another, and with the pepper-and-salt man, whom they called Doctor. But my observations were soon cut short by Peter, who came back with my plate and knife and fork, and a foaming pewter of ale, and I set to work as heartily as the Doctor himself.

"You'll find some of this lettuce and water-cress eat well with your beef, Sir," said he, pushing across a dish.

"Thank you, Sir," said I; "I find that watching the games makes one very hungry."

"The air, Sir, all the downs air," said the Doctor; "I call them Doctor Downs. Do more for the appetite in six hours than I can in a week. Here, Peter, get this gentleman some of your mistress's walnut pickles." And then the good-natured Doctor fell to upon his beef again, and chatted away with the scholars and me, and soon made me feel myself quite at home. I own that I had done my neighbours a little injustice; for they were pleasant enough when the ice was once broken, and I daresay didn't mean to be rude after all.

As soon as I had finished my supper, the shorter of the scholars handed me a large cigar, the first whiff of which gave me a high idea of the taste of my contemporaries of the upper classes in the matter of tobacco.

Just then the verse of a song, in which two or three men were joining, rose from the other end of the tent, from amidst the hum of voices.

"I wish those fellows would sing out," said the short scholar; "I can't make out more than a word or two."

"You wouldn't be any the wiser if you could," said the other; "we have ceased to be a singing nation. The people have lost the good old ballads, and have got nothing in their place."

"How do you know ?" said the short scholar; "I should like to hear for myself, at any rate."

"What sort of ballads do you mean, Sir?" said I to the long scholar.

"Why, those in the Robin Hood Garland, for instance," said he. "Songs written for the people, about their heroes, and, I believe, by the people. There's nothing of the sort now."

"What do you say to 'There's a Good Time coming'?" asked the short scholar.

"Well, it's the best of them, I believe," said the other; "but you know it was written by Mackay, an LL.D. Besides, it's essentially a town song."

"It's a tip-top one, at any rate," said the short scholar; "I wish I could write such another."

"What I say, is, that the popular songs now are written by *litterateurs* in London. Is there any life or go in 'Woodman Spare that Tree,' or 'The Old Arm-Chair'? and they are better than the slip-slop sentimental stuff most in vogue."

"What a discontented old bird you are!" said the short scholar; "you're never pleased with any product of this enlightened century."

"Let the century get a character, then; when it does, we shall get some good staves. I'm not particular; a brave story, or a quaint story, or a funny story, in good rough verse, that's all I ask for. But, where to find one? Here's the Doctor for umpire. I say, Doctor, don't you agree with me, now?"

"Not quite," said the Doctor, looking up from his cold beef. "I dare say you wouldn't think them worth much; but there are plenty of ballads sung about which you never hear."

"What! real modern ballads, written by some of the masses, in this century, for instance? Where did you ever hear one, Doctor? What are they like, now?"

"Well, my work takes me a good deal about in queer places, and at queer times, amongst the country folk, and I hear plenty of them. Will one about Lord Nelson suit you? There's an old patient of mine at the next table who owns a little coal wharf on the canal; he fell into the lock one night, broke his arm, and was nearly drowned, and I attended him. He takes a trip in the barges now and then, which makes him fancy himself half a sailor. I dare say I can set him off, if he hasn't had too much beer."

So the Doctor walked over to a lower table, and spoke to a grisly-headed old man in a velveteen coat and waistcoat, and a blue birdseye-neckerchief, who seemed pleased, and drew his sleeve across his mouth, and cleared his throat. Then there was a rapping on the table, and the old bargee began in a rumbling bass voice:—

THE DEATH OF LORD NELSON.

Come all you gallant seamen as unites a meeting,
    Attend to these lines I be going to relate,
And when you have heard them 'twill move you with pity
    To think how Lord Nelson he met with his fate.
For he was a bold and undaunted commander
    As ever did sail on the ocean so wide;
He made both the French and the Spaniard surrender
    By always a-pouring into them a broadside.

One hundred engagements 'twas he had been into,
    And ne'er in his life was he known to be beat,
Though he'd lost an arm, likewise a right eye, boys,
    No power upon earth ever could him defeat.
His age at his death it was forty and seven;
    And as long as I breathe, his great praises I'll sing;
The whole navigation was given up to him,
    Because he was loyal and true to his king.

Then up steps the doctor in a very great hurry,
    And unto Lord Nelson these words did he say:
"Indeed, then, my Lord, it is I'm very sorry,
    To see you here lying and bleeding this way."
"No matter, no matter whatever about me,
    My time it is come, I'm almost at the worst;
But here's my gallant seamen a-fighting so boldly,
    Discharge off your duty to all of them first."

Then with a loud voice he calls out to his captain,
    "Pray let me, sir, hear how the battle does go,
For I think our great guns do continue to rattle,

Though death is approaching I firmly do know."
"The antagonist's ship has gone down to the bottom,
  Eighteen we have captive and brought them on board,
Four more we have blown quite out of the ocean,
  And that is the news I have brought you, my Lord."

Come all you gallant seamen as unites a meeting,
  Always let Lord Nelson's memory go round,
For it is your duty, when you unites a meeting,
  Because he was loyal and true to the crown'd.
And now to conclude and finish these verses,
  "My time it is come; kiss me, Hardy," he cried.
Now thousands go with you, and ten thousand blessings
  For gallant Lord Nelson in battle who died.

Mourn, England, mourn, mourn and complain,
  For the loss of Lord Nelson, who died on the main.

The short scholar was in raptures; he shouted in the chorus; he banged the table till he upset and broke his tumbler, which the vigilant landlady from behind the casks duly noted, and scored up to him.

I worked away at my note-book, and managed to get all the song, except one verse between the second and third, which I couldn't catch.

"Bravo, Doctor! Here, waiter, get me another tumbler, and some more gin-punch. What a stunning call. Couldn't the old bird give us another bit of history? It's as good as reading 'Southey's Life,' and much funnier," rattled away the short scholar.

"What a quaint old grisly party it is!" said the long scholar; "I shall stand him a pot of beer."

"Well, he won't object to that," said the Doctor, working away at the beef and pickles.

"Here, waiter, take a pot of beer, with my compliments,

over to that gentleman," said the long scholar, pointing to the old bargeman, "and say how much obliged we are to him for his song."

So Peter trotted across with the liquor, and the old man telegraphed his acknowledgments.

"By the way, Doctor," said the short scholar, "as you seem to know a good deal about these things, can you tell me what 'Vicar of Bray' means? I saw two men quarrelling just after the games, and it was all their wives could do to keep them from fighting, and I heard it was because one had called the other 'Vicar of Bray.'"

"It means 'turn-coat' in Berkshire," answered the Doctor. "I didn't think they used the name now; but I remember the time when it was the common term of reproach. I dare say you know Bray, gentlemen?"

"I should think so," said the short scholar; "pretty village just below Maidenhead. I pulled by it on my way to town last June."

"Yes, and it's hard on such a pretty village to have had such a bad parson," said the Doctor.

"I say, Doctor, give us the 'Vicar of Bray,' now, it will set off some of the singing birds at the other end of the booth; I can see they're getting into prime piping order."

"Very good, if you like it," said the Doctor, pushing away his plate, and taking a finishing pull at his pewter, "only the song is in print, I know, somewhere; so you mustn't think you've found much of a prize, Sir," added he to me, for my use of pencil and note-book hadn't escaped him.

"No, Sir," said I; "but I should like to hear it, of all things."

So the Doctor, without further preface, began in his jolly clear voice—

THE VICAR OF BRAY.

In good King Charles's golden days,
    When loyalty had no harm in't,
A zealous High-Church man I was,
    And so I gained preferment.
To teach my flock I never missed:
    Kings were by God appointed;
And they are damned who dare resist,
    Or touch the Lord's anointed.

Chorus.—And this is law, I will maintain
    Until my dying day, sir,
That whatsoever king shall reign,
    I'll be the Vicar of Bray, sir.

When Royal James obtained the throne,
    And Popery grew in fashion,
The Penal Laws I hooted down,
    And read the Declaration;
The Church of Rome I found would fit
    Full well my constitution;
And I had been a Jesuit
    But for the Revolution.
And this is law, &c.

When William, our deliverer, came
    To heal the nation's grievance,
Then I turned cat-in-pan again,
    And swore to him allegiance;
Old principles I did revoke,
    Set conscience at a distance,
Passive obedience was a joke,
    A jest was non-resistance.
And this is law, &c.

When glorious Anne became our queen,
    The Church of England's glory,

Another face of things was seen,
    And I became a Tory.
Occasional Conformist case!
    I damned such moderation;
And thought the Church in danger was
    By such prevarication.
And this is law, &c.

When George in pudding-time came o'er,
    And moderate men looked big, sir,
My principles I changed once more,
    And so became a Whig, sir.
And thus preferment I procured
    From our Faith's great Defender;
And almost every day abjured
    The Pope and the Pretender.
For this is law, &c.

The illustrious House of Hanover,
    And Protestant Succession,
By these I lustily will swear
    While they can keep possession;
For in my faith and loyalty
    I never once will falter,
But George my king shall ever be,
    Except the times do alter.
For this is law, &c.

The short scholar was right as to the effect of the Doctor's song. It was hailed with rapturous applause by the lower tables, though you would have said, to look at them, that scarcely a man of the audience except those close round the singer could have appreciated it. People don't always like best what they fully understand; and I don't know which is the greatest mistake, to fancy yourself above your audience, or to try to come down to them. The little stiffness which the presence of strangers belonging to the broad-cloth classes had at first created amongst the Pastime folk was wearing off, and several songs were started at once from the distant parts of the booth, all of which, save one, came to untimely ends in the course of the first verse or so, leaving the field clear to a ruddy-faced, smock-frocked man, who, with his eyes cast up to the tent-top, droned through his nose the following mournful ditty:—

THE BARKSHIRE TRAGEDY.

A varmer he lived in the West Countree,
 Hey-down, bow-down,
A varmer he lived in the West Countree,
And he had daughters one, two, and dree.
 And I'll be true to my love,
 If my love'll be true to me.

As thay wur walking by the river's brim,
 Hey-down, bow-down,
As thay wur walking by the river's brim,
The eldest pushed the youngest in.
 And I'll be true, &c.

"Oh sister, oh sister, pray gee me thy hand,
 Hey-down, &c.
And I'll gee thee both house and land."
 And I'll, &c.

"I'll neither gee thee hand nor glove,
 Hey down, &c.
Unless thou'lt gee me thine own true love."
 And I'll, &c.

So down she sank and away she swam,
 Hey down, &c.
Until she came to the miller's dam.
 And I'll, &c.

MEMORIES OF THE VALE

The miller's daughter stood by the door,
  Hey-down, &c.
As fair as any gilly-flow-er.
  And I'll, &c.

"Oh vather, oh vather, here swims a swan,
  Hey-down, &c.
Very much like a drownded gentlewoman."
  And I'll, &c.

The miller he fot his pole and hook,
  Hey-down, &c.
And he fished the fair maid out of the brook.
  And I'll, &c.

"Oh miller, I'll gee thee guineas ten,
  Hey-down, &c.
If thou'lt fetch me back to my vather again."
  And I'll, &c.

The miller he took her guineas ten,
  Hey-down, &c.
And he pushed the fair maid in again.
  And I'll, &c.

But the Crowner he cum, and the Justice too,
  Hey down, &c.
With a hue and a cry and a hulla-balloo.
  And I'll, &c.

They hanged the miller beside his own gate
  Hey down, &c.
For drowning the varmer's daughter, Kate.
  And I'll, &c.

The sister she fled beyond the seas,
  Hey-down, &c.
And died an old maid among black savagees.

And I'll, &c.

So I've ended my tale of the West Countree,
And they calls it the Barkshire Trage-dee.
    And I'll, &c.

"'The Barkshire Tragedy', indeed! Now, Doctor, what have you to tell us about this? When did it happen? Who was the lady? Was she drowned in the Thames, the Kennett, or where?"

"Oh, I don't know. All I can say is, she was drowned before my time; for I remember hearing the song when I was a little chap in petticoats. But the story seems a common one. There's a north-country ballad founded on it, I know, but I don't remember the name just now."

"'The Bonny Mill-dams of Binnorie,' is not it?" said the long scholar.

"Aye, that's the name, I think."

"Well, it's very odd, for we've got the same story, all but the miller, and his daughter as fair as any gilly-flower (why are millers' daughters always pretty, by the way?), on the Welsh marshes," said the long scholar.

"Then, Sir, I must call on you to sing it. The call is with me at our end of the booth," said the Doctor. "And, Peter, bring me a little cold gin-and-water, and a pipe. If I must breathe smoke-poison, I may as well make it myself, at any rate."

"Well, singing's rather more than I bargained for. However, I suppose I mustn't spoil sport; so here goes."

THE DROWNED LADY.
Qy. another version of the Barkshire Tragedy?

Oh, it was not a pheasant cock,
    Nor yet a pheasant hen,
But oh it was a lady fair

MEMORIES OF THE VALE

Came swimming down the stream.

An ancient harper passing by
    Found this poor lady's body,
To which his pains he did apply
    To make a sweet melody.

To cat-gut dried he her inside,
    He drew out her back-bone,
And made thereof a fiddle sweet
    All for to play upon.

And all her hair so long and fair,
    That down her back did flow,
Oh he did lay it up with care.
    To string his fiddle bow.

And what did he with her fingers
    Which were so straight and small?
Oh, he did cut them into pegs
    To screw up his fiddle.

Then forth went he, as it might be,
    Upon a summer's day,
And met a goodly company,
    Who asked him in to play.

Then from her bones he drew such tones
    As made their bones to ache,
They sounded so like human groans,
    Their hearts began to quake.

They ordered him in ale to swim,
    For sorrow's mighty dry,
And he to share their wassail fare
    Essay'd right willingly.

He laid his fiddle on a shelf
　　In that old manor-hall,
It played and sung all by itself,
　　And thus sung this fiddle:—

"There sits the squire, my worthy sire,
　　A-drinking his-self drunk,
And so did he, ah woe is me!
　　The day my body sunk.

"There sits my mother, half asleep,
　　A-taking of her ease,
Her mind is deep, if one might peep,
　　In her preserves and keys.

"There sits my sister, cruel Joan,
　　Who last week drownded me;
And there's my love, with heart of stone,
　　Sits making love to she.

"There sits the Crowner, Uncle Joe,
　　Which comforteth poor me;
He'll hold his Crowner's quest, I know,
　　To get his Crowner's fee."

Now when this fiddle thus had spoke
It fell upon the floor,
And into little pieces broke,
No word spoke never more.

"Thank you, Sir," said the Doctor; "that's a queer tune though. I don't know that I ever heard one at all like it. But I shouldn't say all that song was old now."

"Well, I believe you're right. But I can say, as you said of the Barkshire Tragedy, it's all older than my time, for I remember my father singing it just as I've sung it to you as long as I can remember anything."

"And what did he say of it?"

"Well, he said that five out of the first six verses were very old indeed. He had heard them often when he was a child, and always the same words. The rest was all patchwork, he said, by different hands, and he hardly knew which were the old lines, and which new."

"I say," remarked the short scholar, "the Doctor don't seem to be a bad hand at making the smoke-poison."

The Doctor blew out a long white cloud, and was about to reply, when a brawny young carter, at a distant table, took his pipe from his lips, and, in answer to the urgings of his neighbours, trolled out the following little piece of sentiment:—

CUPID'S GARDEN.

As I wur in Cu-bit's gardin
   Not mwoar nor haf an hour,
'T wur ther I zeed two may-dens
   Zittin under Cu-bit's bower,
A-gatherin of sweet jassa-mine,
The lilly and the rose.
   These be the fairest flowers
As in the gardin grows.

I vondly stepped to one o' them,
   These words to her I zays,
"Be you engaged to arra young man,
   Come tell to me, I prays."
"I beant engaged to arra young man,
   I solemnly declare;
I aims to live a may-den,
   And still the lau-rel wear."

Zays I, "My stars and gar-ters!
   This here's a pretty go,
Vor a vine young mayd as never wos

> To sar' all man-kind zo."
> But the t'other young may-den looked sly at me,
>   And vrom her zeat she risn,
> Zays she, "Let thee and I go our own waay,
>   And we'll let she go shis'n."

"Oh, I say, that beats all!" said the short scholar, with a shout of laughter. "I must have the words somehow. Let's see, how did he begin? something about Cubit. What a rum notion to call Cupid, Cubit. What was it, Doctor?"

"You shouldn't laugh, really Sir, at our west-country sentiment," said the Doctor, with astounding gravity. "I don't think I can conscientiously help you to the words, when I know you'll only be making fun of them at some wine-party. They are meant for malt drinkers, not for wine drinkers."

"Fudge, Doctor. Come, now, give us the words, or I shall have to go over and ask the performer for them."

"I think I can give you them," said I, looking up from my note-book.

"What a thing it is to write short-hand!" said the Doctor, glancing at my hieroglyphics; "we don't learn that sort of thing down in these parts."

"I wonder we haven't had more sentimental songs," said the long scholar; "I suppose there are plenty of love stories going about?"

"Oh yes, plenty," said the Doctor; "mostly ballads telling how rich young heiresses disdained all good matches, for the sake of a sailor boy with tarry trousers, or a seductive fogger, thereby provoking their cruel match-making parents. For instance:—

> Says the daughter to the mother, "Your art is all in vain,
> For Dukes and Lords and Earls alike their riches I disdain;
> I'd rather live a humble life, and my time I would employ

Increasing nature's prospects, with my bonny labouring boy."

"What on earth can 'increasing nature's prospects' mean?" asked the long scholar.

"How can I tell?" said the Doctor, laughing; "I don't pretend to construe; I only give you the words. But you must allow the moral to be good. It runs:—

"Success to every labouring boy that ploughs and hoes the ground,
For when his work is over, his home he will enjoy;
So happy is the girl that gets a bonny labouring boy."

"Let's see," said the short scholar, "we've had specimens of patriotic, legendary, and sentimental ditties; but how about drinking songs? All tuneful nations, since the world began, have sung the praises of good liquor."

"I don't know that we have many drinking songs," said the Doctor; "I suppose it takes wine, or spirits at any rate, to make a man write such stuff as 'the glasses sparkle,' or 'a bumper of Burgundy.' The bucolic muse only gets smallish beer. But we must see what we can do for you."

So the Doctor beckoned to Peter, and sent him off to the lower tables with a pot of beer, the speedy result of which mission was the following song:—

TOVEY'S TAP.—Air, "*Derry down.*"

Owld Tovey once brewed a barrel o' beer,
    For he wur a man as loved good cheer,
And zays he, "I'll jest ax a veaw o' my vriends
    To come and try how the likker spends."[40]
Derry down, &c.

---

40 "Spend"—to consume.

There's long Tom Ockle, he shall be one,
    And little Jack Smith, who's as round as a tun,
And owld Gaarge Mabbutt, who's allus a-dry,
    I'll warn'd thay'll make good company.
Derry down, &c.

The barrell wur tapped, and the beer runned well,
    How much they vour drenked I never heard tell;
But zome how or other they one and all
    Did swear as how the drenk wur small.
Derry down, &c.

Owld Tovey at this did look main scrow;[41]
    Zays he, "My vriends, I'd hev'ee to kneow
That my beer has made 'ee as drunk as pegs,
    And not one o' you dree can kip on his legs."
Derry down, &c.

They left the house, and the path they tuk,
    Athert the meadow as leads to the bruk;
And you plainly med zee as every man
    Had a pair o' crooked stockings an.
Derry down, &c.

Zays Mabbott to Ockle, "Owld Tovey wur zurly;"
    Zays Ockle to Mabbott, "I'm uncommon purly;[42]
Be mindful, I zay, vor yer missuses' zakes,
    Which o' them two narrer bridges you takes."
Derry down, &c.

"The bruk is main deep," Gaarge Mabbott then zaid,
    As he looked at the water, and scratted his yead;
"And I owns I should 'mazinly like for to know
    Auver which o' thay bridges you aims vor to go."
Derry down, &c.

---

41   "Scrow"—angry.
42   "Purly"—purblind.

"'Tis a akkerdish place to crass in the night,
    And to stand here till marnin' wouldn't be right;
Taint a mossell o' use to bide stabbleing[43] here,
    Zo let's go back and vinish the barrel o' beer."
Derry down, &c.

"A good cast, Doctor;" said the long scholar; "but you've raised the wrong fish. That isn't what my friend here meant by a drinking song. He expects a bucolic rendering of one of Moore's songs, and you serve him out a queer pot-house tale. Is there no enthusiasm for good drink amongst you?"

"I wish there were less," said the Doctor, with a sigh; "at any rate, less consumption of bad drink. Tippling is our great curse, as it is that of all England; but there's less of it than there used to be. But for a drinking song such as you mean, I'm at fault. The nearest approach to it that I know of is a song of which I only remember two lines. They run—

"Sartinly the sixpenny's the very best I've see'd yet,
I do not like the fourpenny, nor yet the intermediate."

But even here you see, though the poet was meditating on drink, it was in a practical rather than an enthusiastic spirit."

Just then, a stout old yeoman entered the booth, dressed in a broad straight-cut brown coat with metal buttons, drab breeches, and mahogany tops; and, marching up to the bar, ordered a glass of brandy and water; while his drink was being prepared, he stood with his back to our table, talking to the landlord.

"We're in luck," said the Doctor in a low voice, pointing to the new-comer with the end of his pipe; "if he stays, we shall have the best old song in all the west country, sung as it should be."

---

43   " Stabble "—to tread dirt about.

"Who is he?" asked the short scholar.

"An old Gloucestershire farmer from Sutherup way, famous for his breed of sheep. He must be near seventy, and has twelve miles to ride home to-night, and won't think so much of it as you or I would."

"He looks a tough old blade."

"You may say that. But he isn't the man he was, for he has lived pretty hard. He used to be a famous wrestler; and one day, many years ago, an Ilsley dealer came down to buy his flock of two-year olds. They drank six bottles of port over the deal, and got it all straight out except the odd sheep, but they couldn't make out, cipher it how they would, who the odd sheep belonged to; so they agreed to wrestle for the odd sheep in the farmer's kitchen, and somehow both of them got hurt, and the old boy has never gone quite right since."

"What an old sponge! six bottles of port between two of them! no wonder they couldn't do their sum."

"Ah, we mustn't judge of the men of his time by our rules," said the Doctor; "it was part of a yeoman's creed in those days to send his friends off drunk, and to be carried to bed himself by his fogger and carter, or else to sleep under his kitchen-table. They lived hard enough, and misused a deal of good liquor meant to strengthen man's heart, following the example of their betters; but they had their good points. That old man, now, is the best master in all his neighbourhood; and he and the parson keep up the wages in the winter, and never let a man go to the house[44] who will work."

The old farmer turned round, glass in hand, and came and sat down at the table. "Your sarvant, gen'l'men," said he, taking off his broad-brimmed beaver. "Why, Doctor," he went on, recognising our friend, and holding out his great bony hand, "be main glad to zee 'ee."

---

44   *The workhouse.*

"Thank you, farmer," said the Doctor, returning the grip; "we haven't met this long while; I'm glad to see you wearing so well."

"Yes, I be pretty-feteish, thank God," said the farmer. "Your health, sir, and gen'l'men."

After a little judicious talk on the day's sport, the Doctor suddenly began, "Now, farmer, you must do us a favour, and give us your famous old Gloucestershire song. I've been telling all our friends here about it, and they're keen to hear it."

"'Spose you means 'Gaarge Ridler'?"said the farmer.

"Of course," said the Doctor.

"Well, I don't know as I've zung these score o' months," said the farmer, "but hows'mever, if you wants it, here goes."

So the farmer finished his brandy and water, cleared his throat, balanced himself on the hind legs of his chair, cast up his eyes and began—

Thaay stwuns, thaay stwuns, thaay stwuns, thaay stwuns,
Thaay stwuns, thaay stwuns, thaay stwuns, thaay stwuns.

"What's he saying—what language?" whispered the tall scholar.

"Mad old party," murmured the short scholar.

"Hush," whispered the Doctor; "that's the orthodox way to begin; don't put him out."

I couldn't tell what in the world to write, but the farmer went on with growing emphasis—

Thaay stwuns, thaay stwuns, thaay stwuna, thaay stwuns,
Thaay stwuns, thaay stwuns, thaay stwuns, THAAY S, T, W, U, N, S.

There was a moment's pause, during which the Doctor had much difficulty in keeping order; then the farmer got fairly under weigh, and went on—

MEMORIES OF THE VALE

Thaay stwuns that built Gaarge Ridler's oven,
   Oh, thaay cum vrom the Blakeney Quaar,
And Gaarge he wur a jolly owld man,
   And his yead did graw above his yare.

One thing in Gaarge Ridler I must commend,
   And I hold it vor a notable thing;
He made his braags avoore he died,
   As wi' any dree brothers his zons zhou'd zing.

Ther' wur Dick the treble, and Jack the mean,
   Let every mon zing in his auwn pleace,
And Gaarge he wur the elder brother,
And there-voore he would zing the base.

Droo' aal the world, owld Gaarge would bwoast,
   Commend me to merry owld England mwoast,
While vools gwoes scamblin' vur and nigh,
   We bides at whoam, my dog and I.

Ov their furrin tongues let travellers brag,
   Wi' their vifteen neames vor a puddin' bag,
Two tongues I knows ne'er towld a lie,
   And their wearers be my dog and I.

My dog has got his maaster's nose,
   To smell a knave droo' silken hose;
But when good company I spy,
   "Welcome," quoth my dog and I.

When I hev dree sixpences under my thumb,
   Oh then I be welcome wherever I cum;
But when I hev none, O then I pass by;
   'Tis poverty pearts good company.

When I gwoes dead, as it may hap,
   My grave shall be under the good yeal-tap,
Wi' vaulded earmes ther' wool I lie,
   Cheek by jowl, my dog and I.

Just as the farmer was finishing the song, Master George, with Joe and one or two more behind him, came in. He took up the last verse, and rolled it out as he came up towards our table, and a lot of the rest joined in with him; even the overworked Peter, I could see stopping for a moment to shout that he would be buried under the tap; I dare say he meant it, only I think he would like it to be always running.

Master George knew most of the people, and made us all merrier even than we were before; and in the next half-hour or so, for which time we stayed in the booth, I should think there must have been a dozen more songs sung. However, I shall only give the one which seemed to be the greatest favourite, for I find that this chapter is running very long. This song was sung by a queer little man, with a twisted face, and a lurcher dog between his knees, who I believe was an earth stopper. He called it

BUTTERMILK JACK.

Ther wur an owld 'oman as had but one son,
    And thay lived together as you med zee;
And they'd nought but an owld hen as wanted to sett,
    Yet somehow a landlord he fain would be.

"Oh, I've been and begged me some buttermilk, mother,
    Off of an owld 'oman as has girt store;
And I shall well rewarded be,
    Vor she's g'in me haf a gallon or mwore.

"Oh mother, my buttermilk I will sell,
    And all for a penny as you med zee;
And with my penny then I will buy eggs,
    Vor I shall have seven for my penney.

"Oh mother, I'll set them all under our hen,
　　And seven cock chickens might chance for to be;
But seven cock chickens or seven cap hens,
　　There'll be seven half-crownds for me.

"Oh, I'll go carry them to market, mother,
　　And nothing but vine volk shall I zee;
And with my money then I will buy land,
　　Zo as a landlord I med be."

"Oh my dear zon, wilt thee know me,
　　When thee hast gotten great store of wealth?"
"Oh, my dear mother, how shall I know thee,
　　When I shall hardly know my own self?"

With that the owld 'oman she flew in a passion,
　　And dashed her son Jack up agin the wall,
And his head caught the shelf where the buttermilk stood,
　　So down came the buttermilk, pitcher and all.

Zo aal you as has got an old hen for to sett,
　　Both by night and by day mind you has her well watched,
Lest you should be like unto Buttermilk Jack,
　　To reckon your chickens before thay are hatched.

"Well, I must be moving," said the Doctor at last, looking at his watch; "how do you get home, Mr. Hurst?"

"Bless us! near nine o'clock," said Joe, following the Doctor's example; "oh, I ride myself, and my friend here talks of going behind."

"Better not ride double, the night's dark," said the Doctor, hoisting on his over-coat with Peter's help. "If he likes to take his luck in my gig, I can put him down at your gate. What do you say, Sir?"

I thankfully accepted; for I didn't at all like the notion of riding behind Joe on the chestnut, and I can't think how I could ever have been such a fool as to say I would do it. The Doctor had two bright lamps to his gig, which gave us glimpses of the closed booths and camping places of the people who were going to stay on the hill all night, as we drove out of the Castle. I suggested that it must be very bad for the people sleeping out up there.

"For their health?" said he, "not a bit of it, on a fine night like this—do 'em good; I wish they always slept so healthily."

"I didn't quite mean that, Sir!"

"Oh, for their morals? Well, I don't know that there's much harm done. I'm sorry to say they're used to crowding—and, after all, very few but the owners of the booths, and the regular tramps, stay up here. Didn't you see how quiet everything was?"

I said I had noticed this; and then he began asking me about the sports, for he had only got on to the hill late in the afternoon; and when we came to the wrestling and backsword play, I asked him whether he thought they did any harm.

"No," said he, "there are very few serious accidents—in fact none—now that drink is not allowed on the stage. There used to be some very brutal play in out-of-the-way places, where the revels were got up by publicans. But that is all over, at least about this part of the country."

"Then you wouldn't stop them, Sir?"

"Stop them! not I—I would encourage them, and make the parish clerk and constable perpetual umpires." And then he went on to say how he should like to see the young fellows in every parish drilled in a company, and taught all sorts of manly exercises, and shooting especially; so that they would make good light troops at a day's notice, in case of invasion. But he was afraid the great game preservers would never allow this.

And in the middle of his talk, which seemed very sensible, we came to Joe's gate, and I got down, and wished him good night.

I found the family gone to bed, and only Joe and the Parson in the kitchen, and there, over a last pipe, we chatted about the sports.

At last the Parson turned to me and said, "You saw a good deal of the play on the stage; now, would you stop it if you could?"

I thought a minute over what I had seen and what the Doctor had said.

"No, Sir," said I, "I can't say that I would."

"That's candid," said he. "And now I'll make an admission. There's a good deal of the play that wants very close watching. The umpires should be resolute quick men, and stand no nonsense. I saw one or two bouts to-day that should have been stopped."

"You see," said Joe, taking his pipe out of his mouth, "there allus must be."

"We don't admit your evidence, Joseph," interrupted the Parson, "you are a prejudiced witness."

"But you haven't changed your mind, Sir," said I.

"No," said he, "I should be sorry to hear that these sports had died out, but I should like to hear that people took an interest in them who could manage the men thoroughly."

"The Doctor," said I, "as we drove home, said he would have the parish clerk and constable for perpetual umpires."

"They wouldn't be so good as the parson or the squire," said he; "if I were rector of one of the parishes where they are still kept up, I would give prizes for them, but I would always be umpire myself."

"I wish to goodness you was then," said Joe, as we lighted our candles.

"You remember, Sir," said I, "that you promised to write a sermon about the Pastime."

"What! *After* the fair?" said he.

"'Twill do just as well," said Joe, "I should mortally like to hear it."

"Well, it might keep you awake perhaps. He has an hereditary weakness for slumber in church, you must know," said the Parson, turning to me; "when we wanted to alter the sittings in the church six or seven years ago, his father stood out for his old high box so sturdily, that I took some pains to argue with him, and to find out what it was which made it so dear to him. I found out at last that it was a snug corner, which just fitted his shoulders, where nobody could see him, and where, as soon as the text was given out, in his own words, 'I just watches my missus wipe her spectacles, and fix herself to listen, and then I vaulds my arms and thenks o' nothin'.'"

I looked at Joe to see how he would take it, but he only chuckled, and said, "Well, 'tis the parson's business to keep us awake. But a sermon on our sports, just showing folk about the rights on it, is just what I should amazingly like to have by me."

The Parson looked at Joe for a moment very curiously, and then said, "Very well, I will write you one. Good night."

And so we went off to bed.

CHAPTER VII.

Miss Lucy couldn't be spared to go up to the hill on the second day of the Pastime, for there was some great operation going on in the cheese room, which she had to overlook. So Mr. Warton drove me up in the four-wheel. I was very anxious to find out, if I could, whether there was anything more between him and Miss Lucy than friendship, but it wasn't at all an easy matter.

First I began speaking of the young gentleman who had taken my place in the four-wheel; for I thought that would be a touchstone, and that if he were like me he would be glad to get a chance of abusing this Jack. But he only called him a forward boy, and said he was a cousin of the Hursts, who lived in the next parish. Then I spoke of Miss Lucy herself, and he was quite ready to talk about her as much as I liked, and seemed never tired of praising her. She was a thoroughly good specimen of an English yeoman's daughter; perfectly natural, and therefore perfectly well bred; not above making good puddings and preserves, and proud of the name her brother's cheeses had won in the market, yet not negligent of other matters, such as the schools, and her garden; never going into follies of dress in imitation of weak women who ought to set better examples, yet having a proper appreciation of her own good looks, and a thorough knowledge of the colours and shapes which suited her best; not particularly clever or well read, but with an open mind and a sound judgment—and so he went on; and the longer he went on the more I was puzzled, and my belief is, that on this subject the Parson got much more out of me than I out of him, on that morning's drive.

We had a very pleasant day on the hill, but as the sports were all the same as those of the day before (with the exception of jumping in sacks, which was substituted for climbing the pole, and was very good fun), I shall not give any further account of them; especially as the gentlemen who are going to publish my story seem to think already that I am rather too long-winded.

We got down home in capital time for tea, and Joe followed very soon afterwards, in the highest spirits; for, as he said, everything had gone off so well, and everybody was pleased and satisfied; so we were all very merry, and had another charming evening. I couldn't tell what had come to me when I got up stairs alone by myself, for I seemed as if a new life were growing up in me, and I were getting all of a sudden into a much bigger world, full of all sorts of work and pleasure, which I had never dreamt of, and of people whom I could get to love and honour, though I might never see or speak to them.

I had been bred up from a child never to look beyond my own narrow sphere. To get on in it was the purpose of my life, and I had drilled myself into despising everything which did not, as I thought, help towards this end. Near relations I had none. I was really fond of my two friends, but I don't think I should ever have got to be friends with them if we hadn't been in the same office; and I used often to be half provoked with them, and to think myself a very wise fellow, because out of office-hours they would read poetry and novels instead of fagging at short-hand or accounts, as I did, and spent all their salaries instead of saving. Except those two, I knew nobody; and though I belonged to a debating society, it wasn't that I cared for the members, or what they talked about, but that I thought it might be useful to me to talk fluently if I got on in business. Sometimes, and especially in my yearly holidays, I had felt as if I wanted something else, and that my way of life was after all rather a one-eyed sort of business; but I set all such misgivings down as delusions, and had never allowed them long to trouble me. In short I begin to suspect that I must have been getting to be a very narrow, bigoted, disagreeable sort of fellow, and it was high time that I should find my way to Elm Close, or some such place, to have my eyes opened a little, and discover that a man may work just as steadily and honestly—aye, much more steadily and honestly—at his own business, without shutting up his brains and his heart against everything else that is going on in the world around him. However, I can't be too thankful that my teaching came to me in the way it did, for I might have had to learn my lesson in a very different school from Elm Close Farm.

There certainly never was such a pleasant school. For the next two or three days after 'the Scouring,' Mr. Warton was my chief companion. Joe and Miss Lucy both had their work to attend to after breakfast, and so the Parson and I were left a good deal together; and we used to start off to see some of the old men whom he had promised to show me, who could tell me about the old Pastimes. I never liked anything so much as these walks—not even the walks I afterwards used to have alone with Miss Lucy, for they were too exciting, and half the time I was in such a fret that I couldn't thoroughly enjoy them. But there was no drawback in these walks with the Parson. He was full of fun, and of all sorts of knowledge; and he liked talking, and I think rather took a fancy to me, and was pleased to see how I worked at collecting all the information I could about the White Horse, for he took a great deal of pains to help me.

The Parson in our walks set me thinking about fifty subjects which I never cared about before, because I could see that he was himself deeply interested in them, and really believed whatever he said to me. We used to get home by about twelve o'clock, and then I would go away by myself, and think over what we had been talking about till dinner. And, after dinner, Miss Lucy, and sometimes Joe, would come out and walk with us till tea. Sometimes we went to the village school, and I sat at the door and heard them teaching; and as long as Mr. Warton was with us it was all right, but afterwards, when he had gone, I could see that the schoolmistress, a young woman of about thirty, sallow-faced and rather prudish, used to look at me as if I had no business there.

When he left, Mr. Warton gave me a kind invitation to go and see him in town, and added he had no doubt I should come, for he could see I should soon want some such work as he could give me to do.

After he was gone I tumbled fairly head over heels into the net in which I suppose every man "as is a man" (as old Seeley would say) gets enmeshed once in his life. I found it was no use to struggle any longer, and gave myself up to the stream, with all sails set. Now there is no easier thing than going down stream somehow, when wind and tide are with you; but to steer so as to make the most of wind and tide isn't so easy—at least I didn't find it so.

For as often as not, I think, I did the wrong thing, and provoked, instead of pleasing her. I used to get up every morning before six, to be ready to wish her good morning as she went out to the dairy; but I don't think she half liked it, for she was generally in a very old gown tucked through her pocket holes, and pattens. Then after breakfast I used to hanker round the kitchen, or still-room, or wherever she might happen to be, like a Harry-long-legs round a candle. And again in the afternoon I never could keep away, but was at her side in the garden, or on her walks; in fact, to get rid of me, she had fairly to go up to her room.

But I couldn't help myself; I felt that, come what might, I

must be near her while I could; and on the whole, I think she was pleased, and didn't at all dislike seeing me reduced to this pitiful state.

When I was involuntarily out of her sight, I used to have a sort of craving for poetry, and often wished that I had spent a little more time over such matters. I got Joe to lend me the key of the cupboard where he kept his library, hoping to find something to suit me there. But, besides a few old folios of divinity and travel, and some cookery books, and the *Farmer's Magazine*, there was nothing but Watts's *Hymns* and Pollock's *Course of Time*, which I didn't find of any use to me.

Joe used to wonder at me at first, when I refused his offers of a day's coursing, or a ride with him to Farringdon or Didcott markets; but he soon got used to it, and put it down to my cockney bringing up, and congratulated himself that, at any rate, I was pretty good company over a pipe in the kitchen.

The autumn days sped away all too quickly, but I made the most of them as they passed, and over and over again I wondered whether there were any but kind and hospitable and amusing people in the Vale, for the longer I stayed there, the more I was astonished at the kind courtesy of everybody I came across, from the highest to the lowest, and I suppose everybody else would find it the same as I did.

It seemed as if I were destined to leave Elm Close without a single unkind thought of anybody I had seen while there, for even Jack made his peace with me. Only two days before my departure, Miss Lucy gave out at breakfast that she was going to walk over to see her uncle, and wanted to know if her mother or Joe had any message. No, they hadn't. But of course I managed to accompany her.

When we came to her uncle's farm, he was out, and in five minutes Miss Lucy was away with her dear friend and cousin, one of the girls I had seen at the Pastime, and I was left to the tender mercies of Jack. However, Jack at his own house, with no women by to encourage him to make a fool of himself, was a very decent fellow. He walked me about the homestead, and chatted away about the Pastime, and the accomplishments of his terrier dog, whom he had got from the kennel of the Berkshire hounds, and whose father used to run with them regularly. Then he began to inquire about me in a patronising way; how I came to know Joe, what I was, and where I lived. And when he had satisfied his curiosity about me, he took to talking about his cousins.

Joe, I soon found out, was his hero; and he looked forward to the time when he should be able to breed a good horse, like Joe's chestnut, and to go about to all the markets and carry his head as high as any one, as Joe could, as the height of human happiness. As to cousin Lu, if he were looking out for anything of the sort, there was no girl within twenty miles that he knew of to whom she couldn't give a stone over any country. But she wasn't likely to marry any of the young men about; she was too full of fun, and laughed at them too much. "I shouldn't be a bit surprised now, if she was to take to some town chap like you, after all's said and done," said Jack, in conclusion, as we returned to the house.

My last day at Elm Close came swiftly and surely, and the sun rose, and went pitilessly up into the heavens, and sank down behind White Horse Hill, and the clocks went on striking one after another, just as if it had been any other day. What a number of things I had in my head that morning to say to all of them, and above all to her; but one thing or another interfered, and I had said not one quarter of them, and these not in the way I had intended, before it was dark, and tea on the table. But I did go all round the farm and the village, and took a last look at every field and nook and corner where I had been so happy.

The old lady was unusually talkative at tea, and for some time afterwards. The fact that I was not going to leave the house till after midnight, and was to be at business, in London, at nine o'clock the next morning, now that she had realised it, excited her very much, and waked up all sorts of recollections of her own travels; particularly how, when she was a child, she had been a whole day getting to Reading by the stage, and how, even after her marriage, she and father had had to sleep at Windsor, on the occasion of their one visit to London. I was watching Miss Lucy at her work all the time, and thought she seemed a little absent and sorrowful, and when our eyes met every now and then, she looked away directly. We hardly said a word, and left Joe to keep up the talk with the old lady.

Before long she got tired and went off to bed, and then, I thought, if something would only call Joe out—but nothing happened, and so we sat on talking commonplaces, till prayer time; which, however, Joe did consent to put off this evening, because it was my last, till past ten o'clock. The three servants came in, and knelt down as usual; and I, in a place where I could see her, and watch every turn of her figure, and hear every breath she drew. I own I didn't listen to a word that Joe read—I couldn't—and I don't believe any poor fellow in my state will ever be hardly judged, whatever square-toed people may say, for not forcing himself to attend when he hasn't the power to do it. I only know that, though I couldn't listen to the prayers, I could and did thank God for having brought me down there, and allowed me to see her and know her; and prayed, as heartily as was in me to pray, that I might never do anything which might make me unworthy of one so bright, and pure, and good as she.

And too soon Joe shut the book, and got up, and the servants went out, and Joe dived off into the recess; and she lighted her candle and came up to me, holding out her hand, but without saying anything, or looking up in my face. I took the hand which she held out to me in both mine, but somehow, when I thought it might be for the last time, I couldn't let it go. So I stood holding it, my heart beating so that I couldn't speak, and feeling very uncomfortable about the throat. She didn't take it away, and presently I got my voice again.

"Good bye, Miss Lucy," said I, "and God bless you. I can't tell you what my holiday at Elm Close has been to me—and I can't find words to thank you. I'm a poor lonely fellow, with nobody belonging to me, and leading a slave of a life in the midst of the great crowd, with all sorts of temptations to go wrong. You'll let me think of you, and Elm Close, and it will be like a little bright window with the sun shining through into our musty clerks' room. I feel it will help to keep me straight for many a long day. You'll let me think of you now, won't you?" said I, pressing the little hand which I held in mine.

"Why, you see I can't help it if I would," said she, looking up with a merry light in her eyes; but she went on directly, "but, indeed, I'm sure we shall think of you quite as often as you will of us. Joe used to talk so often about you that I felt quite like an old friend before we met, and now you've been here we shall feel so dull without you."

"Now, you two! don't stand talking there all night," said Joe, coming out of the recess, where he had been rummaging out the pipes and a black bottle; "come, come, kiss and part."

I felt the blood rush up to my face, when Joe said that, but I opened my hands with a jerk, and let hers go, I hardly knew why. If I hadn't been so fond that I was afraid of her, I should have taken Joe at his word. But I'm glad I didn't; I'm sure I was right, for I stole a look at her, and saw that she looked vexed, and flushed up to her bright brown hair.

Next moment she held out her hand again, and shook mine heartily, and said, without looking up, "Good-bye, you must come again soon," and then hurried out of the room, and took away all the light with her. Heigh-ho! when shall I see the light again?

Well, as I followed Joe into the kitchen, what between the sinking I felt at having to leave, and the doubt whether I hadn't made a fool of myself at the last with Miss Lucy, I felt half mad, and the first thing I made up my mind to was to have a good quarrel with Joe. So when he sat down on one side of the fire, and began lighting his pipe, I kept standing looking at him, and thinking how I should begin.

"There's your pipe, Dick," said he, puffing away, "on the settle—why don't you sit down and light up?"

"I shan't smoke with you to-night, Joe," said I, "you ought to be ashamed of yourself!"

"Ashamed o' myself," shouted Joe, staring up at me till I could hardly keep from laughing, angry as I was; "what, in the name o' goodness, have I done to be ashamed of?"

"'Tisn't what you've done, but what you've said."

"Said! what in the world have I said? Precious little I know, for you always get all the talk to yourself."

"Why, what you said just now to me and Miss Lucy," said I.

"To you and Lu?" said he, looking puzzled; and then off he went into one of his great laughs. "Oh, I take—well, that's too much! To be blown up by *you* for it! Why, if any one is to scold, I should say it's Lu."

"Do you think I like to be made the means of giving your sister pain?" said I.

"There now, don't be a fool, Dick—sit down like a good fellow, and light your pipe. What I said don't mean anything down in these parts. Well, I'm very sorry. She'll never think twice about it, bless you. And besides, you know, there can't be any harm done, for you didn't take my advice."

Well, I began to get cool, and to think I might do something better than quarrel with Joe the last night; so I took my pipe, and filled it, and sat down opposite him, and he began to mix two glasses of grog, twisting his face about all the time to keep himself from laughing.

"Here's your health, old fellow," said he, when he had done, "and, mind you, we shall always be glad to see you here when you can come; though I'm afraid the place must be terrible dull for a Londoner."

"It's the best place I've ever been in," said I, with a sigh.

This pleased Joe; and he went off about what he would find me to do if I could come down in the winter or the spring; but I didn't listen much, for I was making up my mind to speak to him about his sister, and I was afraid how he might take it. Presently he stopped for a moment, and I thought, 'now or never,' and began.

"I want to ask you, Joe, is your sister engaged to any one?"

"Not she," said Joe, looking up rather surprised; "why, she's only eighteen come Lady-day!"

"What do you think of Mr. Warton? " said I.

"Our Parson!" laughed Joe; "that is a good 'un. Why he has got a sweetheart of his own. Let alone that he'd know better than to court a farmer's daughter."

"Are you sure?" said I; "your sister isn't like most girls, I can tell you."

"Yes, I tell you," said Joe, "he's no more in love with our Lu than you are."

"Then I'm over head and ears in love with her, and that's all about it," said I, and I looked straight across at him, though it wasn't an easy thing to do. But I felt I was in for it, and I should be much better for having it over.

Joe gave a start, and a long whistle; and then a puff or two at his pipe, staring at me right in the eyes till I felt my head swimming. But I wasn't going to look down just then; if he had looked me right through he couldn't have found anything I was ashamed of, so far as his sister was concerned, and I felt he had a right to look as hard as he pleased, and that I was bound not to shirk it.

Presently he got up, and took a turn or two up and down the kitchen. Then he stopped— "Spoke to her, yet?" said he.

"No," said I, "I haven't."

"Come, give us your hand, Dick," said he, holding out his, and looking quite bright again; "I knew you would be all on the square, let be what might."

"Well, I won't deceive you, Joe," said I, " I don't deserve any credit for that."

"How not?" said he.

"Why, I meant to have spoken to her half-a-dozen times, only one little thing or another stopped it. But I'm very glad of it, for I think you ought to know it first."

"Well, well," said he, coming and sitting down again, and staring into the fire, "it's a precious bad job. Let's think a bit how we be to tackle it."

"I know," said I, drawing up a bit—for I didn't feel flattered at this speech—"that I'm not in the same position you are in, and that you've a right to look for a much richer man than I am for your sister, but—"

"Oh, bother that," said Joe, beginning to smoke again, and still staring into the fire; "I wasn't thinking of that. 'Twill be just as bad for we, let who will take her. Here's mother getting a'most blind, and 'mazing forgetful-like about everything. Who's to read her her chapter, or to find her spectacles? and what in the world's to become of the keys? I be no use to mother by myself, you see," said Joe, "and I couldn't abide to see the old lady put about at her time of life; let alone how the pickling and preserving is to go on."

I was very pleased and surprised to see him taking it so

coolly, and particularly that he seemed not to be objecting to me, but only to losing his sister at all.

"Then there's my dairy," said he; "that cow Daisy, as gives the richest milk in all the Vale, nobody could ever get her to stand quiet till Lu took to her; she'll kick down a matter o' six pail o' milk a week, I'll warrant. And the poultry, too; there's that drattl'd old galleeny 'll be learning the Spanish hens to lay astray up in the brake, as soon as ever Lu goes, and then the fox 'll have 'em all. To think of the trouble I took to get that breed, and not a mossel o' use at last!"

"Well, but Joe," said I, "one would think we were going to be married to-morrow, to hear you talk."

"Well, you want to be married, don't you?" said he, looking up.

"Yes, but not directly," said I; "you see, I should like to have a tidy place got all ready before I should think—"

"Why, she mayn't be agreeable after all," interrupted Joe, as if a new light had suddenly struck him; and then he had a good laugh at the thought, in which I didn't join.

"Then, Joe," said I, "I think you don't seem to mind my being a cockney, and not a rich man?"

"I'd sooner have had a chap that knows a horse from a handspike, and something about four-course," said he, "so I won't tell a lie about it, Dick. Put that out of the way, and I'd as lief call you brother-in-law as any man. But you ain't in any hurry you said just now?"

"Well, no," said I; "but of course I should like to write to your sister directly and tell her, and I hope you won't object to that, and won't hinder me if you can't help me."

"Don't have any of that writing," said Joe, "'pend upon it a good-bred girl like Lu wouldn't stand it."

"That's all very well," said I, "but I'm going away to-night, you know, and if I don't write how's she ever to know anything about it?"

"Look here," said Joe; "will you promise, Dick, to give me and mother a year to turn round in from next Christmas—that is, supposing Lu don't say no?"

"Yes, certainly," said I, "Christmas year is the earliest time I could hope to be ready by."

"Then I'll tell you what," said he; "don't you go writing to her at all, and I'll bring her up with me for Christmas cattle show, and you can get us lodgings, and show us some of the sights. You can have it all out with her before we come home, and I shall be by to see all fair."

"No, no, Joe, I couldn't say a word with you by."

"I didn't mean that I was to be in the room, you know, only if anything goes wrong—you understand," said Joe, looking round, and nodding at me with a solemn face.

"Yes, I see," said I; "but somebody else—one of the young farmers now, that I saw on the hill, may be stepping in before Christmas."

"Not they. It's busy times with us these next two months. Besides, I'll look after that. Is it a bargain then?"

"Yes," said I, "only mind, Joe, that you look sharp meantime."

"All right," said he; and then fell to looking into the fire again; and I sat thinking too, and wondering at my luck, which I could hardly believe in yet.

"And now about the pot," said Joe; "suppose Lu says yes, what have you got to keep the pot boiling?"

Then I told him what my salary was, and what I had saved, and where I had put it out, and he nodded away, and seemed very well satisfied.

"Well, Lu has got £500," said he, "under father's will. Parson and I are the executors. You must go and see the Parson when you get back to London; he's an out-and-outer, and worth more than all the chaps at that jawing shop of yours put together. The money is out at interest, all but £200, which we've never raised yet, but for that matter I can pay it up whenever it's wanted."

"Of course," said I, "I should wish all her fortune to be settled on her."

"Yes, I forgot," said he; "I suppose there ought to be some sort of tying-up done for the children. So I'll go and see Lawyer Smith about it next market-day."

"Perhaps you had better wait till after Christmas," said I.

"Aye, aye," said he, "I forgot. We may be running a tail scent after all. But, I say, Dick, if you get married, Lu can never live in those dirty dark streets, and you away all day; she'd mope to death without a place for poultry, and a little bit of turf to cool her feet on."

"Well," said I, "you see I've got a bit of ground under a freehold land society, down the Great Northern line. It's a very pretty place, and only five minutes' walk from a station. I could build a house there in the spring, you know, and have the garden made."

"That'll do," said he; "and if you want £100 or so, to finish it off as should be, why you know where to come for it."

"Thank you," said I, "but I think I can manage it."

"I shall send her up those Spanish hens," said he, looking up again presently from his pipe; "they won't be no use here."

"I wish, Joe," said I, "you wouldn't talk as if it was all quite certain; it makes me feel uncomfortable. Your sister mayn't like me, after all."

"Makes no odds at all," said he; "if she don't have you, there'll be some other chap on in no time. Once a young gal gets a follower it's all over, so fur as I see; though 'tisn't always the first as they takes up with as they sticks to for better for worse."

"Thank you for nothing, Master Joe," said I to myself; and

I smoked away opposite him for some time without saying a word, thinking what a queer fellow he was, and how I had better let things rest as they were, for I couldn't see how to handle him the least bit in the world; and I can't tell whether I was most glad or sorry, when we heard the fogger come to the kitchen door to say the trap was all ready.

Joe knocked the ashes out of his last pipe, took off the last drop out of his tumbler, and then put out his hand and gave me one of his grips.

"It's got to be done," said he, "there's no mistake about that."

"What?" said I, "what's to be done? Don't look so solemn, Joe, for goodness' sake."

"It's no laughing matter, mind you," said he; and he took the candle and went off into the passage, and came back with his whip and two top-coats. "Here, you get into that," he went on, handing me one of them; "you'll find the night rawish."

I buttoned myself into the coat, which was a white drab one, about as thick as a deal board, with double seams and mother-of-pearl buttons as big as cheese-plates, and followed Joe into the yard with a heavy heart.

"Carpet-bag and hamper in?" said he, taking the reins.

"Ees, Sir, all right."

"Jump up, Dick."

I shook hands with the honest fogger, and gave him half-a-crown, which he didn't seem to know how to take; and then I got up by Joe's side, and we walked out of the yard at a foot's pace, on to the grass; he kept off the road to be more quiet. It was bright moonlight, and a streak of white mist lay along the Close. I could hear nothing but the soft crush of the wheels on the rich sward, and the breathing of the great cows as we passed them in the mist. But my heart was beating like a hammer, as I looked back over my shoulder at one window of the old house, until it was hidden behind the elm-trees; and when I jumped down to open the gate into the road, I tore open the great coat, or I think I should have been suffocated.

"It's no laughing matter, mind you," said Joe, looking round, after we had gone about half-a-mile along the road at a steady trot.

"No, indeed," said I. I felt much more like crying, and I thought he was trying to comfort me, in his way.

"Come, you button up that coat again, Dick; I won't have you getting into the train at one in the morning with a chill on you. I won't turn my back," he went on, "on any man in the county at sampling wheat, or buying a horse, or a lot of heifers, or a flock of sheep. Besides, if a chap does get the blind side of me, it's may-be a ten-pound note lost, and there's an end of it. But when you come to choosing a missus, why, it seems like jumping in the dark, for all as I can see. There's nothing to sample 'em by, and you can't look in their mouths or feel 'em over. I don't take it as a man's judgment's of any account when he comes to that deal—and then, if he does get the wrong sort!"

"Thank you, Joe," said I, "but I'm not a bit afraid about getting the wrong sort, if all goes well."

"No, but I be," said he; "why, one would think, Dick, that nobody had to get a missus but you."

Well, that made me laugh out, I was so tickled to find he was thinking of himself all the time; and for the rest of the drive we were merry enough, for he went on talking about his own prospects so funnily that it was impossible to keep sad or sentimental.

We drew up at the silent station five or six minutes nearly before the train was due, and were received by the one solitary porter.

"What luggage, Sir?" said he to me, as I got down.

"One carpet-bag," I answered, "for Paddington."

"And a hamper," said Joe; "you'll find a hamper in behind there. And take care to keep it right side up, porter, for there are some pots of jam in it."

"Who is it for?" said I; "can I look after it, and take it anywhere for you?"

"Why, for you, of course," said Joe; "you don't suppose the women would have let you go back without some of their kickshaws; and I've had a hare and a couple of chickens put in, and some bacon. You must eat the hare this week, mind."

I was quite taken by surprise at this fresh instance of the thoughtful kindness of my Vale friends, and wrung Joe's hand, mumbling out something which I meant for thanks.

"Well, good-bye, old fellow," he said, " I'm very glad to think you've found your way down at last, and now, don't forget it;" and he gave me a grip which nearly crushed all my knuckles into a jelly, and was gathering up his reins to drive off.

"But Joe, here's your coat," I called out, and was beginning to take it off—"you've forgotten your coat."

"No, no," said he, "keep it on—'twill be very cold to-night, and you'll want it in the train. We'll fetch it at Christmas, and the hamper and the jam pots too, at the same time. Lu will be sure to look after them, so mind you don't lose 'em—Hullo! What in the world are you cutting off the direction for?"

"Oh, it's nothing," said I, " but I often fancy parcels go safer with only the railway label on them. Besides, I shall have it in the carriage with me."

The fact was I had caught sight of the direction, which was in her handwriting, and had quite forgotten Joe, as I was cutting it off to put it in my pocket-book.

"Well, that's a rum start," said Joe, "but every one has their own notions about travelling;" and so, with a cheery good-bye to me, off he drove along the dark road; and in another minute the train came up, and I and my luggage were on our way to London.

We went away up through the cold night, eastward, towards the great city which had been my home from childhood. I felt that another man was journeying back from the one who had come down a fortnight before; that he who was travelling eastward had learnt to look beyond his own narrow cellar in the great world-city, to believe in other things than cash payments and short-hand for making his cellar liveable in, to have glimpses of and to sympathise with the life of other men, in his own time, and in the old times before him. These thoughts crowded on me, but all under the shadow of and subordinated to the one great rising hope, in which I had first found and felt my new life. Together they lifted up my heart during the first stages of that night journey, and I opened the window and leant out into the rushing night air, for the carriage was too small for me, and my grand visions and resolves.

But soon it began to feel cold, and I shut up the window, and squeezed myself into a corner with my feet up on the opposite seat, and felt very thankful that I had on Joe's great coat. Then the lamp went out, and it got colder as the dawn came on, and my visions and resolves began to get less bright and firm. The other side of the picture rose up in ugly colours, and I thought of the dirty dark clerks' room, and the hours of oil-lamps and bad air, and the heartless whirl and din of the great city. And to crown all came the more than doubt whether my hope would not fade out and die in the recesses of my own heart. What was I? and what my prospects, that any one should ever give me a thought again of those whom I was so fast leaving behind, much more that she, the flower of them all, should single me out before all others? It was absurd, I should most likely never see Elm Close, or the Vale, or the great mysterious Hill again—I had better make up my mind to live the next twenty years as I had the last. With some such meaning spoke the doleful voices, but I was never much of a hand at looking at the doleful side of things, and I made good strong fight on that night ride; and took out my pipe, and lit it, and pressed my back firmer into my corner.

Well, and if they don't remember me, thought I, I can remember them at any rate—they can't help that; and I will remember them too, and all their kind pleasant ways, and their manlike games, and their queer songs and stories—and the queen of them all, I can carry her in my heart, thank God for that, and every word I ever heard her speak, and every smile I ever saw light up her merry eyes or dimple round her mouth—and the country, too, the fair rich Vale, and the glorious old Hill, they are mine for ever, and all the memories of the slaying of dragons, and of great battles with the Pagan. I wonder whether I shall ever see the old gentleman again who conjured it up for me, and put life into it, and made me feel as if King Alfred and his Saxons were as near and dear to me as Sir Colin Campbell[45] and the brave lads in India!

Just then the train stopped at Reading, and the guard put his head in to say we stopped for three minutes, and I could get a glass of ale. So I jumped out and had a glass of ale, and then another; and stamped about the platform till the train started. And when I got into my corner again, I was quite warm and jolly.

I have been always used to a good night's rest, and I daresay the ale made me more sleepy, and so I fell into a kind of doze almost directly. But in my doze the same train of thought went on, and all the people I had been living with and hearing of flitted about in the oddest jumbles, with Elm Close and White Horse Hill for a background. I went through the strangest scenes. One minute I was first cousin to King Alfred, and try-

---

45 *Commander-in-Chief of British forces during the Indian Mutiny.*

ing to carry his messages over the Hill to Ethelred, only Joe's old brown horse would run away with me along the Ridgeway; then I was the leader of the Berkshire old gamesters, playing out the last tie with a highwayman, for a gold-laced hat and pair of buckskin breeches; then I was married—I needn't say to whom—and we were keeping house under the Hill, and waiting tea for St. George, when he should come down from killing the Dragon. And so it went on, till at last a mist came over the Hill, and all the figures got fainter and fainter, and seemed to be fading away. But as they faded, I could see one great figure coming out clearer through the mist, which I had never noticed before. It was like a grand old man, with white hair and mighty limbs who looked as old as the hill itself, but yet as if he were as young now as he ever had been,—and at his feet were a pickaxe and spade, and at his side a scythe. But great and solemn as it looked, I felt that the figure was not a man, and I was angry with it,—why should it come in with its great pitiful eyes and smile? why were my brothers and sisters, the men and women, to fade away before it?

"The labour that a man doeth under the sun, it is all vanity. Prince and peasant, the wise man and the fool, they all come to me at last, and I garner them away, and their place knows them no more!"—so the figure seemed to say to itself, and I felt melancholy as I watched it sitting there at rest, playing with the fading figures.

At last it placed one of the little figures on its knee, half in mockery, as it seemed to me, and half in sorrow. But then all changed; and the great figure began to fade, and the small man came out clearer and clearer. And he took no heed of his great neighbour, but rested there where he was placed; and his face was quiet, and full of life, as he gazed steadily and earnestly through the mist. And the other figures came flitting by again, and chanted as they passed, "The work of one true man is greater than all thy work. Thou hast nought but a seeming power, over it, or over him. Every true man is greater than thee. Every true man shall conquer more than thee; for he shall triumph over death, and hell, and thee, oh, Time!"

And then I woke up, for the train stopped at the place where the tickets are collected; and, in another five minutes, I was in a cab, with my bag and the great basket of country treasures, creeping along in the early November morning towards Gray's Inn Lane.

And so ended my fortnight's holiday.

APPENDIX.

Note I.

The earliest authentic historical notices of the White Horse are, so far as I am aware,—

1st. A Cartulary of the Abbey of Abingdon, now in the British Museum, of the time of Henry II., the exact date of it being, it is believed, A.D. 1171. It runs as follows: "Consuetudinis apud Anglos tune erat, ut monachi qui vellent pecuniarum patrimoniorum qui forent susceptibiles, ipsisque fruentes quomodo placeret dispensarent. Unde et in Abbendonia duo, Leofricus et Godricus Cild appellati, quorum unus Godricus, Spersholt juxta locum qui vulgo mons Albi Equi nuncupatur, alter Leofricus Hwitceorce super flumen Tamisie maneria sita patrimoniali jure obtinebant," &c.

2dly. Another Cartulary of the same Abbey, of the reign of Richard I. which runs as follows: "Prope montem ubi ad Album Equum scanditur, ab antiquo tempore Ecclesia ista manerium Offentum appellatum in dominio possidet, juxta quod villa X hidarum adjacet ex jure Ecclesiae quam Speresholt nominavit," &c.

3dly. An entry on the Close Rolls, 42 Ed. III., or A.D. 1368-9:—"Gerard de l'Isle tient en la vale de White Horse one fee," &c. See *Archaeologia*, vol. xxxi. p. 290. Letter from William Thomms, Esq. to J. Y. Ackerman, Esq., Secretary.

Coming down to comparatively modem times, it is curious that so little notice should have been taken of the White Horse by our antiquaries. Wise in his Letter to Dr. Mead (1738) regrets this, and then adds, Leland's journey does not seem to have carried him this way, nor does Camden here go out of the other's track; though he mentions upon another occasion, and by the bye, *The White Horse*; but in such a manner, that I could wish, for his own sake, he had passed it over in silence with the rest. For his own account is altogether so unbecoming so faithful and accurate an author, insinuating to his readers that it has no existence but in the imagination of country people. "The Thames," says he, "falls into a valley, which they call The Vale of White Horse, from I know not what shape of a Horse fancied on the side of a whitish Hill."

Much nearer to the truth is Mr. Aubrey, however wide of the mark, who in the additions to the Britannia says: "I leave others to determine, whether the White Horse on the Hill was made by Hengist, since the Horse was the arms or figure in Hengist's standard."

The author of a *Tour through England* is a little more particular, though he leaves us as much in the dark about the antiquity and design of it. "Between this town of Marlborow and Abingdon, is the Vale of White Horse. The inhabitants tell a great many fabulous stories of the original of its name; but there is nothing of foundation in them, that I could find. The whole of the story is this: Looking south from the Vale, we see a trench cut on the side of a high green hill, in the shape of a horse, and not ill-shaped neither; the trench is about a yard deep, and filled almost up with chalk, so that at a distance you see the exact shape of a White Horse, but so large, as to take up near an acre of ground, some say almost two acres. From this figure the Hill is called in our maps White Horse Hill, and the low or flat country under it the Vale of White Horse."

Note II.

SITE OF THE BATTLE OF ASHDOWN.

THERE ARE four spots in Berkshire which claim the honour of being the Aescendun of the chroniclers, where Ethelred and Alfred gained their great victory; they are Ilsley, Ashamstead, Aston in the parish of Bluberry, and Ashdown, close to White Horse Hill. Now it seems clear that Ashdown was, in Saxon times, the name of a district stretching over a considerable portion of the Berkshire chalk range, and it is quite possible that all of the above sites may have been included in that district; therefore, I do not insist much upon the name, though whatever weight is to be attached to it, must tell in favour of the latter site, that of Ashdown. Let us, however, consider the other qualifications of the rival sites.

That of Ilsley is supported, so far as I know, only by Hewitt in his antiquities of the Hundred of Compton (1844); and his argument rests chiefly on the fitness of the ground for the scene of a great battle. He tells us that the detachments of three Waterloo regiments, marching through Ilsley in 1816,

when they came to the spot, stopped and called out, "Waterloo! Waterloo!" to one another. He also states that the name Ilsley is, in fact, "Hilde laeg," the field of battle; but as he has no tradition in his favour, and cannot, so far as I know, point to any remains in the neighbourhood in support of his theory, I think his case must fail, and only mention it to show that I have not overlooked the claim.

Ashamstead, situate five miles to the south-east of Ilsley, is named by the Lysons in their topographical account of Berkshire as the probable site of the battle, but they give no reasons, and are unsupported by tradition or remains.

Aston has a stronger case. It is situate between Wallingford and Ilsley. The range of chalk hills rises just above it, and one detached hill is here thrown out into the Vale, on which are still visible considerable earthworks. There is a chapel called Thorn Chapel on the eastern slope of this hill, and I am told there is a tradition that this chapel was built on the spot where some Saxon king heard mass on the morning of a battle. It is suggested by Mr. Lousley and others, that the Saxons occupied this outlying hill, the Danes the opposite range; and that the battle was fought in the valley between, where, when the road was recently altered, a number of bones were found, apparently thrown in together without care, as would be the case after a battle. There are, however, no regular barrows or other remains. Bishop Gibson is in favour of this spot, on account, as it would seem, of a passage in the *Saxon Chronicle* for the year 1006, which runs as follows: "They" (the Danes) "destroyed Wallingford, and passed a night at Cholsey." Then they "turned *along Ashdown* to Cwichelmes Low."

The bishop says, that Cwichelmes Low (the *low* or hill of King Cwichelm, who reigned in these parts, and died in the year 636 A.D.) is Cuckhamsley Hill, or Scuchamore Knob, as it is generally called; a high hill in the same chalk range, about ten miles east of White Horse Hill; and he argues that, as the Danes went *from* Wallingford, *by* Ashdown, *to* Cwichelmes Low, we must look for Ashdown between Wallingford and Cuckhamsley Hill. Now Aston lies directly between the two, therefore Aston is Ashdown, and the site of the battle. But the place now called Ashdown is on the further side of Cuckhamsley Hill from Wallingford—therefore the Danes could not have passed it in getting from Wallingford to Cuckhamsley Hill—therefore the modern Ashdown cannot be the site of the battle.

To this I answer, *First,* the Bishop *assumes* that Cwichelmes Low is Cuckhamsley Hill, without giving any reason.

Secondly, assuming Cwichelmes Low and Cuckhamsley Hill to be identical; yet, as Ashdown was clearly a large tract of country, the Danes might go from Wallingford, *along* a part of it, *to* Cwichelmes Low without passing the battlefield.

Thirdly, the name Aston is written "Estone" in Domesday Book; meaning "East town," or enclosure, and not "Mons fraxini," the "Hill of the Ash-tree."

Fourthly, Ethelred and Alfred would have kept to the hills in their retreat, and never have allowed the Danes to push them out into the Thames-valley, where the Pagan cavalry would have been invaluable; but this must have been the case, if we suppose Aston to be the site of the battle. Lastly, all the above sites are too near to Reading, the farthest being only sixteen miles from that town. But Ethelred and Alfred had been retreating three days, and would therefore much more probably be found at Ashdown by White Horse Hill, which is ten miles farther along the range of hills.

Ashdown, the remaining site, and the one which I believe to be the true one, is the down which surrounds White Horse Hill, in the parish of Uffington. On the highest point of the hill, which is 893 feet above the level of the sea, stands Uffington Castle, a plain of more than eight acres in extent, surrounded by earthworks, and a single deep ditch, which Camden, and other high authorities, say are Danish.[46]

There is another camp, with earthworks, called Hardwellcamp[47], about a mile W.N.W. of Uffington Castle, and a third smaller circular camp, called King Alfred's camp, about a mile to the S.W., which may still be made out, close to the wall of Ashdown Park, Lord Craven's seat, although Aubrey says, that in his time the works were "almost quite defaced, by digging for the Sarsden stones to build my Lord Craven's house in the Park."

Wise suggests that the Danes held Uffington Castle; that Ethelred was in Hardwell-camp, and Alfred in Alfred's Camp. A mile and a half to the eastward, in which direction the battle must have rolled, as the Saxons slowly gained the day, is a place called the Seven Barrows, where are seven circular burial-mounds, and several other large irregularly-shaped mounds, full of bones; the light soil which covers the chalk is actually black around them. The site agrees in all points with the description in the chroniclers; it is the proper distance from Reading; the name is the one used by the chroniclers,— "Ashdown," "Mons Fraxini," "Aescendun;" it is likely that Ethelred would have fought somewhere hereabouts to protect Wantage, a royal burg, and his birthplace, which would have been otherwise at the mercy of the enemy; and lastly, there—and not at Cuckhamsley Hill, or elsewhere—is carved the White Horse, which has been from time immemorial held to be a monument of the great victory of Ashdown.[48]

---

46 *The fort is now considered to date from the early Iron Age, with underlying Bronze Age traces.*

47 *Also now considered Iron Age, though this does not preclude it being used by later forces.*

48 *White Horse Hill may or may not be the site of the Battle of Ashdown, but the figure itself is now considered Iron or Bronze Age.*

Note III.

WAYLAND SMITH'S CAVE.

WISE thinks he has discovered the place of burial of King Bas-reg, Bagseeg (or whatever his name might be, for it is given in seven or eight different ways in the chroniclers), in Wayland Smith's cave, which place he describes as follows:—

"The place is distinguished by a parcel of stones set on edge, and enclosing a piece of ground raised a few feet above the common level, which every one knows was the custom of the Danes, as well as of some other northern nations. And Wormius observes, that if any Danish chief was slain in a foreign country, they took care to bury him as pompously as if he had died in his own. Mr. Aubrey's account of it is this: "About a mile [or less] from the Hill [White Horse Hill] there are a great many large stones, which, though very confused, must yet be laid there on purpose. Some of them are placed edge-wise, but the rest are so disorderly that one would imagine they were tumbled out of a cart."

The disorder which Mr. Aubrey speaks of is occasioned by the people having thrown down some of the stones (for they all seem originally to have been set on edge), and broken them to pieces to mend their highways. Those that are left enclose a piece of ground of an irregular figure at present, but which formerly might have been an oblong square, extending only north and south.

"On the east side of the southern extremity stand three squarish flat stones of about four or five feet over each way, set on edge, and supporting a fourth of much larger dimensions, lying flat upon them. These altogether form a cavern or sheltering-place, resembling pretty exactly those described by Wormius, Bartholine, and others, except in the dimensions of the stones; for whereas this may shelter only ten or a dozen sheep from a storm, Wormius mentions one in Denmark that would shelter a hundred.

"I know of no other monument of this sort in England; but in Wales and the Isle of Anglesey there are several not unlike it, called by the natives Cromlechs. The Isle of Anglesey having been the chief seat of the Druids, induced its learned antiquary to ascribe them to the ancient Britons; an assertion that I will not take upon me to contradict, but shall only at this time observe, that I find sufficient authorities to convince me that ours must be Danish.

"Whether this remarkable piece of antiquity ever bore the name of the person here buried is not now to be learned, the true meaning of it being long since lost in ignorance and fable. All the account which the country people are able to give of it is, 'At this place lived formerly an invisible smith; and if a traveller's horse had lost a shoe upon the road, he had no more to do than to bring the horse to this place, with a piece of money, and leaving both there for some little time, he might come again and find the money gone, but the horse new shod.' The stones standing upon the *Rudgeway*, as it is called (which was the situation that they chose for burial monuments), I suppose gave occasion to the whole being called Wayland Smith, which is the name it was always known by to the country people.

"An English antiquary might find business enough who should attempt to unriddle all the fabulous traditions of the vulgar, which ascribe these works of unknown antiquity to demons and invisible powers.

"Leaving, therefore, the story of the invisible smith to be discussed by those who have more leisure, I only remark, that these stones are, according to the best Danish antiquaries, a burial altar; that their being raised in the midst of a plain field, near the great road, seems to indicate some person there slain, and buried, and that this person was probably a chief or king; there being no monument of this sort near that place, perhaps not in England, beside."

I have given Wise's statement of his own case, but the better opinion amongst antiquaries seems to be that he is wrong, and that the cromlech called Wayland Smith's Cave is of much earlier date than 871 A.D.[49]

Note IV.

As an illustration of one of the methods by which traditions are kept up in the country, I insert some verses written by Job Cork, an Uffington man of two generations back, who was a shepherd on White Horse Hill for fifty years.

> "It was early one summer's morn,
> The weather fine and very warm,
> A stranger to White Horse Hill did go
> To view the plains and fields below.
>
> "As he along the hill did ride,
> Taking a view on every side,
> The which he did so much enjoy
> Till a shepherd's dog did him annoy.
>
> "At length an aged man appeared,
> A watching of his fleecy herd,
> With threadbare coat and downcast eye,
> To which the stranger did draw nigh.

---

49   *Hughes was right: Wayland's Smithy is now considered to be a*
      long barrow with chamber tomb dating from the Neolithic.

MEMORIES OF THE VALE

"'O noble shepherd, can you tell
How long you kept sheep on this hill?'
'Zeven year in Zundays I have been
A shepherd on this hill so green.'

"'That is a long time, I must own,
You have kept sheep upon this down;
I think that you must have been told
Of things that have been done of old.'

"'Ah, Zur, I can remember well
The stories the old voke do tell—
Upon this hill which here is seen
Many a battle there have been.

"'If it is true as I heard zay,
King Gaarge did here the dragon slay,
And down below on yonder hill
They buried him as I heard tell.

"'If you along the Rudgeway go,
About a mile for aught I know,
There Wayland's Cave then you may see
Surrounded by a group of trees.

"'They say that in this cave did dwell
A smith that was invisible;
At last he was found out, they say,
He blew up the place and vlod away.

"'To Devonshire then he did go,
Full of sorrow, grief, and woe,
Never to return again,
So here I'll add the shepherd's name—

JOB CORK."

There is no merit in the lines beyond quaintness; but they are written in the sort of jingle which the poor remember; they have lived for fifty years and more, and will probably, in quiet corners of the Vale, outlive the productions of much more celebrated verse-makers than Job Cork, though probably they were never reduced into writing until written out at my request.

Job Cork was a village humorist, and stories are still told of his sayings, some of which have a good deal of fun in them; I give one example in the exact words in which it was told to me:—

"One night as Job Cork came off the downs, drough-wet to his very skin, it happened his wife had been a baking. So, when he went to bed, his wife took his leather breeches, and put 'em in the oven to dry 'em. When he woke in the morning he began to feel about for his thengs, and he called out, and zed, 'Betty, where be mee thengs?' 'In the oven,' zed his wife. Zo he looked in the oven and found his leather breeches all cockled up together like a piece of parchment, and he bawled out, 'O Lard! O Lard! what be I to do? Was ever man plagued as I be?' 'Patience, Job, patience, Job,' zed his wife; 'remember thy old namesake, how he was plagued.' 'Ah!' zed the old man, 'a was plagued surely; but his wife never baked his breeches.'"

Other shepherds of the Hill have been poets in a rough sort of way. I add one of their home-made songs, as I am anxious to uphold the credit of my countrymen as a tuneful race.

> "Come, all you shepherds as minds for to be,
>   You must have a gallant heart,
> You must not be down-hearted,
>   You must a-bear the smart;
> You must a-bear the smart, my boys,
>   Let it hail or rain or snow,

MEMORIES OF THE VALE

For there is no ale to be had on the Hill
Where the wintry wind doth blow.

"When I kept sheep on White Horse Hill
 My heart began to ache,
My old ewes all hung down their heads,
 And my lambs began to bleat.
Then I cheered up with courage bold,
 And over the Hill did go,
For there is no ale to be had on the Hill
 When the wintry wind doth blow.

"I drive my sheep into the fold,
 To keep them safe all night,
For drinking of good ale, my boys,
 It is my heart's delight.
I drove my sheep into the fold,
 And homeward I did go,
For there is no ale to be had on the Hill
 When the wintry wind doth blow.

"We shepherds are the liveliest lads
 As ever trod English ground,
If we drops into an ale-house
 We values not a crownd.
We values not a crownd, my boys,
 We'll pay before we go,
For there is no ale to be had on the Hill
 When the wintry wind doth blow.'

THE END.

Part Three

SCRAPBOOK.

Author Thomas Hughes, as depicted in Vanity Fair, *8th June 1872.*

THOMAS HUGHES (1822–1896) was born in Uffington. His family had been vicars of Uffington for five generations and lived at The Hall on the site of the present primary school.

After Oxford University, he studied law and was called to the bar in 1848. He joined the Christian Socialists and, in 1854, became a founder member of the Working Men's College, of which he was principal from 1872 to 1883. A committed social reformer, Hughes was elected to Parliament as a Liberal for Lambeth (1865–68), and for Frome (1868–74).

In 1847, Hughes married Frances Ford, daughter of Rev. James Ford, and they settled in 1853 at Wimbledon. While living at Wimbledon, Hughes wrote his literary masterpiece, *Tom Brown's School Days*, in which the hero grew up in the Vale of the White Horse. In the novel, which was published in April 1857, Hughes describes Uffington in detail through the eyes of his hero Tom Brown.

The small stone building pictured below is the Tom Brown's School Museum in Uffington, pictured around 1960. It is open from 2pm to 5pm each Saturday, Sunday and Bank Holiday Monday from Easter until the end of October. There is no charge for admission during normal opening hours.

Above: Kingston Lisle Park, home of the "Squire", Mr Edwin Martin Atkins at the time of the 1857 Scouring. Below: Mr Martin Atkins' obituary in Jackson's Oxford Journal, *Saturday May 14th 1859.*

DEATH OF EDWIN MARTIN ATKINS, ESQ.

(From a Correspondent at Weston-super-Mare.)

The death of Mr. Martin Atkins, of Kingston Lisle, near Faringdon, has cast a gloom over our town. The lamented gentleman had only arrived here a few days since on a visit, as we have been informed, to his son, a pupil in the scholastic establishment of Mr. Elwell. His death, which occurred on Friday the 6th instant, was not occasioned by diphtheria, as by some stated, but from the effects of a tubercular affection of the throat, which produced suffocation. He was attended throughout his distressing illness by Dr. Symonds, of Clifton, Dr. Pritchard, of Bristol, and by the most experienced medical attendants in our town, who were united in opinion that his case afforded but little hope of recovery.

The Three Magpies, Hounslow Heath: (right) in 1906; (middle) in 1912; (below) today. Thomas Gibbons' account of his highwayman great-grandfather (see page 168) does appear to cross-reference with the sources available today.

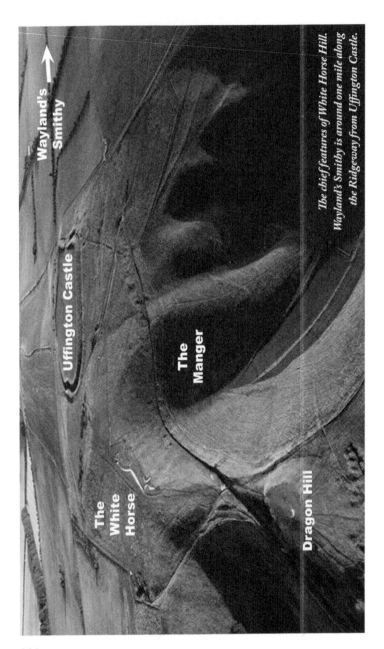

Wayland's Smithy

Uffington Castle

The Manger

The White Horse

Dragon Hill

The chief features of White Horse Hill. Wayland's Smithy is around one mile along the Ridgeway from Uffington Castle.

Above: Emily Mary, Countess Craven, née Grimston, (1815–1901) and William Craven, 2nd Earl of Craven (1806–1866). The Earl was already ill by the time of the Pastime. He died nine years later aged 57. Below: Ashdown House, thought to have been built by William Craven, 1st Earl of Craven (1608–1697) for Charles I's sister Queen Elizabeth of Bohemia.

PRIZE-FIGHTER John Shaw (see page 88) was born on a farm between Cossall and Wollaton in 1789. He worked as a carpenter on Lord Middleton's estate at Wollaton Hall. At just over six foot and weighing almost fifteen stone, Shaw was an imposing figure. He was particularly adept at protecting his face from punishment by using his left hand to cover his retreat from an opponent's attack.

According to the *Nottingham Date Book* for 1815, "He was a tremendous pugilist, fought several times in the ring and was never beaten." Like many of his contemporaries Shaw supplemented his income by body modelling for the sculptor Benjamin Haydon. It is reported that during one of these sessions Shaw encountered the writer Sir Walter Scott, who would play a significant role in the destiny of Shaw's skull after the Battle of Waterloo.

In 1807, during a visit to the Nottingham Goose Fair at the age of 18, Shaw joined the 2nd Life Guards. His first and last taste of action was at Waterloo. Early in the battle his regiment charged a body of French cuirassiers and drove them back until the two units mingled in a confused melee where the strength and skill of the individual soldier was key.

Shaw's training with the regiment and in the ring meant that he excelled at this form of conflict. Indeed his training with the sabre had made his sword arm 'strong and flexible as a bar of steel.' However, Shaw's size made him an obvious target. Although surrounded by as many as nine cuirassiers, he fought valiantly many of his opponents before his sword snapped. In desperation he used his helmet to defend himself, but in vain. He was unhorsed and left, terribly mauled. It appears that he was able to make his way to La Haye Sainte farmhouse and was still alive when found under a wall, but he died sometime during the night.

His body was recovered and buried near La Haye Sainte. A few years later Sir Walter Scott arranged for the return of Shaw's remains to Britain. Scott's fascination with the great man inspired him to retain Shaw's skull in his library at Abbotsford, where it remains to this day. A plaster cast of the skull is on display at the Household Cavalry Museum.

householdcavalrymuseum.co.uk
waterloo200.org
thorotonsociety.org.uk

This plaster cast of Shaw's skull was made by his comrades, and can be seen in the Household Cavalry Museum in London.

THE BLOWING STONE is a 3-foot tall sarsen pierced with several naturally-occurring holes, from one of which issues a Y-shaped channel.

Closing the hole over completely with the mouth and then blowing hard produces a note that resonates across the Downs, sounding something like a calf lowing for its mother. Supposedly it can be heard as far away as Faringdon church, some six miles distant.

Legend says the stone once stood high on Kingstone Down and was used by King Alfred the Great to summon the local militia to fight at the Battle of Ashdown. While this story is probably a myth, it has been suggested that the stone could have been used by the local Iron Age tribe in a similar manner. According to another legend, anyone capable of making the stone sound a note that is audible from the top of Uffington White Horse Hill will become king of England.

The parish smith brought the stone down into the valley, in around 1750, and set it up outside his smithy. By 1809, this building had become the 'Blowing Stone Inn' and the landlord entertained his customers by blowing the stone for a small fee. The stone still lies in the garden outside the cottages which used to be the Blowingstone Inn on a lane called Blowing-stone Hill close to the Uffington White Horse. The owners

The Blowing Stone: looking remarkably similar to Doyle's sketch (page 81).

There is now a new Blowing Stone Inn, and the stone itself sits in a private garden.

allow access to the stone and a leaflet and postcard can be purchased on the site.

The name the 'Blowing Stone Inn' is now used by another public house elsewhere in the village of Kingston Lisle.

Blowing Stone Hill, Kingstone Lisle.

Above: The former Blowing Stone Inn at the turn of the 20th century. Below: The same view today. The stone can still be seen a few yards from its original site.

WOMBWELL'S Menagerie was a popular touring attracting throughout the nineteenth century. An ever-changing line-up of exotic animals thrilled a public thirsty for novelties brought back by merchant ships from faraway corners of the British Empire.

George Wombwell first took his travelling menagerie on the road in 1805. He had adored his childhood pets, and looked after them with tender care. But now lions, tigers, elephants and snakes were his business. From his premises in the Commercial Road, his

293

January 1850: the shocking death of Wombwell's "Lion Queen" Ellen Bright.

horse-drawn caravans of beasts rumbled out to fairs all over the country. Apart from offering a delicious frisson of fear, the exhibits were considered to be educational, and their keepers purveyors of knowledge and symbols of the mastery of Mankind over Nature. Sadly for one keeper, during a show in January 1850 one of her tigers gave onlookers a bit more of an education than they were expecting by eating her (above). Wombwell's niece Ellen Bright, the "Lion Queen", was only 17 when the animal savaged her. She died within minutes.

George Wombwell died peacefully in his caravan in 1851.

THE RIDGEWAY is an ancient track extending from Wiltshire along the chalk ridge of the Berkshire Downs to the River Thames at the Goring Gap. For thousands of years the Ridgeway formed part of a reliable trading route stretching from the Dorset coast across the south to the Wash in Norfolk. The high, dry ground made travel easy and gave travellers a commanding view, warning against potential attacks.

The Bronze Age saw the development of Uffington White Horse and the stone circle at Avebury. During the Iron Age, inhabitants took advantage of the high ground by building hill forts along the Ridgeway to help defend the trading route. Following the collapse of the Roman Empire in Western Europe, invading Saxon and Viking armies used it. In medieval times and later, the Ridgeway was used by drovers bringing livestock from the West Country and Wales to markets in the Home Counties and London.

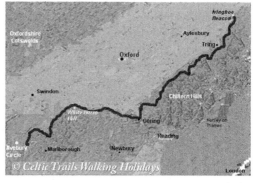

Also by Julie Ann Godson

THE WATER GYPSY
How a Thames fishergirl became a viscountess
AT DUSK on a snowy evening in 1766 a tired young couple made
out the welcoming lights burning in the windows of creaky old
Shellingford Manor in the Vale of the White Horse, the house that
was to be their home. He was Viscount Ashbrook, she was Betty
Ridge, daughter of a humble Thames fisherman. Earlier that day
they had been married in a little village church, and now Betty—a
real-life Cinderella—was embarking on a new life in the alien
world of the aristocracy.

ON THIS DAY IN OXFORDSHIRE
PICK ANY DAY of the year, and something interesting will have
happened somewhere in Oxfordshire. The county has experienced
its share of events of national importance: rioting, civil war,
archaeological finds and life-changing inventions. And at the
same time, ordinary people have struggled through their own
dramas. With only alcohol to soothe their exhaustion and worries,
inevitably conflict broke out behind closed doors too. But, in times
of world war, the people of Oxfordshire have displayed humbling
dedication. This book offers a daily snapshot of their lives from the
seventh century through to modern times.

SCANDAL IN HIGH SOCIETY
OXFORDSHIRE
Twenty tales of toffs in trouble
SECRET LOVE affairs, murder, blackmail, poisoning and
extortion: most of us enjoy a good scandal. And it's even more
fun when it involves our so-called 'betters'. This book tells twenty
tales of Oxfordshire toffs in trouble, from the Tudor period right
up to the modern age. Few readers will fail to be impressed by the
sheer variety of ways in which the upper classes of the county have
contrived over the centuries to behave badly—and often to get
away with it.

OUR BOYS 1914–1918
Who were the fallen f one Oxfordshire valley?
ACTS OF REMEMBRANCE relating to the First World War
often conjure up images of stone monuments, solemn churchyards,
and ranks of gravestones marching across foreign fields. Forty-eight
men from the Lower Windrush Valley in Oxfordshire are listed
on the village memorials of Northmoor, Standlake and Stanton
Harcourt. This book attempts to provide a glimpse of them in the
villages, farms, and lanes where they lived and worked – with their
families, plying their trade as craftsmen, or labouring in the fields.
On their days off they would play with their children, promenade
with their sweethearts, or just wink at the girls, like young men
throughout the ages have always done.

1066: OXFORDSHIRE &
THE NORMAN CONQUEST
Why it all started and finished in our county
IT CHANGED the country forever. And from the birth of
a prince to the formal surrender after the Battle of Hastings,
Oxfordshire frequently provided the background for the board-
room take-over that was the Norman Conquest of England.

FREE SPIRITS OF OXFORDSHIRE
Twenty true lives from history
IGNORING THE RULES is all very well if you have a
background sufficiently affluent to disregard the consequences.
This book celebrates those like the Woodstock hatter who became
a pirate, the country parson who joined a tribe of Aboriginal
Australians, and the Banbury baker who took up pedestrianism.
And let us never forget the much-loved Donkey Man who opted
out of society to take his flea circus on the road.

Available at Amazon.com
www.julieanngodson.com
Facebook @julieanngodson

Printed in Great Britain
by Amazon